W9-CGO-281

Straight Through Processing for Financial Services Firms

Edited by

Hal McIntyre

Text and art copyright © 2004 by The Summit Group Publishing, Inc. All rights reserved. No part of this book may be reproduced or transmitted in any form, by any means, without the prior written permission of any of the authors.

ISBN: 0-9669178-5-5

Printed in the United States of America

Published and distributed by The Summit Group Press, a division of The Summit Group.

For general information on The Summit Group Press or for permission to photocopy items for corporate, personal or educational use, please call our Wall Street office at (212) 328-2500.

Limit of Liability/Disclaimer of Warranty: The authors and publisher have used their best efforts in preparing this book. The Summit Group, The Summit Group Press and the authors make no representations or warranties with respect to the accuracy or completeness of the contents of this book and specifically disclaim any implied warranties of merchantability or fitness for any particular purpose. Neither The Summit Group, The Summit Group Press nor the author shall be liable in any event for any loss of profit or any other damages, including but not limited to special, incidental, consequential, or other damages.

Cover and Photo Design by Lee Titone.

FORWARD

The editor would like to thank the staff of The Summit Group and Securities Operations Forum for their support, and would especially like to recognize the continuous editing and feedback provided by Ledia Koka and Ari Sternberg, as well as the efforts of the Publisher, Scott Porter.

The editor would also like to thank the following authors for providing their time and expertise to help develop this book:

Simon Cleary, Head of Securities Markets & Business Solutions, SWIFT

Ignace R. Combes, Deputy CEO, Euroclear Bank

Robert M. Curtis, Director of Product, CSS Q Middle

Lee Cutrone, Managing Director of Industry Relations, Omgeo

Craig S. Dudsak, Director Relationship Management Americas, Clearstream

David Flinders, Head of Securities and Derivatives, City Networks Limited

James T. Leman, Co-Chairman US Business Practices Committee (FIX Americas)

Tom McMackin, CEO & Partner, Open Information Systems

Peter Patch, Director of Market Research, The Summit Group

Gert Raeves, Business Development Director, HelioGraph

Joe Rosen, Senior Technology Consultant

Ken Scheinblum, CEO of ii Solutions, LLC

Frederick Stanley, Executive Vice President, Evare LLC

Scott E. Vey, Chief Architect, SunGard Asset Management Systems

Larry Wentz, Managing Partner of Wentz Consulting LLC

The contributions of all of these people were invaluable in producing a book of this scope.

June 1, 2004

Hal McIntyre, Managing Partner

hal.mcintyre@tsgc.com

The Summit Group

48 Wall Street / 4th Floor

New York, NY 10005

(212) 328-2500

CONTENTS

INTRODUCTION

This book contains a series of specific articles from leading industry experts, consultants and vendors that address the issue of Straight Through Processing. The articles not only define the issues, but they also identify available solutions to a broad range of the problems that face all segments of the industry.

Identifying the solutions has been difficult in the past because people throughout the securities industry look at Straight Through Processing from a number of different viewpoints: by instrument, by geography, by processing area and by different types of firms. These different views result in some different definitions of just what STP really is and the confusion over the definition wastes time and energy. In The Summit Group we try to simplify these varying views by focusing on what is truly important and define STP as Client-to-Client Automation.

Whatever we call the process; most managers recognize that there are two primary problems facing our industry: cost-efficient processing and risk management. Both of these can be solved by continuously evaluating the processes that are used by the firm and the infrastructure. The evaluation process itself produces ideas for improvement that could be small incremental steps (which is all the industry has had an appetite for in the last two years) or for sweeping changes that could make fundamental adjustments to connectivity and to the infrastructure.

The Securities Industry Association has been working to re-direct energy away from T+1 now that it has been delayed and towards incremental improvements. Some industry consultants are saying that STP is dead or are trying to jump start spending by changing the buzz-phrase to Securities Process Automation (SPA).

Early in 2004, the SEC began the process of resurrecting T+1 by asking for comments on a Concept Release that included questions about the viability of shortening the settlement cycle.

Despite the confusion over the definition and the lack of a single co-ordinated effort, many solutions have evolved from firms, vendors and the infrastructure. These solutions are presented in this book.

SECTION I - INTRODUCTION TO STP

In this section, we present background information about STP and the how it relates to activities in the securities industry.

- The first chapter looks at the business forces that drive the financial industry and describes how we got to where we are today. The chapter also presents a definition of STP and looks its impact on several areas.

- Peter Patch, TSG's Director of Market Research presents the results of some recent proprietary research that was conducted by TSG. Peter compares STP to SPA (Securities Process Automation), a new buzz-phrase, and identifies the recent processing trends.

- The third chapter looks at industry trends from a different perspective, describes how these trends could affect the industry in general and STP specifically and presents a 'Vision of the Future.'

- Ted Stanley, in Chapter IV, makes the case that many of the tools needed to implement STP are available today and there is no need to wait for a magic bullet.

As these chapters point out, the industry needs to improve processing efficiency, and whether we call the process STP or SPA, or even redefine STP to mean Strengthening Transaction Profitability, we must do something. Big bang or incremental improvements, in-house coding or building on vendor products, the methodology is unimportant. Firms must do something today to improve their processing efficiency and reduce costs or they won't be here tomorrow.

CHAPTER I - WHAT'S DRIVING FINANCIAL FIRMS TODAY?

By Hal McIntyre, Managing Partner, The Summit Group

Introduction

Most securities processing firms, while facing the on-going threat of an industry shakeout, are trapped by their own inertia and are not effectively implementing an appropriate business or technical strategy. Critical mass is essential in this computer-based processing business, but size alone will not guarantee profitability. There are several firms with over $100 million in revenue that have minimal earnings.

Most firms spend a small portion of their planning time considering exit strategies during their annual budget exercises. This causes a few businesses to be in play each year. Most firms ultimately decide not to exit from specific product lines because the revenue helps to cover corporate overhead that will not go away, and the interrelations of different aspects of the securities processing business limits the potential expense reduction. Various product lines share clients, systems and often operations. Eliminating an unprofitable product might improve profits for that segment of the business, but could negatively impact other areas of the firm.

For years, shrinking margins, increased competition and the continual threat of disintermediation have caused many industry observers to believe that a huge shakeout will occur in the securities processing industry. There have been some mergers of large institutions which have effectively reduced the number of players, but the securities processing business itself was seldom the driving force behind the merger. Since the massive size of the industry continues to offer the potential for large annual returns for the successful participants, even marginal businesses are unwilling to exit gracefully, and some other fringe service providers would still like to become players.

Large firms believe that they need to be in all segments of the securities processing industry; however, many of the most successful firms have been those that focused on any one aspect of the business, and then expanded. There are very few examples of firms that successfully grew all aspects of the business simultaneously.

Just when firms need the most from their employees, they are getting less. Productivity is up; loyalty is forgotten.

Naturally, firms need competent people in their jobs, but the fear of becoming redundant is constraining creativity and aggressiveness. The historical employment covenant between an employer and employee in financial services has been completely broken. There are increasing examples of people being moved aside, in spite of their success. New senior managers are tending to look more at what needs to be done, rather than what has already been accomplished by the staff they inherited, and new senior managers are given shorter time frames in order to perform. This causes them to bring in a few key people who they already know and trust, and who in turn cause more disruption. The introduction of a new senior manager can paralyze a firm for 3-6 months.

The focus on expense control is necessary, but is often unfocused. Firms would have more impact by cutting a few marginal businesses than by decreasing costs across the board by 10% and suffocating all businesses. Downsizing without changing the process only reduces the number of people available to perform the work. This often has a short term financial benefit, but usually results in a de-motivated staff, missed opportunities, rework, and in some cases, a loss of operating control. Process reengineering offers a much better solution, but is not a quick fix. Process reengineering requires people with general business knowledge, imagination, and skills in project management and change management. Reengineering is not a one-time project; it becomes a way of life and the process of downsizing will continue year after year. This increases the need for firms to consider outsourcing.

Outsourcing offers a tantalizing opportunity to pass off responsibility while reducing costs. In fact, responsibility can never be delegated and outsourcing decisions must be carefully analyzed to ensure that short term cost savings will not result in unanticipated long term costs and loss of control. When you outsource a process to a firm in another country, the laws of that country will be used to resolve disputes, so issues such as intellectual capital, staff changes and monetary repatriation need to be carefully considered.

Each year's budget process is long and potentially dangerous. Very little progress is usually made by firms from August to November, and virtually nothing starts again until after January 1st. By May, managers will have to start thinking about their "new" strategy for next year.

The desire for quick solutions in strategy and expense control is also affecting the use of technology. New technologies offer the promise of faster development, lower operating costs, and easier, more efficient enhancements. What's missing is an understanding by senior managers that establishing the environment (staff, tools, and process), and developing the expertise to use the new technologies is not quick or cheap. Technology managers know that they need to deliver software in smaller pieces, as quickly as possible; but in many cases the transition from massive, complex legacy systems makes this an extremely difficult task.

In addition, mobilizing users to define their requirements and develop a vision of the future in a complex business is a major task. The users with the detailed knowledge are seldom the same people who can establish the details of the vision that will satisfy the business and take advantage of the new technologies.

The search for a technical magic bullet has caused firms to fail to stay the course on valid strategies and spend major dollars and effort on the grail.

The staff is increasingly internally focused and defensive, and it is not being rewarded for taking chances. Today, a good batting average is not enough, and striving for error free activities limits the incentive to innovate.

How Did We Get Where We Are?

Before we can talk about improving our current process, we should look at how we got where we are and why the industry is organized the way it is.

Role of Financial Intermediaries

The role of financial intermediaries is one of bringing together borrowers and lenders in a regulated environment.

In the United States, we have a regulatory environment, managed by the SEC, which establishes our rules and processing requirements. As a result of the regulatory environment, we have established an infrastructure of depositories, exchanges and clearinghouses, all of which are designed to help participants in the industry work together more efficiently and economically. All the participants in the industry are constantly involved in a process that is designed to bring together the borrowers and the lenders. We establish new products that will entice investors and satisfy the intermediate- and long-term needs of the borrowers. As a result of these new products and inner mediation process, we create a number of increasingly complex transactions in the U.S. and across borders.

In this process, we have to bring together all of the participants in the entire trade value chain. The value chain consists of the following steps:

- Issuance
- Pre-trade
- Trade
- Post-trade
- Clearance
- Settlement
- Issue servicing

The infrastructure and all the industry participants have different roles to perform throughout the investment value chain. There are several roadblocks to successful implementation of Straight Through Processing. These include several generic issues, such as standards, inertia and demand, the difficulty involved in establishing STP because of separate learning curves, and the overall expense of implementation. There are usually a variety of internal issues that firms have to overcome, which can include ownership issues as well as application deficiencies.

There are always external issues to resolve between the firms and with the infrastructure.

Even if we only consider internal Straight Through Processing, we find that there are a variety of processing issues to resolve. Almost every firm is saddled with a large number of legacy applications that frequently involve complex undocumented code and sometimes even the lack of object code.

There are almost always multiple platforms and technologies involved in these legacy applications and most of them are very batch oriented. Many firms are still in a paper-based environment that often requires the input of information into multiple systems. And finally, not all the data that is required in order to successfully interface externally is in the required electronic form.

New managers often look at a firm's IT architecture and ask who designed the 'mess'. Clearly, no rational person would design the architecture that most firms work with every day – and the answer is that no one designed it – it evolved. Each day, managers made decisions that were logical and reasonable given the goals and constraints that existed that day. The new manager should begin to re-direct the evolution towards more useful and efficient architectural goals.

Evolution of Operations and Technology

Front Office vs. Back Office

The DTCC was originally designed to support the Back Office and has done a very good job supporting operations. The Back Office staff sees DTCC as dependable and thorough. This includes DTCC services such as software, networking and operations.

However, the Front Office generally does not have any direct knowledge of the DTCC other than portions of TradeSuite, which is usually used by Trading Assistants.

Today, firms typically use separate systems for their Front Office activities and their Back Office activities, so the technology and support staff works within two very different environments.

		FRONT OFFICE	BACK OFFICE
PEOPLE		Responsiveness	Control
		Flexibility	Efficiency
		Transaction Oriented	Process Oriented
TECHNOLOGY		Goal Driven	SDLC Driven
		Real Time	Batch
		Distributed	Mainframe

Figure 1 – Generic Characteristics

Most products go through a life cycle that consists of several phases:

PHASE	CHARACTERISTICS					
	VENDORS	VENDOR STYLE	STANDARDS	COST	PROFITS	PRODUCT DIFFERENTIATION
PRODUCT INTRODUCTION	Many	Entrepreneurial	None	High	High	High
RAPID GROWTH	Fewer	Entrepreneurial	Few	Medium	Medium	High
MATURITY	Very Few	Corporate	1- 2	Low	Low	Medium
DECLINE	1	Corporate	1	Low	Medium	Low
PHASE-OUT	1	Corporate	1	Low	Low	Low

Figure 2 – TSG Vendor Maturity Model

Within the securities industry, one of the areas that have experienced rapid growth is connectivity between firms. Connectivity is either still in the rapid growth phase, or is beginning to enter the maturity phase. Although the Back Office is clearly in the maturity phase, the Front Office may be either at the end of a period of rapid growth, or it may be just entering maturity.

Life Cycle of the Back Office

The Back Office is in a mature phase, and very little differentiation between firms can exist in the area of efficient clearing and settlement.

Life Cycle of the Front Office

If the connectivity aspect of Front Office systems is still in a phase of rapid growth, the market place will continue to look for quick solutions from specialized vendors; however, if these areas are entering a mature phase, then DTCC's strengths apply and the market will demand commodity processing and standards.

The Front Office has had its breakthrough products and is ready to consolidate in a new phase of maturity, which is typically characterized by:

- Control/reliability
- Decline in number of products
- Decreased change
- Ease of operations
- Higher barriers to entry
- Increase in number of products
- Low barriers to entry
- Maturity

- Multiple solutions
- Occasional surprises
- Process efficiency
- Product introduction
- Quick response
- Rapid change

There are other factors that indicate that connectivity in the Front Office is entering a phase of maturity:

- Consolidation of operations
- Outsourcing of processes

Middle Office

The Middle Office usually consists of functions such as:

- Investment Accounting
- Risk Management
- Decision Support
- Trade Processing
- Client Services, etc.

There are no single, generally accepted lines that divide the front from the middle, from the back; however, the goal of the Middle Office is to bring together the best features of the front and the back.

The Front Office has been known for responding quickly and satisfying the immediate needs of the firm, often by using emerging technologies in a creative way.

The Back Office has typically satisfied the firm's long term processing needs, with a highly structured systems development process, and an efficient and controlled processing environment.

There is no single definition of the Middle Office, and different people have identified at least three different reasons for creating this new function:

- Establish some operations and technical support under the direct control of the Front Office.
- Combine the best of the existing Front Office and the Back Office methodologies and processes. This includes flexibility, speed of development, as well as control of response time and processing time.
- Support the long-term growth of Middle Office as by automating existing manual functions that are currently performed by the Front Office or the Back Office.

Whatever the reason for this new organizational unit, the characteristics and objectives are usually the same and much of the responsibility for supporting the shorter settlement cycle falls on the staff of the Middle Office.

Preparing for the Future

To combat the endless shifting of priorities and the downward spiral that results from continuous introspection and second-guessing, firms need to focus on three activities: Stability, Strategy and Sales.

Stability

Stability involves establishing an effective environment (People, tools and process) and doing so in a controlled and high quality manner. Internal staff is focusing more and more on relationship management, planning, and crisis management. Routine projects and day-to-day activities can be outsourced to firms that are more focused and more efficient.

Strategy

There are a limited number of strategies that are available for the securities processing business manager today. After determining whether or not you really want to be in the business, the trick is to select the strategy that best matches your objectives, strengths and weaknesses. A multi-product firm with an integrated offering needs a significant competitive advantage in order to compete with firms that are very focused on a particular product, target market, or geography, and with smaller firms that can react more quickly to sporadic opportunities. Firms with the same basic strategy will different themselves by the tactics they employ.

Sales

Sales will come through the implementation of the strategy and the tactics. As the plan progresses, some modifications will be necessary, but knee-jerk reactions that are based upon management changes, re-organizations, and strategic shifts should be avoided. There is no quick fix in this business if the result is going to be a radical, effective and non-disruptive to clients.

To succeed in this industry, firms must establish effective environments, select an appropriate business and technology strategy and implement it well, and move towards Straight Through Processing.

STP in the Securities Industry

Each firm in the securities processing industry realizes that it must implement Straight Through Processing if it is going to succeed. However, there are very few common definitions of just what STP is, and the view is even more different when we consider how trust and custody banks see STP, versus how brokers and investment managers view it.

Most brokers and investment managers have tended to see STP as a process that integrates trade flow from initiation through to settlement. They were primarily concerned with the connectivity of internal applications within their firm, and are only now actively seeking connectivity to external applications as a critical priority.

This resulted from the constant flood of improvements in Front Office technology. Whether building internally or buying applications, brokers and managers have been evolving rapidly for the last ten years as they try to optimize their Front Office systems and stay ahead (or at least even) with their competition. These new applications have usually taken advantage of newer technologies, and have created an architecture based upon heterogeneous platforms. Not only have these firms had to integrate data across multiple databases and files, they have also had to move the data as seamlessly as possible across multiple technical platforms.

As individual applications were created, each better than the past, firms found themselves in an ever shifting technical environment and also found it difficult to integrate these systems with their in-house resources. By looking to external systems integrators for technical support, firms were able to acquire "best of breed" technology and still move data from one application to another; but as soon as another "best" system was identified, another round of integration was initiated.

Custodians and Trust Banks, on the other hand, generally had a single processing system but have many interfaces to their clients and to the industry infrastructure. These firms have focused on external connectivity as a priority. However, the new round of mergers and consolidation has required banks to work actively to integrate the various applications that they obtained as the two firms are integrated.

All of these changes created an opportunity for some vendors to develop or assemble suites of integrated applications that support firms from front to back, and which require a minimum of sophisticated systems integration experience, and for other vendors to support technically complex internal application integration.

What is STP?

STP is a major topic at industry conferences and in numerous articles, yet there is no single definition of what constitutes Straight Through Processing. Some of the interpretations are:

- Processing without human intervention
- End-to-end computing
- Paperless processing
- Exception-only processing

Each of these interpretations is valid, depending upon the viewpoint of the reader. However, regardless of which of these interpretations are adopted, one overriding question remains: When does STP begin and end? To answer this question we need to know:

- Does STP include pre-trade processing and trade processing as well as post-trade processing?

- Does STP consider only firm-to-firm interfaces, or does it also include the processes within a firm?

- Are the interfaces with the client also included?

At The Summit Group, we believe that for the industry to effectively have Straight Through Processing, both internal and external connectivity will have to be established, from the initiation of the transaction by the client all the way to reporting the completed transaction to the client. At TSG, we regard STP to be 'Client-to-Client Automation'.

Many firms were moving actively towards STP throughout the 1990's. This focus was diverted in the last few years as business slowed and investment was reduced. Recently, we are seeing indications that investment is being reconsidered and firms are looking to improve processing efficiency and quality by re-examining the concepts behind STP. STP can fundamentally change the way the securities industry conducts business:

- Eliminate different processing methods, and eliminate any differentiation between firms based upon processing ability

- Focus on exception processing, not on transaction processing

- Implement continuous reconcilement

- Significantly reduce errors

After full implementation of STP, the only remaining operational functions should be:

- Risk Management

- Reconcilement Reviews

- Exception Processing

- Database Management

- Workflow Rules Management

- Client Investigations

- New Product Development

Based upon this, the acronym STP could begin to stand for Strengthening Transaction Profitability.

Why is STP Needed?

STP primarily requires an Information Technology focus. The key issues that must be overcome are:

- Resolving the multiple standards that are used in the industry today, either by converging the standards or by using technology to make the differences transparent.
- Most firms in the industry use faxes and manual intervention throughout some aspects of the process, especially for international trade confirmations. This is expensive and error prone.

The three major reasons why the industry needs to implement STP are:

- Increased client demands for efficiency, timeliness and quality
- Changes in regulatory requirements
- Increased competition

The industry's need for managing risks and controlling costs has led regulators to begin moving their markets towards shorter settlement cycles. To attain this goal, each market has begun a series of initiatives that will identify and implement the necessary changes; one of these initiatives is STP.

What Is Needed to Implement STP?

There is no shortage of potential solutions. Brokers, Banks and Investment Managers all have unique as well as overlapping problems and are working together, as well as independently, on industry-wide solutions. Vendors are actively looking for ways to extend their existing products and develop new niche opportunities, and the infrastructure has mobilized to offer wide-ranging solutions.

Investment Manager Requirements

Investment Managers need many of the systems that are required by Brokers, and have some similar processing needs at every step in the Securities Processing Value Chain (Figure 4.). While, in general, they have less of a requirement for high volume clearing and settlement systems, Investment Managers still perform a critical role in ensuring efficient trade processing. Their primary need is for internally integrated systems and secondarily for connectivity with external entities.

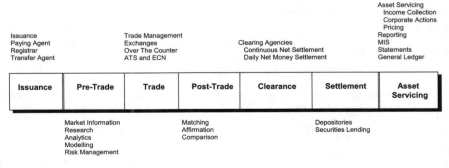

Figure 3 - Securities Processing Value Chain

Several vendors are trying to create solutions that will support the Managers' internal end-to-end needs. These solutions all share the same primary characteristic: they are working to establish a single set of seamless applications. Most Investment Managers tend to see STP as a process that integrates trade flow from initiation through affirmation. They are primarily concerned with the connectivity of internal applications within their firm, and see connectivity to external applications as an important, but secondary priority.

This is a result of the constant flood of improvements in Front Office technology. Whether they build internally or buy applications, Brokers and Managers have been evolving rapidly for the last ten years as they have tried to optimize their Front Office systems and stay ahead (or at least even) with their competition. These new applications have usually taken advantage of newer technologies, and have evolved within an architecture based upon heterogeneous platforms. Not only have these firms had to integrate data across multiple databases and files, they have also had to move the data as seamlessly as possible across multiple technical platforms.

As individual applications were created, each better than the last, firms found themselves in an ever shifting technical environment and also found it difficult to integrate these systems with their in-house resources. By looking to external systems integrators for technical support, firms were able to acquire "best of breed" technology and still move data from one application to another; but as soon as another "best" system was identified, another round of integration was initiated. In the past, technology focused on specific product areas or instrument types, and since there were multiple databases, the integrity of the data was always suspect.

This created an opportunity for vendors to develop or assemble suites of integrated applications that support firms from front to back, and which require a minimum of sophisticated systems integration experience.

Broker Requirements

A small number of vendors are each trying to present single integrated Back Office processing solutions for small- to medium-size Brokers.

Another solution for small- to mid-size Brokers trying to attain seamless processing without a major capital investment has been to outsource through Correspondent Clearers. Correspondent Clearers typically sell themselves as complete solutions, and provide an integrated system that will support all aspects of trade processing, from pre-trading through settlement and record-keeping. This solution has a particular appeal for firms that do not see their value added in processing.

The problem for large Brokers is different. In addition to trying to integrate their applications, they have a large number of older legacy systems that need to be modernized, and due to their volumes, need increased efficiency in processing street side information for clearing and settlement. In this area, large Brokers are similar to the Banks, which are discussed next.

Banking Requirements

The environment for the major custody Banks is very different from the Managers and most Brokers. Banks have built up large, complex systems that are basically already internally integrated. Since there have been fewer Front Office demands and opportunities to use modern technology, the Banks have been able to continuously improve their internal interfaces. While their systems are old and less flexible, they are stable.

Banks typically have many different sets of applications that support different target markets.

The Banks' problem has been with application redundancy as well as interfacing to their clients and to the street. This external connectivity goal has been difficult to achieve since the Banks cannot unilaterally impose processes or standards. When they tried to do this by creating proprietary formats in the late 1980's, their clients rebelled and demanded a single set of standards, which resulted in standards from SWIFT, ISITC and FIX.

Since the Banks saw their proprietary formats as a way to control their clients, they initially resisted common standards, but eventually gave in to industry pressure. Banks have now embraced these standards as the long-term solution to their processing needs, but still see a need to manage the process and are now actively involved in the initiatives. Banks hope that by receiving clean data electronically, they will be able to efficiently use their large processing infrastructures at increasingly lower unit costs, and can continuously lower their prices and avoid disintermediation.

STP for Equities

Investment managers and brokers who attempt to implement Straight Through Processing have found that there are different problems associated with the different instrument categories. For instance, STP for Equities is easiest for DTCC-eligible securities and more difficult for non-eligible securities and international trades. The high volumes associated with equity processing create other interface issues since there is very little time available to correct errors that are associated with cancels and corrects.

Since most Mutual Funds are based on Equities, the Mutual Funds need for fast and accurate reporting of transactions and positions has stressed the industry's ability to process these instruments.

Although the primary settlement period in the U.S. is three days, Mutual Funds need to process their transactions through to their custodians by the end of trade date in order to ensure that the accounting being used to determine net asset value is completed in a timely fashion.

STP for Fixed Income

Straight Through Processing for Fixed Income instruments varies for each of the different debt instrument types. The periodic nature of many of these instrument types creates problems since the instruments are not processed on a daily basis. There are also many categories of same day trades within Fixed Income processing that have to be accommodated, as well as pair off and turnaround transactions.

It is only in the last two years that the users' demand for Fixed Income solutions has matched the products available from a few selected vendors.

What Generic Roadblocks Must Be Overcome?

But despite the amount of effort that has already been expended, industry-wide STP will not arrive without a significant amount of additional work by firms throughout the industry and by the industry's infrastructure. There are many roadblocks that must be overcome to make this change come true, including:

Inertia

As with the settlement cycle, many industry participants would prefer to avoid STP changes and keep things as they are, following the philosophy "If it ain't broke…"

Segmentation

Different types of firms (Brokers, Banks, and investment Managers) each place a different emphasis on what needs to be improved first.

Expense

Implementing STP will be a significant expense to many firms that have fallen behind their peers in automation and process optimization. The pressure to invest may force many firms to consider outsourcing.

Difficulty Due to Separate Learning Curves

Different firms have different knowledge bases and sometimes find it difficult to effectively communicate between themselves.

Implications of STP

STP will increase the industry's efficiency and capacity, and will have an impact on every firm and vendor.

Some firms will benefit and some will lose ground.

- Custodians will need to make many changes to survive in an STP world, but could lose clients to depositories as the depositories add services, and this will result in another round of custodian consolidation. The survivors of this trend will be those that provide more than the basic services, and will probably provide more information about the client's accounts and more credit services.

- Brokers could lose clients as their competitors offer faster and more responsive customized services. Electronic connectivity is now at the top of the automation priority list for brokers.

- Investment Managers face increasing pressure on administrative and processing costs, and are finding that good investment results are no longer enough to guarantee success.

About the Author

Hal McIntyre has 30 years of management experience in securities operations and technology. He founded The Summit Group in 1991 by consolidating the business activities of BIBLOS Technology, Inc., and Parsec Information Corporation.

Prior to establishing The Summit Group, Hal managed numerous banking and securities functions in a sixteen year Citibank career in New York and Europe, including marketing, operations, and technology. He worked for four years in Zurich as the head of Operations and Technology for Citibank's Swiss Investment and Private Banks, and was the Chief Administrative Officer for Citicorp Investment Bank. During his last four-year assignment, he managed a division of over 300 technologists who supported Citibank's worldwide securities processing applications.

Hal is the Managing Partner of The Summit Group, which was recently listed by Crain's New York Weekly as one of the Top 25 Management Consulting firms in New York, for the third year in a row. TSG, with over sixty employees, is active in consulting to major banks, brokers and investment managers, and provides comprehensive services in Management Consulting, Market Research, and Systems Integration.

Hal has a Bachelor of Arts in Industrial Psychology from Miami University, an MBA from Southern Illinois University, and was an officer in the USAF. He has taught graduate and undergraduate courses at Fairleigh Dickinson University, and he has been a guest lecturer at the University of Massachusetts. He is frequently quoted in publications such as American Banker, Investor's Business Daily and Institutional Investor, and is a regular speaker at securities industry conferences around the world such as ABA, SIBOS and ISITC.

Hal has written three books for the securities industry: *How the US Securities Industry Works*, the *Securities Operations Glossary,* and *Software Testing for Financial Services Firms*. Hal is the editor of this book, *STP in Financial Services*. The books can be ordered from TSG's website, www.tsgc.com, or from Amazon.com.

hal@tsgc.com

CHAPTER II - SECURITIES TRENDS SURVEY

By Peter Patch, Director of Market Research, The Summit Group

Introduction

The market for securities technology is caught between two conflicting and powerful forces: the pressure for market participants to move towards higher levels of automation and security in supporting securities transaction processing, and the financial constraints imposed by reduced volumes, revenues and profits.

Both forces are compelling. Both demand attention. Together, however, they create a conflicting set of priorities for participants in the industry, demanding increased investment at the same time that spending must be curtailed.

The pressures created by these forces will result in different patterns of response in the short, intermediate- and longer-term. The short-term response will address the need for security and efficiency with incremental, tactical fixes, funded by modest increases in technology budgets. In the intermediate-term, there will be increased investment in cost reduction through centralization, standardization and automation.

Over time, this investment in application and architecture will lead to larger structural changes in the industry. There will be consolidation of the industry in each segment, and greater reliance on third parties and industry utilities to provide services. In selected functional areas and securities industry segments, there will be greater reliance on outsourcing as a fundamental response to the adverse economics of long-term maintenance and development of the securities processing infrastructure.

The Major Theme: Securities Process Automation

Apart from the immediate focus on Disaster Recovery, the overriding focus of the securities industry is on Straight Through Processing (STP), which is evolving into the more broadly defined move towards Securities Process Automation (SPA). SPA spans the Front Office, the middle and Back Office, and the connectivity to other market participants and industry utilities.

The essential difference between STP and SPA is at once subtle and fundamental.

STP has focused on entering trade details once for each transaction, achieving more complete reliance on the interconnectivity of firm and industry systems to enrich the trade, and moving through clearance and settlement without manual intervention. The distinguishing features are three:

- Single entry of trade data
- Interconnectivity and interoperability of systems

- Lack of manual intervention in trade processing through clearance and settlement

STP is achieved largely by linking existing elements of infrastructure, and allowing the trade to pass through to settlement without further intervention. Timely settlement, reduction of fails, and reduction of manual intervention are the hallmarks of STP.

Securities Process Automation aims for the same vision, and shares the same objectives, but focuses on these priorities in reverse order. The primary focus of SPA is reduction in cost through automation of activities - or better yet, obliteration of those activities.

Where STP would focus on linking existing elements of infrastructure, SPA will force, in the near term, a 're-engineering of those processes,' which will lead, in the intermediate- to longer-term, to a 're-architecting of the underlying infrastructure.'

In the short run, SPA appears as a host of relatively modest spending initiatives, a tinkering with a broad array of elements of that infrastructure. These initiatives will be described in some detail within this report. They range from refining exception management processes to automating reconcilement, and from automating indications of interest to addressing issues in legal and regulatory reporting.

In the longer term, SPA will change what activities are done, and who performs those activities. This will require the consolidation of applications, the centralizing and standardization of functions (such as maintaining the central securities database), leveraging the potential of network based technologies (web browsers, corporate portals), and moving key elements of the firm's infrastructure to third parties to manage and maintain, through outsourcing and ASP services.

The near-term technology focus of securities industry participants should be viewed through this larger, longer-term prism.

Additional Themes: Connectivity, Data Management and Client Focus

External and internal connectivity is a priority that spans the industry. While this can be viewed as one of the primary building blocks to achieve SPA, connectivity - along with the standardization of communication protocols such as FIX - stands out as a priority for brokerage, banking and buy-side firms. Enhanced connectivity and standardization are important to allow increased automation of processes, interoperability of systems, reduction of errors (by reducing manual intervention), and acceleration of transaction processes.

Database Management, with a particular emphasis on central securities reference data, is another broad priority. It is self-evident that if the trade data is not accurate, the trade cannot clear and settle on a timely basis.

The issue here is not just the accuracy of the data, but the consistency of the data throughout the organization as it is used to enrich transactions on a near real-time basis.

The sharpening focus on the client is pervasive and sustained. This includes both improving access to client data for representatives within the firm (that is, supporting client services), and providing the client access to their own data over the Internet (that is, obliterating client services). While the larger firms have long invested in this capability, those investments are ongoing and increasing. Smaller firms are likewise expanding their investments in this area.

Application Focus: Front Office, Core Processes and Support Applications

The critical Front Office applications are order management and trade management, supported by order routing and trade reporting. Portfolio management and accounting are also important in support of Front Office operations, with portfolio management increasing in significance with the expanded emphasis on asset accumulation across the industry.

Clearance and settlement systems are the principal focus of attention, along with the core transaction engine, within the Middle and Back Office. Trade confirmation and database management are viewed as important, but somewhat less salient as current areas requiring attention in brokerage and banking. In asset management, however, trade confirmation is viewed as equally important, and database management almost as important as the settlement system and the core-processing engine.

Among support applications, disaster recovery is receiving the most attention, followed by automated reconciliation and Straight Through Processing. Central reference data and the central securities database are additional areas of concern. Other important support applications include client access and client relationship management, along with exception processing and application security.

In brokerage, automated reconcilement is of particular concern, whereas banking has more attention on Straight Through Processing and disaster recovery. In asset management, disaster recovery and automated reconcilement are of primary concern, followed by Straight Through Processing and client relationship management.

Securities Technology Spending Patterns: Growth Areas within a Constrained Budget

The primary focus of securities technology spending is on an array of activities and applications in support of Straight Through Processing, evolving towards the more broadly defined Securities Processing Automation (SPA). The companion theme is disaster recovery, followed by client relationship management and client connectivity.

The STP/SPA focus encompasses an array of activities, which include:

- Improving order management and trade management in the Front Office
- Strengthening the clearance and settlement system
- Addressing concerns with regard to central securities data and reference data management
- Improving internal and external connectivity and communications
- Cleaning up the applications architecture through application consolidation and messaging/middleware
- Capitalizing on the opportunity represented by the internet, including browser based applications and corporate portal development and expansion

With regard to spending, overall budget increases are generally modest, within the single digit range (under 10%). Even within specific areas of concern, most increases are modest and incremental and will likely remain so until there is a recovery in the economy and financial markets.

Nevertheless, the directional signals reflect a sharpening focus on how to achieve improved automation of securities processes from the Front Office through the Back Office. Efforts will be characterized by incremental investment more than dramatic breakthroughs, with most firms increasing spending, even in priority areas, by limited amounts – more typically by single- or low double-digit percent increases than through blockbuster investments.

Given the high level of attention on securities process automation, security, improved client relationship management and market connectivity, and the more modest increments to investment in these areas, the picture is one of responding to a system under stress with limited, interim solutions.

This stress is likely to play out in two ways over the coming months and years: First, modest accelerations in spending as market conditions improve, and second, more dramatic and cost-reducing solutions over the intermediate time frame.

One such solution that is increasing in importance, and is likely to accelerate further over coming years, is the outsourcing option. Outsourcing is viewed as an important but often as a secondary alternative across a number of applications in each sector of the securities industry. At present, it is a fallback position for more firms than a preferred option. This should evolve over time into a more economic solution to the cost pressures associated with the maintenance and development of securities processing infrastructure.

Detailed Findings: Securities Technology - Market Themes

The principal focus of securities technology spending is on Straight Through Processing (STP), which is expanding to encompass Securities Process Automation (SPA). In the post-T+1, post GSTPA world, each firm is defining its individual priorities with the objectives of reducing cost, reducing risk, and increasing accuracy by automating specific elements of the process.

In addition to STP/SPA, and in support of that underlying development, there is an array of interdependent themes that are governing market priorities as well as spending patterns. In this section, the set of themes that are driving securities market technology are described.

Disaster recovery is the other pressing theme: In the post 9/11 world, both industry participants and industry regulators are examining where the exposures are, what backup capabilities are required and moving to ensure these are addressed in a reasonable and timely fashion.

The third major theme is improving client access and client relationship management. Institutional and individual investors drive and determine the requirements of the broker-dealers, who in turn collectively drive and determine the requirements of the custodial banks and the industry utilities. At each stage of the value chain, the motivation is to provide a technology platform that supports the client's requirements and provides easy access to the information the client requires.

The fourth major theme is connectivity and communications. Connectivity is required both externally, to link to clients, service providers and counter-parties, and internally, to link related applications across geographies. This connectivity is required to achieve Straight Through Processing, let alone more compete realization of securities process automation. To achieve SPA, there must ultimately be a high degree of interoperability throughout the industry, which in turn requires standardization of messaging protocols (such as FIX and FIXML).

The fifth major theme is data management. The promise of securities process automation cannot be achieved without reference data - in particular, the securities reference data - which is accurate and consistent throughout the enterprise. This requires the combination of a well-defined and yet flexible data model, implemented through a central securities database, which is accurate and updated on a (near) real time basis. This central securities database must then support the processing of the transaction as it moves through its life cycle.

The sixth major theme is achieving efficiencies through automation of individual activities and processes. This includes automating such activities as reconcilement, and corporate actions, and minimizing the effort associated with exception processing. Workflow management tools will serve to integrate these activities, and help to achieve additional economies and reduce risk by monitoring the status of individual transactions within the system.

The seventh major theme is capitalizing on the technologies of the web, including web browsers and corporate portals. In contrast to the mania of a couple of years ago, however, this is viewed more as a cost saving - and value adding - tactic, which serves both short-term and longer-term objectives than a strategy that is justified in its own right.

Over time, these web-related technologies will become a defining influence on how certain activities are conducted and how certain applications are developed because of multiple efficiencies:

- Efficiencies in application development
- Efficiencies in application maintenance
- Efficiencies in the dissemination of information, which leads to
- Efficiencies in supporting, training and developing the operating team within the organization

Industry Issues: Survey Data

The importance of these issues receives validation in survey responses from industry participants in brokerage, banking and asset management. Respondents indicated which issues are of high importance, medium importance or low importance. (The weighted survey response on issue importance was based on 3 points for a response of high importance, 2 points for medium importance, and 1 point for low importance.)

The issues identified as most important are presented in Figures 4 and 5. The chart provides two measures: The weighted average importance of each issue, and the percentage of respondents identifying the issue as being of 'high importance.'

The most highly rated issues are Front Office and Middle and Back Office systems, along with Straight Through Processing and systems security. Related themes that are components of achieving securities processing automation were next most heavily weighted: reference data and database management, communications capabilities (especially external communications) and workflow management.

	FRONT OFFICE SYSTEMS	CRM-CUSTOMER RELATIONSHIP MANAGEMENT	MIDDLE AND BACK OFFICE SYSTEMS	STRAIGHT THROUGH PROCESSING	REFERENCE DATA MANAGEMENT	INTERNAL COMMUNICATIONS	EXTERNAL COMMUNICATIONS	DATA BASE MANAGEMENT
Weight	2.74	2.32	2.65	2.62	2.40	1.97	2.22	2.25
% Highly Important	75%	38%	65%	64%	46%	18%	39%	39%

Figure 4 - Issues in Securities Technology (1)

Other issues identified as important include client relationship management, as well as architectural issues (systems consolidation and messaging and middleware), and web technologies (web and browser based application as well as corporate portal development).

	MESSAGING & MIDDLEWARE	GROUP DECISION MAKING	SYSTEMS CONSOLIDATION	WEB & BROWSER BASED APPS	CORPORATE PORTAL DEVELOPMENT	SYSTEMS SECURITY	ENTERPRISE RESOURCE PLANNING	WORKFLOW MANAGEMENT
Weight	2.26	1.71	2.26	2.28	1.95	2.62	1.83	2.27
% Highly Important	41%	11%	41%	40%	21%	64%	9%	41%

Figure 5 - Issues in Securities Technology (2)

Critical Industry Themes and Trends: Survey Response

Survey respondents identified which themes and trends would most impact the securities industry this year. For each theme, the survey response is characterized by two values: the importance 'weight', and the percentage of respondents finding the theme important.

The importance 'weight' is the weighted average response, where the weights are 3 points for a 'critical area,' 2 points for a 'very important' factor, and 1 point for a 'moderately important' factor. No points are awarded for factors that are deemed 'somewhat important' or 'not important.' The total points received by each factor are then divided by the number of respondents to that issue.

The '% Important' value is simply the percentage of respondents who rated the factor as either a critical area, very important, or moderately important. The importance of key industry themes is summarized in Figure 6.

Industry Response: Survey Findings

Overall, the themes identified as most important were Disaster Recovery and Straight Through Processing (STP). Disaster Recovery received a weight of (2.17), with 100% of respondents identifying it as important. Disaster Recovery is critical in the near-term, as the industry responds to the events of 9/11, and the potential for future events.

The other major factor, and the factor reflected most broadly throughout the survey, was Straight Through Processing. STP received a weight of (2.12), which 95% of respondents deemed an important theme.

	EXCEPTION PROCESSING	CONSOLIDATION	CYBER TERRORISM	EXTERNAL CONNECTIVITY	INTERNAL CONNECTIVITY	INTERNET	OUTSOURCING	STP	DISASTER RECOVERY	LEGAL / REGULATORY REPORTING
Weight	1.98	1.80	1.54	1.92	1.90	1.36	1.53	2.12	2.17	1.72
% Important	100%	86%	86%	100%	95%	86%	86%	95%	100%	95%

Figure 6 – Industry Themes

Factors identified as being of next highest importance are external and internal connectivity, with weights of about (1.90), which were rated important by 100% and 95% of participants, respectively. Exception processing and consolidation of applications also received high weightings.

Legal regulatory reporting, outsourcing, cyber-terrorism and the Internet received somewhat lower weightings. With values between (1.72) and (1.36), these factors are deemed by most participants to be either moderately important or very important, but somewhat lower on the list of priorities than the factors identified above.

This general pattern was reflected across industry segments of brokerage, banking and asset management with relatively minor variations. All segments rated STP and Disaster Recovery as the principal areas to address, although for brokerage and asset management, Disaster Recovery received a slightly higher weighting than STP. In banking, STP was the principal concern.

Exception processing and connectivity were the next most important factors across the board. Banking and brokerage were both particularly concerned with regard to exception processing, and brokerage was almost equally concerned with legal-regulatory reporting. Brokerage reported a somewhat higher level of concern with regard to both cyber-terrorism and the Internet than the other sectors, whereas banking and asset management showed a somewhat higher level of interest in outsourcing than brokerage.

Front Office Applications

The Front Office applications that are receiving the most attention are trade management and order management. These were rated, on average, to be very important, with between 88% and 98% of respondents identifying them as important areas to address. Trade reporting and order routing followed closely in importance with more than five out of six respondents identifying each area as important.

	Indications (IOI)	Order Management (OMS)	Order Routing	Trade Mgmt	Trade Reporting	Portfolio Mgmt	Attribution Systems	Accounting Systems	Connectivity
Weight	1.27	2.17	1.93	2.27	2.21	1.67	0.99	1.81	1.55
% Important	78%	88%	84%	98%	98%	82%	74%	93%	87%

Figure 7 – Front Office Applications

Portfolio management and accounting systems are additional areas deemed important by participants. The focus on portfolio management ties closely to the increased emphasis on asset accumulation across all sectors of the industry.

The implication is that respondents across the board believe there is considerable work to do on Front Office systems. Indeed, by one measure, as many as three out of four deemed Front Office systems a 'critical area,' and the area within the firm which requires the most attention and investment. This focus on the Front Office can be traced to a number of factors:

- Emphasis on protecting and strengthening the Front Office as the revenue generating part of the business

- Need to provide for both efficient processing of trades including the need to achieve 'best execution'

- Desire to provide automation at the Front-end which can simultaneously facilitate client access and reduce the time and effort required to support the client

This applies differently to large block transactions that must be actively managed, as distinguished from smaller, high volume transactions that must be automated.

Across sectors, the focus on the Front Office is most pronounced in the brokerage industry; due in large measure to the combined pressures associated with the extended bear market and reduced trading volumes. In brokerage, trade reporting is viewed as important as trade management, due in large measure to the increased attention on regulatory scrutiny within the industry. Connectivity and indications of interest (IOI) likewise receive greater attention within brokerage, reflecting its role as an intermediary pressured to increase trade volumes and the ease of trading, while reducing the cost of processing transactions.

Asset managers are expressing more concern and attention on their Front Office activities than the banking sector, with order routing, trade management, connectivity, portfolio management and accounting systems receiving more attention than for their banking counterparts. By contrast, banking shows more attention on order management, and less attention on order routing, and shows less concern with regard to Front Office connectivity than the other sectors.

Core Processing Applications

The core processing applications are almost universally viewed as being very important, both across applications and across sectors. Among these applications, clearance and settlement and the core transaction-processing engine are receiving the most attention. Database management is likewise viewed as highly importance, with trade confirmation following closely behind. Each of these factors was deemed to be important by more than 95% of respondents.

	CORE PROC ENGINE	TRADE CONFIRM (ETC)	CLEAR & SETTLEMENT	DATABASE MGMT
Weight	2.33	2.06	2.39	2.14
% Important	96%	97%	98%	97%

Figure 8 – Core Processing Applications

Brokerage and banking have particular attention on the clearance and settlement process, as well as the core transaction-processing engine. Asset management has more attention, relatively speaking, on the trade confirmation process. Understandably, electronic trade confirmation is also an important focus for brokerage. Database management is a particular concern in brokerage, although banking also rates database management as highly important.

Primary Support Applications

Among the support applications that are receiving particular attention are Straight Through Processing, disaster recovery, and automated reconcilement. As indicated above, although disaster recovery received a marginally higher weight than Straight Through Processing, this will likely prove a specific, near-term focus, whereas a large group of related applications reflect the ongoing and sustained attention directed at securities process automation.

	Auto Reconcilement	Customer Relationship Management	Data Base Mgmt	Disaster Recovery	Exception Processing	Straight Through Processing (STP)
Weight	2.22	2.12	1.95	2.26	2.05	2.22
% Important	98%	97%	97%	97%	96%	99%

Figure 9 – Primary Support Applications

Automated reconcilement and exception processing are good examples of the several applications receiving increased attention, which reflect the overall focus on securities process automation. Client relationship management is an additional major focus, which should receive sustained and growing attention over the next few years.

Straight Through Processing and disaster recovery are of particular concern to both banking and brokerage, while brokers are particularly focused on the reconcilement issue.

Although asset managers rate these application areas as somewhat less critical to their operations, they nonetheless view them as very important. Disaster recovery and automated reconcilement are receiving particular attention, followed by Straight Through Processing and client relationship management.

Securities Technology Spending Patterns: Detailed Findings

Spending patterns on securities technology mirrors the pattern of concerns the industry expressed, as summarized above. The move towards securities process automation is reflected in the areas of spending within the Front Office, across the core transaction processing applications and among the set of support applications essential to securities operations.

Front Office Spending

Within the Front Office, roughly half of respondents indicated that spending would increase on trade management and trade reporting, with spending by these respondents rising on average by between 8% and 13% (See Figure 10). Note that the left scale indicates % change in spending by those increasing or reducing their budgets, while the right hand scale indicates the overall percent change in spending within that application area.) Spending on order management and order routing is projected to increase by almost half of respondents, with increases again in the low double-digit percentages (12%-13%).

	INDICATIONS OF INTEREST	ORDER MGMT SYSTEMS	ORDER ROUTING SYSTEMS	TRADE MGMT SYSTEMS	TRADE REPORTING SYSTEMS	PORTFOLIO MGMT SYSTEMS	ATTRIBUTION SYSTEMS	ACCOUNTING SYSTEMS	ATS CONNECTIVITY
Average % Rise	10%	13%	12%	13%	8%	14%	11%	11%	10%
Average % Fall	-12%	-11%	-12%	-11%	-11%	-8%	-9%	-9%	-13%
Average % Chg	-1%	4%	3%	4%	2%	3%	0%	1%	2%

Figure 10 – Front Office Spending

Portfolio management and connectivity to alternative trading systems are two other areas showing growth, with roughly two out of five respondents increasing spending, on average by percentages of 10-14%.

Accounting systems and indications of interest are areas where spending appears to be flattening, with little or no growth anticipated in these areas overall.

Across the market, however, the primary challenge for technology firms will be to identify those pockets of growth, by identifying those firms that are at the Front-end of the investment cycle in upgrading these applications. While growth in Front Office spending overall will be modest, at least one-quarter to one-third of respondents - and as many as one-half - indicate that spending on specific Front Office applications is expected to increase.

Core Process Spending

Within the core process applications, spending is projected to increase most for clearance and settlement systems, with almost three out of five respondents indicating that spending will increase by double-digit percentages on average (See Figure 11). The core transaction-processing engine is followed closely by electronic trade confirmation processing, with roughly half of respondents indicating an increase in each area, with the typical increase of the order of 10% in each case. Database management systems show a slightly smaller proportion of respondents indicating an increase in spending - roughly two out of five - with the spending increase again of the order of 10%.

As for the Front Office, the challenge is to identify those firms that are increasing their spending in each area. Identifying those prospects early in their investment cycle is equally important in order to respond to the needs of these market participants. However, the rather dramatic proportion of firms which are increasing spending in at least a couple of these areas, if not all of them, reflects the magnitude and breadth of the need to upgrade the core processing systems within the industry.

	CORE PROCESSING ENGINE	ELECTRONIC TRADE CONFIRM SYSTEMS	CLEARANCE & SETTLEMENT SYSTEMS	DATABASE MGMT SYSTEMS
Average % Rise	11%	11%	12%	10%
Average % Fall	-11%	-9%	-13%	-9%
Average % Chg	4%	4%	6%	3%

Figure 11 – Core Process Spending

Support Application Spending

Across the broad array of support applications, Straight Through Processing and disaster recovery are among the leaders both with regard to the proportions of respondents planning increased spending, and the overall spending increase reported for these applications (See Figures 12 and 13). Close to three out of four respondents report increased spending in both areas, with average spending increases of 12% to 15%, with the result that spending in these areas is projected to grow at or near double-digit rates.

	AVERAGE % RISE	AVERAGE % FALL	AVERAGE % CHANGE
Automated Reconcilement	11%	-8%	5%
Investigations	10%	-14%	0%
Central Reference Data	15%	-11%	4%
Central Securities Database	14%	-11%	4%
Corporate Portal Development	12%	-10%	3%
Customer Access	10%	-13%	3%

	Average % Rise	Average % Fall	Average % Change
Customer Relationship Management	15%	-12%	5%
Data Base Management	9%	-11%	2%
Disaster Recovery	12%	-13%	8%
Exception Processing	13%	-10%	5%
Enterprise Resource Planning	6%	-10%	-1%
External Communications	9%	-14%	2%
External Connectivity	9%	-13%	3%

Figure 12 – Support Applications (1)

There are a set of related application areas, including external & internal connectivity, central reference data management, exception processing, automated reconciliation and workflow management, all of which are building blocks of more complete automation of the securities processing chain of activities. Each of these are areas where spending is increasing, with one-third to one-half of respondents reporting planned increases which average between ten and fifteen percent. Overall spending growth in these areas is more modest - typically in the mid-single digit percentages - which reflects the overall constraint on technology spending in the current market environment.

While the individual initiatives may appear fragmented in the near term, in that they are addressing areas where human intervention is more pervasive and the trade processing chain is either inefficient or broken, the collective impact will be gradually evolving toward a new application architecture, and ultimately a new paradigm with regard to securities processing.

In the near term securities applications are largely particular, ad hoc, boot-strapped solutions to common securities processing requirements. Over time, this will evolve to a structure in which first communications will become more homogeneous, by adopting common communications protocols and increased use of industry utilities to address common requirements, and then applications solutions will become fewer, operating on fewer discrete platforms, with greater leverage in applications maintenance and development resulting from the larger use of shared approaches in solving common challenges.

At present, this shows up in the relatively modest growth in web and browser based applications, and the similarly modest growth in corporate portal development. The investment in messaging and middleware is a related trend, which is noteworthy for the large number expanding expenditure (almost three out of five) and the relatively modest amounts short-term expenditure is growing (just under 10%). At the same time, a markedly smaller number of participants (about one out of eight) report a significant reduction in spending, averaging 20%. As a consequence, spending in this area is growing, albeit at a modest rate. The intermediate-term should see some acceleration in spending, assuming the near-term investments prove productive.

Client relationship management and client access are areas of sustained growth despite the economic environment, and areas in which not quite half of respondents report expenditures will grow. Almost as many respondents indicate spending will be flat, while about one out of six sees spending falling from existing levels.

	AVERAGE % RISE	AVERAGE % FALL	AVERAGE % CHANGE
Group Decision Making	5%	-14%	-4%
Historical Data or Archives	10%	-10%	0%
Internal Communications	6%	-7%	1%
Internal Connectivity	7%	-7%	2%
Messaging & Middleware	8%	-20%	2%
Professional Productivity	9%	-12%	0%
Reference Data Management	13%	-11%	4%
Straight Through Processing	15%	-15%	10%
Consolidation of Applications	14%	-13%	7%
Application Security	13%	-10%	6%
Web/Browser Based Applications	14%	-13%	6%
Workflow Management	14%	-8%	6%

Figure 13 – Support Applications (2)

Conclusion

There is a direct relationship between the areas where management shows the most concern regarding securities processing, and where spending is continuing to grow, even in this challenging economic environment. In no small measure, the weakness in the securities markets and the related decline in transaction volumes, along with the outside threats to the system, are dictating where and how management is allocating its constrained technology budget.

Apart from the immediate pressure to address concerns with regard to disaster recovery and security, the focus of attention is on the nexus of applications that support Straight Through Processing and securities process automation. At present, the increases in spending on an array of applications addressing front, middle and Back Office processing will incrementally increase efficiencies, while simultaneously adding value to participants, and will ultimately support the evolution to a highly automated process across the full span of activities required to complete securities transactions.

These activities, which range across the Front, Middle and Back Office, will enhance the efficiency of trades from indications of interest through clearance and settlement, as well as maintaining and servicing client and principal positions, and as well as addressing risk and security concerns, in the pre- and post-trade environment.

About the Author

Peter Patch is Director of Research at The Summit Group. Mr. Patch has more than 20 years experience developing market strategies for established and emerging firms, with a focus on financial services, technology, consumer products and retail trade. His geographic experience has included extensive work in Europe, Latin America and Southeast Asia, as well as the United States and Canada.

Areas of particular interest include accelerating business development in such markets as global securities services, financial technology, information-intensive industries and the outsourcing of systems infrastructure. He has done extensive research on the role of technology in financial services, retail credit, and corporate banking. He is the author of numerous articles and a frequent speaker on the relationship between corporate strategy, business development, and technology policy.

Mr. Patch received his B.A. with honors in Applied Mathematics and Economics from Harvard University, and his M.B.A. from Stanford University, where he was a Miller Scholar. He completed the course requirements with distinction for the Ph.D. in Business Economics at Harvard University. He has been an instructor and speaker on business strategy and economic analysis at Harvard University and Northeastern University.

Mr. Patch has served as lead instructor at numerous executive development programs in the United States and around the world. For example, he conducted programs in marketing and strategic management sponsored by the European Bank for Reconstruction and Development, as well as for major global corporations, for executives from the United States, Eastern Europe, Latin America and Asia Pacific.

Peter.Patch@tsgc.com

CHAPTER III - VISION OF THE FUTURE

By Hal McIntyre, Managing Partner, The Summit Group

Securities Industry Trends

STP is an inevitable change since it is being driven by a number of forces in the industry, such as trends, events and business drivers.

There are several categories of trends, such as worldwide trends, industry trends, and technology trends that are causing the need for Straight Through Processing, and there are a number of industry events that are making it a necessity.

Based upon research projects that have been performed by The Summit Group, we believe that there are several worldwide trends that are driving the securities industry. These trends are the result of the recommendations made by international groups such as the Group of Thirty, as well as fundamental economic, political, and social changes that are occurring worldwide.

There are six basic trends that affect every participant:

- Commoditization of the basic securities processing services
- Changes in client requirements
- Increased settlement efficiency in each country
- Lower margins on the basic services
- Securitization of assets
- Shifting sources of cross-border investment

Many firms are reacting to these basic trends by reevaluating their position and role in the industry. This is causing:

- Shifting alliances in the infrastructure
- Increased competition
- Increasing disintermediation of the traditional players

Finally, as firms develop their on-going strategies, they have to consider three other trends in order to develop their implementation plans:

- Shifting regulatory and geopolitical environments
- Increase in the use of standards
- Availability of new technologies

These trends are creating new opportunities for securities processing intermediaries, and will also create numerous potential pitfalls. If intermediaries fail to adapt to the new realities of the securities business and do not solve their clients' problems, disintermediation will be hastened, not postponed.

To avoid disintermediation, the last two fundamental trends (Standards and Technology) support the need for services message standards that make paperless processing possible and for the technology to implement this concept.

These trends are creating new opportunities for securities processing intermediaries, and will also create numerous potential pitfalls. If intermediaries fail to adapt to the new realities of the securities business and do not solve their clients' problems, disintermediation will be hastened, not postponed.

Each of these trends has some specific implications.

Commoditization

Basic services in the securities processing industry are becoming commodities:

- The concept of commoditization changes as mechanical control is replaced by computer control
- Firms are now moving from a production orientation ("any color so long as it is black") to customization for each client, using a common base, and towards one-to-one customized contact for clients
- As the overall market becomes more complex, clients will look for additional simplicity and efficiency, which will probably be made possible by complex technology

Client Needs

Clients' needs are changing rapidly:

- Clients' quality and service requirements are steadily increasing
- All trends require cost leadership (but other firms will soon match the leader)
- Ownership of the client becomes critical in mature markets
- The clients' focus on risk is increasing, but it is uninformed
- Clients expect price reductions, and need revenue/income enhancement

Disintermediation

Traditional participants in the securities processing industry are trying to disintermediate each other and are at risk of being by-passed by new players:

- Participant's reactions to change in the infrastructure and the technology are fairly predictable
- As markets mature, every participant in the value chain looks to disintermediate the other players

Efficiency

Increasing efficiency in settlement processing in emerging countries, and in all facets of the industry:

- Countries will continue to mature and become more efficient, but compliance with industry-initiated recommendations will continue

slowly
- Greater efficiency is a mixed blessing for clients, since the ultimate in efficiency would reduce the role of banks and brokers
- Market cycles move from infancy to maturity with a predictable set of mid-life changes, and different countries are at different stages of their life cycle
- SWIFT, FIX and other standards help to accelerate this evolution, but market inertia and parochial resistance slow it down
- The pressure for low unit costs in a mature market will drive the largest institutions to push for utility processing and depository linkages, which could ultimately be self destructive

Competition

Competition is increasing from the traditional players who wish to remain profitable, or increase their profitability, and from new entrants:
- There are limited opportunities to differentiate today, and future differentiation will be even more difficult
- Existing global custody competitors are reconsidering their options
- New categories of non-traditional competitors are gaining momentum, and threatening to take market share

Lower Margins

Profit margins are coming under increasing pressure throughout the securities processing industry:
- Plain custody is increasingly a low margin business; but, the size of the market makes it remain interesting
- Some institutional market characteristics make it difficult for new global custodians to enter the market
- There is a potential to significantly leverage costs by increasing volume, and firms throughout the value chain are striving to reduce costs
- Decimalization has significantly affected brokers' margins
- Automation, personalization and connectivity, which force cost competition and investment, have become expected by clients
- To prepare for the unattained critical mass strategies, firms have build significant capacity that now exceeds their needs.

Securitization

Assets are becoming increasingly securitized and internationalized:
- Risk management has led to securitization, which is creating new buying opportunities and attracting investors
- There is an increasing internationalization of business by a small number of firms

- Financial engineering will continue to create new types of instruments, and the global demand for derivative continues to grow
- Increases in the complexity of the available instruments cause institutional and individual investors to look for professional money management; but, there are a limited number of successful cross-border and derivative advisors
- Development of international instruments will follow the US's pattern of maturation

Shifting Alliances

Alliances are shifting throughout the securities processing industry

- Conflicts over infrastructure leadership are increasing
- Local and central depositories are developing new linkages
- Many large and small participants are examining potential alliances

Sources of Investment

Sources of investment capital are shifting throughout the industry:

- The total amount invested in pension funds is growing and changing in character, and the sources and uses of pension fund assets will continue to change over the next few years
- Mutual funds continue to grow rapidly, and expand their services
- Private Banks and private trust are growing internationally and rapidly
- Insurance will not grow their international investments rapidly, and will continue to match assets and liabilities in local markets

Standards

Increasing use of standards throughout the securities processing industry:

- New standards are creating opportunities for new centers of power
- SWIFT is the message standard adopted by banks and investment managers worldwide for post-trade processing
- FIX is the message standard adopted by brokers and investment managers worldwide for pre-trade and trade processing
- SWIFT and FIX will continue to evolve towards each other through the increasing use of ISO 15022 and XML

Technology

Application of technology is fundamental to the securities processing industry:

- The use of technology is constantly improving in all areas
- Improvements in technology make time compression possible
- Client demand for service delivery automation continues to increase, and technology allows high tech to provide high touch service

- The increasing focus on the client causes technology goals to shift
- Improvement in the underlying technologies increases the potential uses of technology
- New technologies will encourage firms to modify their organizations
- This organizational shift should make firms more agile unless they remain locked into legacy applications
- There are several fundamental paradigm shifts in technology that could affect other clients. Because of these shifts, firms establish technology strategies that support their business plans.
- Strategies based solely on technology will not have a long-term advantage
- Technology often stimulates the infrastructure to change in unexpected ways
- Constant advances in technology favor the new entrant, since the entrenched firms have legacy systems which prevent rapid changes

Regulatory

- Regulations are changing slowly in developed countries due to operational and cultural barriers, while emerging countries are liberalizing faster and becoming magnets for investment
- There are numerous barriers to entry for cross-border processors; but, due to the obvious revenue potential, more firms are finding new ways to enter the marketplace

Business Drivers

As we work together to define how Straight Through Processing will work in the future, we need to constantly ask ourselves what is driving the movement towards STP, and what do we think the future will be like? The forces that are driving us towards STP are the same ones that shape our businesses on a daily basis. The four classic business drivers are: Client Requirements, Regulations, Technology and Competition.

Client Requirements

Our clients are constantly challenging us to improve our processing services, just as they are challenged within a shifting marketplace. We are all affected by factors such as the shifting sources of capital, shifting investment alternatives, and the need for efficiency and control. There are several major changes in how individuals and institutions invest. In the US, the shift from defined benefit programs to defined contribution continues, the baby boomers are beginning to save, and US Social Security might eventually have some privatized component. Internationally, investment in US securities is preventing inflation despite a significant trade deficit, and the Chinese have become the single largest country investing in US Treasuries.

From an investment perspective, we know that there is a slow, but steady movement towards cross-border investments, and additional instruments are constantly being developed. Our clients know that they need to improve their own processing, and are looking to us to help them become more efficient. And with all of the news in the last few years about serious losses that have resulted from a lack of internal processing controls, our clients are concerned about managing processing and settlement risk more than ever.

Regulations

Our processing today and our plans for the future are seriously affected by the way our industry is regulated. While the worldwide trend is towards less restrictive regulations and a more open market, there will always be many government regulations that we have to consider as we process.

As regulations change in the U.S. and other countries, the need for STP increases. For instance, the changes in government regulations, and in the rules, structure, and customs of the marketplace is, and local politics, will require us to consider improvements in processing that will require more efficiency and less risk.

The Patriot Act and Sarbanes-Oxley establish additional regulations that must be efficiently integrated into existing processes in order to comply without adding excessive costs.

Technology

Everyday brings new technologies for us to consider, and many of them actually offer solutions to our current and future problems. Technology should be bringing us more efficiency, and every new technology opens the door for some new products and services. And those very new products and services stimulate the technology industry to stretch even further to bring us new technologies. The cycle seems endless.

Changes in technology cause us to look for new opportunities to employ that technology and as we continue to employ that technology we see new ways to employ it. Overall the increase in the use of technology supports the industry's drive for efficiency and will require firms to employ technology with one of two major strategies. One is the drive to critical mass, which causes firms to ant to increase their volume. And the other trend is to create processing boutiques that focus on niche opportunities because a small firm with a big idea can affect the industry more so than in the past with technology as the enabler

Competition

Since we are all trying to serve our clients, we are in a state of constant competition. Thinning margins, the threat of disintermediation and the need to differentiate ourselves, has caused us to behave differently towards our competitors than was traditional in the past. Although there are still some traditional animosities, we see a steady stream of mergers and acquisitions, new partnerships and evolving alliances. Today's competitor could be tomorrow's partner, at least for a while.

Vision of the Future

In 1998, The Summit Group evaluated the implications of the trends that are driving the market and established a five-year vision of the future for securities processing. Since that forecast was so prescient, the process was repeated again in 2003 and a summary of our forecast for the next five years is presented here.

Marketing

The volume and complexity of instruments traded in the US markets will continue to grow dramatically as the US economic recovery continues throughout the balance of the decade. The major risk to this period of prosperity is terrorism.

Twenty-four hour markets will increasingly be implemented around the world, with additional non-US firms wanting to actively trade US stocks in their own domestic time zones. Alternative electronic exchanges will challenge the traditional exchanges and NASDAQ, and force major changes in how trading is conducted.

NASDAQ and the NYSE will not merge, but the NYSE will evolve towards NASDAQ's negotiated model and retain limited floor-based auctions.

Utilities such as exchanges, depositories and clearinghouses will increasingly compete in order to remain relevant. Although they are positioning themselves to compete with each other, their primary risk comes from vendors. Vendors will provide new low-cost electronic alternatives that will challenge the dominance of the traditional infrastructure.

Trading days will increase in length; decimalization will continue to reduce trading profits and shorter settlement cycles will increase the pressure on traders.

Firms will increasingly use technology applications such as Client Relationship Management and client portals to provide one-to-one marketing and personalization, which will use high tech solutions to achieve high touch relationships with clients.

Highly automated processes will reduce costs and control risk, but clients will increasingly require customized and individualized solutions that will ultimately require more innovation and automation.

Markets for different instruments in different regions and countries will become increasingly homogenous, and the retail market will act more and more like the institutional market, with the exception of block trades.

Despite slow-downs in Asia, crises in the Middle East and risks in emerging markets, the world economy will continue to move towards deregulation, as capitalism becomes even more pervasive. This will increase competition from traditional as well as non-traditional participants.

Fewer, stronger players will struggle constantly to differentiate themselves but standardized processing will force firms to differentiate in non-traditional ways. A few global mega-players will emerge to dominate the securities processing environment, but their very size will create opportunities for boutique firms seeking niche opportunities.

Processing

Discussions regarding T+1 resumed in 2004 and a shorter settlement cycle will be implemented in the US after another period of discussion and planning, probably in 2007. After T+1 is implemented, fewer process steps will be required to complete transactions due to automation. This will continue the industry's evolution away from clerical staff towards technically proficient people at all levels, who will be in increasingly short supply.

Outsourcing will become essential as firms are forced to focus their best talent and energy on their core competencies in order to compete successfully. The pace of outsourcing will increase as firms realize that non-strategic functions should be removed from the firm.

The traditional operations functions will disappear as settlement cycles are shortened and outsourcing is used. The best people will be refocused into areas such as risk management, technology evolution, client satisfaction, reconciliations, exception processing and new product development.

Firms will continue to oscillate between centralization and decentralization to reduce cost as they realize that there is no optimal solution. Some firms will be moving towards one end of the pendulum's swing while others move towards the other end as firms increasingly understand that they obtain their benefits from the process of managing change and activities such as TSG's Continuous Process Improvement^{TM}, not from any one organizational philosophy.

The increased use of standards, from pre-trade through settlement, will make more connectivity possible and increasingly necessary. Increased connectivity will reduce re-keying of data, increase the use of exception-only processing, and establish the opportunity for outsourcing. Businesses that used to make their best margins from inefficient markets will have to change their product mix in order to survive.

The Internet and Alternative Trading Systems will increase the potential for automated end-to-end connectivity, where the client is the start and the finish of a transaction.

The Internet and other forms of electronic distribution of information to consumers will continue to reduce the need for paper documents, speed up the process, and change the traditional role of brokers in the retail market.

About the Author

The author's biography was included in Chapter I.

CHAPTER IV - STP NOW! DON'T GIVE UP ON IT

By Frederick Stanley, Executive Vice President, Evare LLC

Introduction

Right now, information and link management services provide a workable, cost-effective answer to the STP riddle, because they remove the need for system and process modification and for the adoption of and strict adherence to any particular messaging standard. But after decades of interoperability struggles and years of STP disappointments, the buy-side has abandoned T+1 and the industry has been left searching for the rationale and cost justification for any STP solution. Even though the reasons for adopting an STP strategy have been well documented by the SIA and recently by the Tower Group, and the value is widely understood, the cost of interoperability, both internal and external, and the perception of an interminable technology project have brought the industry to an impasse.

Before we examine the current situation, let's review some of the history of interoperability, from both the business and the technical perspectives. An understanding of the ups and downs of how we got to where we are today may shed some light on the current reluctance to move forward with STP. Then we'll explain how information and link management services can get the industry to STP now.

The Emergence of Business Automation

As an institutional bookkeeper for Bache, Merrill, and Wainwright in the 1960s, I spent a lot of time managing multiple copies of forms, especially trade tickets and confirms. I used copies of forms for my tickler file of settlement day checks, for dividend announcements and other corporate action reviews, and for other activities throughout the Purchase and Sale (P&S) functions. I required the same data for internal operations and as the basis for matching, researching DKs, and ultimately posting to ledgers the results of working with counterparties on each item. Using copies of the same form was the best way to get to interoperability at that time, mainly because the data for everyone was from the same source. In that era, the major problems everyone in the Back Office dealt with were trying to read the form copies and making errors in ledger entries.

Automation changed things by eliminating most of the manual errors. The first automated functions that I implemented were at the Boston Stock Exchange, where we developed assembler functions to track dividends on the early mainframes (IBM S360). Automation removed errors from our internal process, and we wanted our partners to use the same technology in order to reduce problems between companies. So in the interest of spreading interoperability, we shared these functions and others with the Philadelphia and Toronto Exchanges.

Then came the next big thing. At the NASD/NCC in the early 1970s, we first had the dream of a "National Electronic Stock Exchange," based on the

NASDAQ 3-tiered system and on PCE's net-by-net system, soon to become the CNS or Continuous Net Settlement System. This scheme would eventually eliminate most of the process problems between counterparty brokers and market makers for domestic Equities, but it took 20 years and a lot of bumps along the way - fear of losing the trading floor, the sale of NCC to Bradford and finally to DTC where it fulfilled its mission, so that today, NASDAQ is opting for exchange status and iNet is getting market share on SuperMontage.

Our processing problems in the domestic equity market have been significantly reduced, and our National Electronic Stock Exchange has been realized with the 'National Market.' Unfortunately, other instruments have not fared so well. For example, Fixed Income departmental budgets were notoriously ignored during the 'over exuberant' equity and IPO love fest of the 1990s. And for some years now our attention has focused on global clearing and settlement, even after the death of GSTPA. Eventually, the move will be to maximize global liquidity and to create a Global Electronic Stock Exchange, linking in all local exchanges, dealers, and market makers - an ECN of ECNs will be implemented by necessity.

We need to work towards including all asset classes in this glowing future, and by bringing STP to those operations, achieve the same gains, across all borders and boundaries and at much lower costs.

Technical Progress Towards Interoperability

From the technological perspective, the early computing model reflected a fully integrated process and data integrity based on serialized access to shared states. Within the computer, everything was interoperable. Outside the computer, we struggled with forms and reports.

The solution in the 1970s was homogeneous (single vendor) technology. Everything *kind of* worked together (at least, we were told, it would in the next release). However, with the growth of the relational database model we saw the first real extensible standard become adopted by the industry. Relational technology was designed to protect the integrity of data. This meant that data could be distributed without risk. Hierarchical and networked data structures worked faster and more efficiently, but the relational model was designed to support the real business needs of the 1960s and 1970s - ad hoc queries and business reports.

The relational model took 10 years to develop and 10 years to adopt. Competition meant that one database's SQL was not portable to another's. Regardless, the 1980s saw the growth of data-driven system designs, culminating in the notion of Objects, defined as self-sufficient units of process. With these capabilities as a foundation, the OMG promulgated the CORBA standard, and it seemed we were close to interoperability on an application interface level between companies, although networks and security lagged behind.

In parallel, from the 1970s on, distributed departmental processors took hold for accounting and analytics, and the dream of open systems that could talk to each other, share information and work, was born. However, the first UNIX implementation quickly generated 16 different UNIX operating systems from a wide variety of vendors. After 10 years or so, well into the 1980s, computing (with the exception of Microsoft) had accepted the Open Systems Foundation model, supported by relational databases. As we moved into the 1990s, we began to see actual implementations of Open Systems standards.

In the 1990s, we also saw the growth of process-driven design, the rediscovery of the flowchart and workflow, and a major effort to create better, business-oriented systems that were more responsive to change. Even the mainframes began to see the value of open systems standards.

Then the Internet emerged. As a result, the first consolidation around a network standard, TCP/IP based on the OSI layers of the open systems standard, finally began taking hold. By the end of the 1990s, as open systems began to communicate via the Internet, they became web and application servers. In the last few years, process-driven design found Web Services for systems integration and browsers as the ubiquitous human interface, adding standards as functionality increased. Now real standards are finally emerging on the technology front, and once stabilized, should provide a loosely coupled model that will adapt more readily and cost-effectively to technological change, while being able to be more agile in support of business needs. Unfortunately, the combination of financial services business requirements and technology has not solved the interoperability problem.

STP Disappointments

STP is the dream, first really articulated in the 1990s, of risk reduction via elimination of human handling in the post-trade process, primarily for cross-border trades where the DK rate was 10-12% and rising. A whole slew of STP 'solutions' have been floated, attempted, and ultimately failed to deliver.

Let's begin with messaging standards. EAI (Enterprise Application Integration) and messaging vendors, who needed common APIs to be useful and competitive, and industry groups trying to make utilities available for at least DTCC-eligible securities to all of their member firms, drove the adoption of internal and external standards to support STP, especially counterparty communications for central trade matching and settlement. And many companies have relied on those standards - only to find that they are not, in fact, standard. For example, I gather that some 70% of FIX users are on version 1.1, while the standard has moved on to version 4.4, with its support of allocations and Derivatives. A golden horde of consultants and IT folks may sync every system in a firm over time (and over budget), but they cannot possibly sync all clients', counterparties', and suppliers' systems as well. Therefore, in even the best scenario, STP stops at the door because it is virtually impossible to have all systems, internal and external, on the same version of a standard, or even on a standard at all, at the same time. As a result, many firms have found it easier to standardize on the lowest common denominator, such as FAX and comma-delimited files, especially for Fixed Income and Derivatives processing. These tools have worked fine for a long time at low volumes, but don't scale well, and certainly create difficulties for counterparties using more sophisticated methods.

Real standards historically take many years to adopt because their business benefit must be proven empirically, not simply intuitively. Even TCP/IP, with an obvious business benefit, took many years to be adopted, especially on the mainframe. For the same reason, real standards take years to change as well. IP v.6, with its increased address space and ability to carry voice traffic, has taken many years to adopt because the business benefit hasn't been critical enough to force change. When we run out of Internet addresses, there will be a race to adopt IPv.6. Adoption of data standards has been somewhat easier, due to the business need for common identifiers (CUSIP, ISIN, SEDOL, BIC, etc.). With the additional need for process and transaction descriptors, more complexity was introduced, with SWIFT and FIX becoming New Age trade tickets and confirms. Of course, all of this is at great cost, and fundamentally cannot provide a universal standard.

Integration consultants have attempted to tackle STP from a different angle, by forcing a re-engineering of business processes in support of a collaborative work-oriented design. Some vendors of EAI and work process management systems even sell tools that claim to manage the entire critical path in the trade cycle, from decision support to account reconciliation. They have come closer to the solution by rationalizing data semantics among systems, but process redesign is inevitably followed by major development efforts, as firms struggle to connect their systems in a straight through process, standardize data for all systems of record, and transform all systems to speak the same data language. However, if any changes are required in the source systems, the goal is not much closer. Also, links must still be built to the external environment, and rather than work with custom transformational engines, they tend to depend on standards and defined APIs.

Many companies attempt to implement real-time or store-and-forward schemes, requiring significant modification and re-programming of systems to deal with message handling. For example, TIBCO's Rendezvous typically requires a daemon process running on each server with a business application. The daemon talks to the application through a socket connection. MQSeries requires the application to talk to a Queue Manager. In both cases, the application must be rewritten to handle these communications and new data handling routines. All such hard-wired architectures are vendor-serving, and typically require a development expenditure of years and millions of dollars to automate all critical path functions. Certainly these capabilities have valuable specific uses, but hardwiring business processes from beginning to end is not the best use of these tools.

There is also an inherent assumption that the systems of record themselves are badly designed due to their specific functional concentration (i.e., pipe-stacked asset-class based trading silos), and therefore must be 'improved' so they can embrace generic business functions and communication. In medicine, this type of thinking would eliminate the value of specialists, in favor of general practitioners. Obviously, both generic and specific knowledge are critical at different stages of a process.

In a nutshell, history shows that the problem of interoperability has been major. But lessons have been learned. The advantages of operational efficiency are now much better understood. The value of STP outside the T+1 business driver has been accepted by the industry, for domestic as well as cross-border trades and in all asset classes. Business, like nature, goes with what works. New standards are like mutations that may add positive characteristics favoring adaptation to the environment, or they may not. It is important that standards are only adopted when they work for everyone. This takes time and patience. In the financial services business, change in markets, and regulatory, political, and technology changes drive standards. They are not adopted overnight, and then only when they save money and time, improve business, or reduce risk.

The Right Approach for STP Now

Revamping processes and modifying systems is incredibly complex, time-consuming, and expensive, and ultimately cannot lead to industry-wide STP based on ubiquitous standards. In the near-term, the industry has settled for a practical 80/20 approach, accepting the reality of a split of standard and non-standard counterparty communications, with an eye towards higher adoption rates of technology and semantic/taxonomic standards over the next 10-20 years. *We have a way to go, but giving up the benefits of STP today is unnecessary.*

Contrary to what you may have heard, to take advantage of STP does not require the re-engineering of business processes; nor does it require the abandonment or reprogramming of systems; nor does it require adoption and adherence to a specific messaging standard. In fact, systems, message form or formats, and processes do not have to change at all. A reliable information and link management service will allow the industry to achieve internal STP and to integrate counterparties into processes with the systems, formats, and processes that are already in use.

The solution is to evaluate custom linking engines and work on the links between systems rather than on the systems themselves. Although many firms have attempted this level of integration internally, most have found it too expensive. And even if some firms manage to create EAI internally, most links externally are point-to-point, must be built one at a time, and are a costly management headache.

Link management is the approach taken by Evare and a few other firms, which provide outsourced information and link management services to broker/dealers, asset managers, custodians, and their respective clients. If STP has not been accomplished in-house, then a link service can pull together the distributed internal environment. Externally, a link service can integrate the larger system of counterparties, clients, suppliers, and utilities through the cost-effective reuse of links for everyone. In the long run, the hope is to have the industry step up to the linking issue by creating common utilities as they have done with trade matching and settlement.

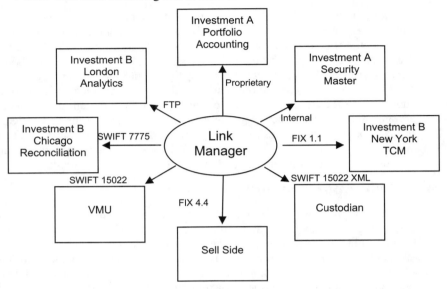

Figure 14 – Creating the STP Distributed System

In this scenario, established transaction processing systems and systems of record, selected on the basis of unique value propositions, do not have to be modified in order to communicate with one another, regardless of the data formats each uses. Rather, the information is transformed in-process from any format to any format, and transmitted from one to one, one to many, many to one, or many to many systems. The information/link management approach works equally well for internal STP and connections to counterparties, including Virtual Matching Engines, Settlement Instruction Databases, and Concentrators/Routers. More importantly, all asset classes can be accommodated in this design.

In all cases, proprietary formats can be transformed to standard formats, and vice versa, on the fly. The transformations are rules-based and state-driven. Concentration and aggregation are performed and managed on a generic level. Traffic is managed as a just-in-time enrichment process. Systems of record at both ends are 'plug and play', doing whatever they do best in a loosely coupled, fault-tolerant, borderless, distributed architecture. Over time, component systems within this environment can be replaced by more effective systems as they become available and business needs require them, creating an adaptable infrastructure that is sensitive to business transformations and that supports the sunset of dysfunctional components and the introduction of new ones.

As an example of how this approach works in the real world, the following diagram of Evare's service reflects the collection of data in multiple formats and from multiple source systems on the left, and then the process within the service that maps, transforms, and aggregates the data into information. This information is then transformed again into a format useful to downstream systems, shown on the right, and delivered via an agreed-upon method/protocol.

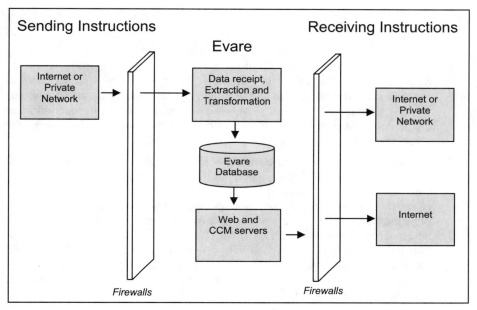

Figure 15 –Evare's Transformation Process

Thus, a link management service such as that provided by Evare may be the most efficient and cost-effective way possible to achieve STP today and evolve systems tomorrow, integrating the whole value chain of unique internal applications, counterparties, liquidity pools, VMUs, and other global information sources and services. Equally important, this type of service allows firms to outsource an expensive, resource-consuming headache so that they can once again focus on their core competencies.

Conclusion

The industry has been reluctant to move forward with STP strategies of late, largely because of a perception that interoperability projects are cost-prohibitive and never really solve the operational risk problem, let alone the core buy-side goal of increasing assets under management. History shows us that innovation and change take time; more recent lessons have taught us that neither standards, process re-design, nor systems re-engineering can provide the ultimate solution the industry hoped for any time soon.

In an ideal world with a ubiquitous global network, data would be motionless at its source, maintaining absolute data integrity. When data is required by a process, a view would be aggregated from all of the systems of record, leaving the source intact and providing the most useful, current, and immediate data in whatever way it is needed. This solves the problem of operational risk, and through increased service offerings, can help with the assets under management issue. Until that time arrives, information management and linking services are the closest approximation, and the best chance of achieving STP.

About the Author

Mr. Stanley is the Executive Vice President of Evare. He has led many successful technology ventures within the financial services industry, in a wide range of leadership roles. In particular, he has extensive experience in enterprise architecture design and development, the transformation of mission-critical systems and business work practices from legacy to process-driven, distributed and web-based architectures, and in global architectures for securities industry services delivery.

Mr. Stanley made his initial contributions to the industry at the Boston Stock Exchange and NASD/NCC, where he was involved in creating the first automations in the financial services industry. As President of several companies in the 1980s, Mr. Stanley led the strategic development and implementation of software products that were the first of their kind in a broad range of industries. In the 1990s, Mr. Stanley ran the Transfer Agency for Putnam Investments, and then, as VP of Application Architecture, transformed the firm's infrastructure from legacy to client server to the web, creating extraordinary efficiencies that helped the organization support a doubling in assets under management.

Most recently, Mr. Stanley provided broad leadership for Computer Sciences Corporation's Financial Services Group. As VP of Securities Industry Architecture, he created industry visibility and capability for CSC by managing the GSTPA, SIP, and ADF bids, by helping provide managed utility services to 40 financial services clients, and through consulting engagements supporting global initiatives with many major Wall Street firms.

ted@evare.com

SECTION II - INDUSTRY SOLUTIONS

Solutions have been identified by vendors, individual firms and from industry-owned organizations. In this section, we will present solutions from several of these leading associations and vendors.

- Chapter VI introduces the Best Practices that have been developed by ISITC and which are being implemented by their members around the world. By establishing a code of best practices, ISITC is helping firms identify what needs to be done and what they can do to process more efficiently.

- In Chapter VIII SWIFT's Simon Cleary describes the various messaging and network solutions that it developed and how it works with industry leaders to support efficient processing between firms. SWIFT feels that there will probably never be a single seamless process flow and the best way to achieve STP is in linking together the various elements to the processing chain through efficient telecommunications.

- In Chapter IX, Jim Leman explains the history of the FIX Protocol and describes how it can be used to support trade processing activities between firms, including the use of FIX for Fixed Income processing.

- Euroclear's Deputy CEO, Ignace Combes, describes how the various markets across Europe are working together to improve cross-border processing.

- In Chapter XI, Craig Dudsak, Clearstream's Director of Relationship Management for the Americas, talks about their product (Vestima) to support mutual fund processing.

All of these authors present the reasons why some solutions are needed and then describe one alternative solution for the problem they defined.

CHAPTER V - ISITC-IOA MARKET PRACTICE GUIDELINES

By Genevy Dimitrion

Introduction

ISITC-IOA has been focused on STP and standards since inception in 1991. This work culminated in the run up to the successful implementation of ISO 15022 standard in November 2002 during which time ISITC-IOA was extremely active defining market practice for the US. Within the ISITC-IOA organization we have several working groups that focus on Market Practice. Additional groups are added based on the industry and membership direction. Each working group has either two or three co–chairs representing the various industry constituents who are responsible for leading the discussions, documenting the market practices and getting industry sign-off.

Across the various market practice working groups a similar work structure is applied. First the business case/need is determined. This is typically done based on member firms recommending a need for standardization in a product/message flow. Meetings are than held both at the quarterly conferences and in between to begin to highlight the workflow and define the data elements for each flow. The data model is than compared to the ISO15022 data dictionary to determine if an existing message can be used. If no message exists than ISITC-IOA will work with ISO's registration authority to have the new message registered. If a message does exist SWIFT will work with SWIFT to identify the enhancements/changes that need to be made to the messages in order to support the business. SWIFT has a very structured maintenance process so changes to messages are very timely. In cases were the business need is immediate the working group will identify short-term recommendations to satisfy the problem, as well as work with SWIFT to determine a long-term solution.

Most important all the work addressed in the working groups is distributed globally through the Securities Market Practice Group (www.smpg.info). This provides ISITC-IOA with the opportunity to align the work being done in the US with the global institutions.

The following section will provide you with the details of each Market Practice working group and the development and standards that have been defined to date. The work done by ISITC-IOA is very detailed with the goal in providing guidance to firms and individuals who are looking to automate their technology infrastructure. All detailed documentation and templates can be found on the website at www.isitc.org within each working group section under the document tab.

Trade Initiation and Confirmation

This group is responsible for highlighting the market practice between the Buy-Side and Sell-Side Firms.

The Trade Initiation and Confirmation Working Group is documenting the US National Market Practice for:

- Orders
- Notices of Execution
- Allocations
- Confirmations
- Net Proceeds
- Status Messages

The group is reviewing all products traded in the US, is protocol neutral, and has representation from various industry participants. This working group is aligned with the SIA Code of Practice Market Practice Group to support a single standard. The initial focus of the group is to address Equity and Fixed Income products. This will ensure that market practice recommendations satisfy all industry participants.

For the above message flows the working group has defined the mandatory, optional and conditional data elements necessary to communicate the information in an automated environment. Each product type supported will have a separate flow created to support the business need. For example, an order for a Fixed Income product will contain different data elements than that of an Equity. For details on the data elements please visit www.isitc.org Market Practice – Trade Initiation and Confirmation Document repository.

Settlements – Securities, Treasury, and Cash

This group is responsible for highlighting the market practice between the:

- Buy-Side and Global Custodian
- Global Custodian and Sub-Custodian / Depository / International Depository
- Sell-Side and Clearing Institution/Depository / International Depository

The Settlement, Treasury and Cash working group is focused on the following:

- **Settlement and Confirmation Messages across all security types** - This includes the MT54x messages.
- **Treasury messages** - This includes the MT304 Third Party Foreign Exchange, MT380 Bank to do Foreign Exchange and MT381Foreign Exchange Confirmation.
- **Cash messages** - This includes the MT202Financial Institution Transfers and MT210 Notice to receive.
- **Status Messages** - This includes the MT548 Status and Processing Advise.
- **Derivatives** – Futures and Options

The working group has been successful in defining US Market Practice for all of the following product types:

Bankers Acceptance	FHA	Strip
Certificate of Deposit	FHLMC	Student Loan
Commercial Paper	FNMA	Time Deposit
CLO	GNMA	TIPS
CMO	Ioette	TNBD
Corporate	Municipal	Warrant
Equity	Private Placement	Zoo

Figure 16 - Security Types Covered by the Settlement, Treasury, and Cash Working Group

The group has also defined the market practice for the following transaction types:

- Pair-off
- Turnarounds
- TBA
- Book Transfers
- Block Trades
- Free Trades
- Repos

For the above message flows the working group has defined the mandatory, optional and conditional data elements necessary to communicate the information in an automated environment. Each product type supported will have a separate flow created to support the business need. For details on the data elements please visit www.isitc.org Market Practice – Settlements, Treasury, and Cash Document repository.

Reconciliation

This group is responsible for highlighting the market practice between the Global Custodian and Buy-Side; Global Custodian and Sub-Custodian/Depository/International Depository; Sell-Side and Clearing Institution/Depository/International Depository.

The Reconciliation Working group is focusing on the review, documentation, and market practice recommendations for the following reconciliation message types:

- **Holdings** – MT535 – Statement of Holdings – Accounting vs. Custody
- **Posted Transactions** – MT536 – Statement of Transactions
- **Pending Transactions** – MT537 – Statement of Pending Transactions
- **Cash Activity** – MT950 – Bank Statement

The working group has aligned itself with the Settlements working group and has been successful in defining US Market Practice for all of the following product types:

Bankers Acceptance	FHA	Strip
Certificate of Deposit	FHLMC	Student Loan
Commercial Paper	FNMA	Time Deposit
CLO	GNMA	TIPS
CMO	Ioette	TNBD
Corporate	Municipal	Warrant
Equity	Private Placement	Zoo

Figure 17 - Security Types Covered by the Reconcilement Working Group

For the above message flows the working group has defined the mandatory, optional and conditional data elements necessary to communicate the information in and automated environment. Each product type supported will have a separate flow created to support the business need. For further details please visit www.isitc.org Market Practice – Reconciliation Document repository.

Corporate Actions

This group is responsible for highlighting the market practice between the Global Custodian and Buy-Side; Global Custodian and Sub-Custodian/Depository/International Depository; Sell-Side and Clearing Institution/Depository/International Depository.

The primary purpose of the group is to review ISO15022 standards and enhance the Corporate Action message content between account owner and account servicer. This involves working on assigned examples of U.S. Corporate Actions, ensuring that data elements for each message have been incorporated and recommending enhancements where key elements are missing. Once required enhancements have been identified, the group provides their feedback of U.S. best practices to SWIFT and the Global SMPG. Additionally, the group offers members the opportunity to discuss issues concerning Corporate Actions in an open forum.

Securities Lending

The Securities Lending Group provides a forum to allow lenders, borrowers and custodians to address standardization of communication for all data flows relating to domestic and international securities lending.

Claims and Compensation

The scope of the Claims and Compensation initiative is losses and claims caused by failed financial transactions (securities trades, payments, foreign exchange, etc.) as a result of errors made by parties to these transactions, or by their agents. The objective is to provide our industry with a set of recommendations and best practices that participants can agree to implement voluntarily with each other in any context (such as the cross-border market) where no other compensation practices prevail by the force of regulation and law.

Reference Data

The objective of the working group is to identify issues and recommend solutions to the challenges created by the same security trading in more than one location and settling in multiple geographically and jurisdictionally dispersed custody locations.

Technology and Standards

The purpose of this group is to:

- Provide insights and technology education, (including current underlying technologies for Straight –Through Processing), to ISITC-IOA members and the financial services industry to better leverage technology.

- Research and recommend methodologies and standards which promote better and more consistent communications among financial services participants.

The current focus is on standards migration and interoperability.

For more information about the ISITC-IOA Market Practice activities, go to either www.smpg.info or www.isitc.org.

CHAPTER VI - SWIFT AND STP

By Simon Cleary, Head of Securities Markets & Business Solutions, SWIFT

Introduction

For SWIFT, Straight Through Processing (STP) is essentially about community – or, more precisely, about bringing together participants and solutions to resolve the fragmentation that so complicates the business of securities processing. Rather than a single seamless flow, we have a series of links that together comprise a long and complex chain, an amalgamation of processes, vendors and standards that have emerged over the past thirty years in a largely uncoordinated manner to address shortcomings in the trading and post-trade environments.

Consequently, the cherished ideal of one overarching industry 'solution' for STP remains but a distant prospect – indeed, such a grand design will in all likelihood never materialize. Rather a global solution for STP is a matter of incremental steps, an evolutionary process of streamlining and automating individual links within the securities processing chain – from trade execution through to settlement – and then ensuring interconnectivity and common standards are in place to allow these different solutions to work together as a seamless whole.

This scenario will require an institution or entity that can help draw together these disparate elements. As an industry cooperative, wholly owned and driven by its members, SWIFT finds itself in a unique position – at once both a messaging infrastructure provider and the registration authority for ISO 15022, we are ideally placed to act as the 'glue' between participants, processes, standards and market practice.

Having been a provider of global connectivity and messaging solutions to the financial industry for three decades, SWIFT is now in the process of implementing a single window approach for the industry in the shape of our secure IP-based network (SIPN), SWIFTNet. The platform offers one point of access to an ever-increasing range of value added business solutions spanning the entire transaction lifecycle.

The development of industry standards on behalf of ISO will remain an essential element of our efforts within the securities markets. SWIFT's priority is to drive standards convergence, but additionally, SWIFT is also active when it comes to efforts to harmonize market practice. Perhaps most significantly, SWIFT is a provider of value added services in the form of key business solutions – we are deepening and broadening our activities, covering more instruments, servicing more clients and supporting more business solutions across the entire transaction lifecycle

The Challenges

While many securities firms have successfully implemented STP internally, when it comes to communicating with their counterparties – be they brokers, custodians, fund managers or the market infrastructures that serve them – the situation remains far from ideal. A lack of automation and standardized connectivity between counterparties leads many firms to resort to insecure electronic mechanisms, fax or telex, which introduce errors and inefficiency and impact negatively on costs and risk.

Messaging is an important element of STP efforts, and SWIFT has played a central role – originally within the payments space and, subsequently, in other areas of the banking and securities businesses – in the proliferation and uptake of messaging standards, most recently with the advent of the new ISO 15022 standard. However, while ISO 15022 is widely acknowledged as a major step forward, it remains only a partial solution. In particular, there remains a significant disconnect between the pre- and post-trade spaces within the equity and Fixed Income markets, with the Front Office-developed FIX protocol on one side, and downstream settlement and custody activity, predominantly employing ISO standards, on the other.

Efforts have already been made to address inefficiencies within these parts of the securities processing chain. These include the original Electronic Trade Confirmation (ETC) efforts during the early 1990s, such as those supported by FMC Net and Thomson OASYS; subsequent central matching initiatives by GSTPA and Omgeo; initiatives driven by the emergence of FIX in the Front Office; and enhanced downstream settlement automation and message standardization, including ISO 7775 and, subsequently, ISO 15022. However, there has been little cohesion between these varied initiatives, and as a result the processing chain remains essentially fragmented.

Meanwhile, a dearth of automation and standardization threatens to derail the expansion of the mutual funds industry in Continental Europe and Asia. As the open architecture model for distribution gains traction, so the need for a scalable, secure and standardized platform for communication becomes more pressing. The additional effort associated with managing orders and reporting on a manual basis is estimated, by SWIFT, to be costing the industry between one and five billion dollars annually in Europe alone. These costs, and the related operational risks, must be aggressively reduced for the investment funds industry in these regions to remain competitive and respond to the growing regulatory focus on operational risk management.

The US-driven initiative to standardize securities markets on a T+1 settlement cycle was seen as an important catalyst to drive forward the global STP effort. It has been suggested in some quarters that the Securities Industry Association's decision to postpone the US T+1 transition has caused many securities firms to put their own STP initiatives on the back burner.

The reality is that, T+1 or no T+1, STP must be a priority – without investment in wider STP solutions, firms will be more expensive and will bear more risk than their peers, and, hence, will struggle to stay competitive. Moreover, individual institutions will find themselves facing capacity issues once global markets rebound, which could have a serious knock-on effect on the industry as a whole. If firms do not begin to implement STP solutions now, the chances are that they will find themselves unable to catch up in the future. Darwinism, red in tooth and claw, is alive and well in the securities industry, and, going forward, only those who adapt will survive.

The depressed state of global capital markets over the past two years has hit securities firms hard, and, as a result, a robust business case for new initiatives, demonstrating a clear value proposition, is now imperative if institutions are to be persuaded to invest the necessary time and resources. Furthermore, such business cases have to demonstrate a short-term return on investment (ROI). As the demise of the GSTPA initiative last year demonstrated all too clearly, three year ROIs are no longer regarded as acceptable to cash constrained firms, who are obliged by shareholders to achieve tangible payback within months rather than years.   Accordingly, institutions are gravitating towards smaller projects – incremental steps on the road to STP.

The SWIFT Model

SWIFT's overriding goal is to provide the platform that enables end-to-end STP, facilitating both the alignment of that platform with standardization efforts and connectivity to diverse end points.

In an ideal world, where all the goals currently being pursued by the industry have been attained, institutions would connect to SWIFT and be able to communicate with all parties to a trade – fund managers; brokers; custodians; facilitators such as Omgeo; FIX engines and FIX applications; and market infrastructures such as exchanges, central counterparties and central securities depositories.

The securities industry is often characterized as a collection of distinct vertical silos – banking, treasury, securities – and as a result, it is too often overlooked that SWIFT, originally via our FIN store-and-forward messaging service, links together this diverse range of processes that underpin the business.

For a fund manager, a securities transaction comprises not merely a FIX message to its broker and a settlement message to its custodian, it is also a foreign exchange instruction and a payment instruction to those, or potentially other, counterparties. Accordingly, SWIFT is not merely focused on securities solutions, it is seeking to provide solutions for securities firms – and that is a much wider remit. We do not expressly look to develop and provide applications; rather, we offer connectivity to value added applications and providers looking to support STP initiatives.

As an industry utility/cooperative, SWIFT is not a commercial player; nor do we merely focus on one part of the transaction chain – indeed, SWIFT is the only entity looking at STP along the entire transaction lifecycle.

SWIFT and Standards

The standardization of content and connectivity is central to the SWIFT model. We are active on three fronts within the standards arena for securities – our role as registration authority on behalf of ISO 15022; our active involvement in supporting and promoting standards convergence; and our participation in the harmonization of market practice around the globe.

Registration Authority

As the ISO 15022 registration authority, SWIFT has been appointed by the International Organization for Standardization (ISO), to act as the guardian of the ISO 15022 central database. SWIFT, acting on behalf of ISO, interfaces with the message developers and users, and is responsible for making the database publicly available and ensuring compliance, quality and consistency in respect of the contents of that database.

Standards Convergence

Convergence of financial standards end-to-end, from a business and technical perspective, remains our primary mandate and objective. This convergence will enable communication interoperability between our members, their market infrastructures and their end-user communities while simultaneously benefiting the industry at large, streamlining wider communications, and reducing related investment still further.

In addition, the use of common standards greatly facilitates interoperability between platforms such that, for example, SWIFT members can more easily communicate to counterparties employing processing mechanisms other than SWIFT's own.

SWIFT's standards convergence strategy has three strands:

- The definition and promotion of a common standardization methodology
- A common standardization process
- A common repository for financial message standards

It is vital that as many standardization initiatives as possible harmonies their objectives if the industry is to avoid the emergence of inconsistent, non-interoperable and overlapping standards. At the same time, it is important that there is sufficient freedom to allow new standardization initiatives to prosper.

SWIFT is well placed to take on the role of neutral and pro-active standards organization and registration authority. SWIFT Standards department are already engaged in standardization activities initiated by international standards bodies, such as ISO and UN/CEFACT, with financial standards bodies within the securities, treasury, Derivatives, payments and trade finance areas – including FIX Protocol Ltd, ISDA, ISITC-IOA, Omgeo and Bolero.Net – and 'external' standards bodies active in sectors such as the insurance industry.

While the existing ISO 15022 standards offer great opportunities to enhance automation, they only become available within the securities processing chain at the point of trade and, thus, do not cover the complete transaction lifecycle. The disconnect between Front and Back Office remains, with the two camps essentially speaking different languages – the latter typically using ISO 15022, the former FIX, which comes in a variety of versions, the latest being FIX 4.4. ISO 15022 XML is the instrument through which the industry is looking to converge all financial standards into a single common language, and SWIFT supports that effort both directly, through our standards work under the ISO umbrella, and indirectly, via business solutions on SWIFTNet.

In looking to expand the coverage of ISO 15022, two approaches to bridging the Front/Back Office divide presented themselves. From SWIFT's perspective, the first option could have been to extend ISO 15022 by modeling all those processes in the pre-trade space as a stand-alone exercise. However, that would have involved the costly duplication of the work already capably done by FIX Protocol Ltd (FPL) and would have pitched ISO 15022 into direct competition with a well-established and supported standard in the shape of FIX itself. Given that the industry is seeking standardization, it would have made no sense to propagate fragmentation.

Far better, in SWIFT's view, is to work with other industry bodies, such as FPL, to combine their substantial intellectual capital and business expertise in the Front Office space with SWIFT's technical standards resources and capabilities in order to incorporate FIX functionality into the ISO 15022 data dictionary. Accordingly, FPL has become the business owner of ISO 15022 XML within the pre-trade arena, dictating how the business flows should be defined, while SWIFT implements technical standards work underpinning those flows.

This is a model SWIFT and ISO would very much like to propagate throughout the transaction lifecycle, integrating the efforts of standards bodies such as FpML, MDDL and others to ensure that these principles are accepted and adopted throughout the industry.

Market Practice

SWIFT is actively engaged in Securities Market Practice Group (SMPG) activities. Essentially, our role is centered on three areas. In the first instance, we collate the requirements for business transactions as ISO 15022 is developed and enhanced (message scenarios, for instance). Secondly, we directly support the documentation of market practice, its subsequent usage, and the industry's compliance to that market practice. Finally, we act as a neutral reference body for practitioners. This last point, in conjunction with the industry's Global Market Practice initiative, is particularly important when it comes to ensuring harmonization across markets by challenging divergent business requirements raised by local markets so as to drive towards a common template for market practice globally.

SWIFT Business Solutions

For over a decade SWIFT has been expanding its role in securities markets. Whereas 10 years ago we were very much focusing on settlement activities around custodian banks, we have gradually moved in both directions along the transaction lifecycle, during which time we have taken on new participants such as investment managers, brokers, transfer agents, insurance companies and the market infrastructures mentioned earlier.

BANKS	CENTRAL BANKS	BROKER/ DEALERS	REGISTRARS / TRANSFER AGENTS	ETC PROVIDERS	INFRASTRUCTURE SYSTEMS AND PARTICIPANTS	MARKET DATA VENDOR
		Exchanges	Subsidiary Providers of Custody /Nominee Services	Proxy Voting Agencies	Fund Administrators	
		CSDs	IMIs		Insurance Companies	
		Clearers			Government Institutions	
					VMU	
1977	1982	1987	1992	1997	2002	2004

Figure 18 – Evolution of SWIFT Members and Participants

In 1999, SWIFT embarked on a fundamental evolution of its business model, and a central component of this reengineering is SWIFTNet. SWIFTNet is a highly resilient, reusable architecture that comprises an IP-based messaging platform and the infrastructure that provides access to multiple SWIFTNet business solutions.

The platform itself comprises three components – SWIFTNet connectivity, SWIFTNet messaging services and SWIFTNet interfaces. SWIFTNet messaging services enable secure and reliable exchange of information and transactional data within a closed user group (CUG) or amongst the wider financial community. Three complementary services – FileAct, InterAct and Browse – provide secure real-time and store-and-forward messaging and file transfer, together with a secure browsing capability.

The forerunner of today's business solutions approach is FIN, SWIFT's store-and-forward financial messaging service. While it is a platform in its own right, FIN has long represented SWIFT's support for its users' various business processes. Originally designed to support payment, foreign exchange and treasury activities, since the early 1980s FIN has evolved to support specific securities activities, beginning with settlement flows, moving downstream, to encompass custody services such as corporate actions and holdings and transaction statements, and upstream, in support of ETC processes.

It should be noted that the use of FIN by securities firms continues to expand by some 20% per annum - an enviable rate of growth given the current economic environment. At this point, securities messaging on FIN accounts for approximately 36% of SWIFT's overall traffic, not including the payment and treasury messaging that directly results from securities activity.

Having operated on SWIFT's private X.25 transport network since 1977, our store-and-forward FIN financial messaging service is now being migrated to SWIFTNet, providing users with a single point of access not only to existing services but also allowing them to leverage a new range of functionality framed within the context of SWIFTNet business solutions. These business solutions act to remove a number of critical barriers on the road to STP, examples of which can be found below, and are linked to services such as FIN to pull together previously disparate parts of the securities transaction lifecycle into a seamless flow.

SWIFT views business solutions as the marriage of platform, community and industry standards to satisfy users' specific business requirements. Within SWIFT, much effort is employed in evaluating the value proposition for specific users in advance of the roll-out of business solutions. We have a dedicated Value Proposition team working with potential users to evaluate their existing procedures; analyze possible areas in need of process enhancement; and, most importantly, to assist in calculating the likely ROI associated with the implementation of SWIFT's business solution for that user.

Some examples of business solutions designed specifically for securities industry users are detailed below:

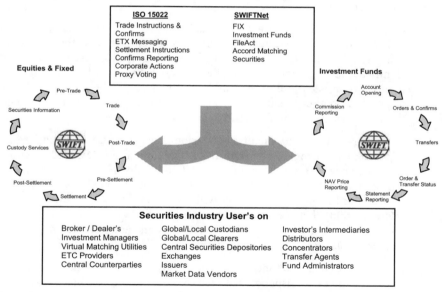

Figure 19 – Processing Lifecycle

SWIFTNet FIX

SWIFT recognizes that creating a standard is only part of the solution – the real challenge is ensuring adoption of that standard across the market. The signing of a Statement of Understanding in 2001 saw SWIFT and FPL begin to work together on developing and promoting ISO 15022 XML for the Front Office.

It was clear that many users had already invested heavily in, and were receiving great benefits from, existing solutions based around the FIX protocol. Current FIX users would only migrate over time to an ISO 15022 XML version of the standard if they could retain communications with their existing counterparties. Equally, new users of standards in the pre-trade space would only adopt ISO 15022 XML if by doing so they would be able to communicate directly with existing FIX users.

The only way to encourage take up of a new standard in this space is to provide tools and solutions that support interoperability or co-existence with legacy standards. With this in mind, SWIFT undertook industry research to identify what value it could bring to users in the shape of a new business solution. Feedback from firms in this space underlined the importance of not merely replicating what existing providers offered, but in offering a service that brought additional, enhanced functionality to the table.

To this end, SWIFT has introduced the SWIFTNet FIX business solution, featuring a centralized hub developed in conjunction with Financial Fusion, a major provider of FIX engine services and other process flow applications. Managing a firms' communications with every other institution connected to it, the hub is essentially a routing mechanism that offers upfront support for various standards.

One of the big challenges with FIX has been that, for every end point to which a firm is directly connected, that firm has to manage both the platform it is using to make the connection and the ongoing session itself. Additionally, significant testing with counterparties is required prior to live activity in order to ensure consistent use of the standard. While very large firms with hundreds of point-to-point connections may be able to justify the expense of automating these processes, most will have to employ staff to manage it.

As well as significantly facilitating session management, the centralized aspect of a hub mechanism greatly simplifies the addition of value added functionality to the end user. As and when documentation is fully available, SWIFTNet FIX will be enhanced to support the output of the ISO 15022 XML convergence effort. Furthermore, the solution will incorporate tools designed to facilitate interoperability between the new standard and both existing FIX and ISO 15022 messaging in the pre-trade space, thus encouraging the adoption of the converged standard across the industry.

A program to enhance functionality is already in place. We have added a layer of certification that dispenses with the traditional need for bilateral agreements to resolve interpretation issues between firms using different versions of FIX. Another obstacle for would-be FIX users has been the need to connect the FIX engine to an expensive order management system, an investment many institutions in Continental Europe or Asia may not yet be in a position to make. This is one of the reasons why institutions still rely on manual processing and the use of communication tools such as fax or telex, and has been a major barrier to the take-up of the FIX protocol in those regions. We are therefore rolling out a 'lite' order entry mechanism as part of the SWIFTNet FIX solution, enabling pre-trade and trade communication, using industry standards, without the need for major development work at the client site.

Funds Processing and Distribution

The increased fragmentation of distribution channels is posing huge problems for the investment funds industry in Europe and Asia. The whole process of subscription, redemption, registration, transfer and settlement of mutual fund transactions is plagued by inefficiencies.

There are no universally adopted industry standards in terms of the content and no central infrastructure to support the flows between different players in that market. Distributors often utilize faxes to settle with their transfer agents, and the lack of a US-style Fed Funds mechanism leads to problems reconciling payments with the relevant asset transfer. The problem of different providers in different locations using different communications formats and processing mechanisms is further compounded by the existence of multiple money transfer systems across Europe.

As previously stated, SWIFT has estimated that, in Europe alone, there is in excess of $1billion in additional direct costs currently being spent on manual processing within the sphere of mutual fund distribution, rising as high as $5bn if indirect costs are factored into the equation. The volume of messages exchanged in this space are immense – indeed, in 2003 we estimate the number of messages to be in the region of 600 million if we include both domestic and cross-border flows. This message exchange is predominantly transacted in non-standard fashion, often, as suggested above, by manual means such as fax.

There is thus a burning need to bring order to this chaos. It is clear that the benefits of STP need to be better aligned with the business priorities of the investment funds industry. There is a pressing need to demonstrate that investment in STP will facilitate the industry's open architecture model, allow firms to reduce costs and errors, and enable them to increase the level of orders and monies flowing into their funds.

In 2000 SWIFT already sought to address the lack of standardization in this space through the 'templating' of a number of key securities messages – MT502 (buy or sell), MT509 (trade status), MT515 (confirmation) and MT535 (reconciliation) – to allow mutual fund participants to automate the order routing process. New code words were added to meet their requirements in respect of subscription and redemption orders, switches and statements of holdings for investment funds.

Use of this facility is currently doubling on a quarterly basis and now stands at over two million messages per annum but it was nonetheless only designed to be a stop-gap solution. We are in the process of creating bespoke XML-based funds message types from scratch that treat investment funds as a wholly isolated asset class with its own distinct processes. Whereas the 'templated' messages only offer support for cross-border flows within Europe and Asia to a limited degree, the new XML messages are much broader in scope, encompassing the entire transaction flow and covering both domestic and cross-border flows.

Modeled on the ISO15022 structures, these XML messages will additionally cover activities such as account openings and maintenance, NAV and tax reports and commission statements in respect of both domestic and cross-border funds. We have worked closely with major players in Europe and Asia on modeling investment fund flows – which cover everything from an account opening to a trade subscription or redemption through to settlement and NAV reporting – and have come up with some 40 separate messages.

We will begin to publish the formal documentation relating to these standards during the first half of 2004, from which point we will support their take-up by establishing a dedicated business solution on SWIFTNet, SWIFTNet Investment Funds, following the SWIFTNet FIX example in providing tools to support interoperability with the order templates already in use on FIN. The solution will leverage both interactive and file transfer capabilities on SWIFTNet within a closed user group designed to facilitate automation and STP for the entire investment fund distribution process.

Corporate Actions

Corporate actions are a good illustration of how market practice initiatives can benefit automation efforts and how SWIFT's efforts intersect with our involvement in market practice groups, both local and global. Corporate actions processing is plagued by complexity, ambiguity and a lack of standardization, and these characteristics have ensured corporate actions have, for the most part, resisted attempts at automation that have so far been essayed.

The protracted nature of the corporate actions chain does not help matters, encompassing the announcement of an event by the issuing company; discovery of that event by the custodian or its agent; client notification; receipt of the client's response; and distribution of the resultant resource or consideration. At the same time, firms must deal with a bewildering diversity of procedures, message formats and national nuances – indeed, even basic terminology varies from market to market.

Accordingly, processing corporate actions remains, on the whole, a highly manual business predicated on labor-intensive practices such as telexing, faxing and the rekeying of information. The inherent inefficiencies in this area result not only in additional costs, but in a significant level of risk, as missing an event, processing it incorrectly, or missing a holding, can, in a worst case scenario, entail a massive liability, both financial and reputational.

A study published in January 2003 by the Group of Thirty (G30) – Global Clearing and Settlement: A Plan of Action[1] – stressed that "corporate actions, across the market, are the major source of financial losses attributable to operational failure". Volume II of the Giovannini Group report subsequently

---

[1]   Highlites of this report are included in Part VI.

urged European regulatory authorities to harmonies their rules on corporate actions.

Quantifying the overall corporate action losses caused by inaccurate or incomplete announcement data, missed deadlines, human error or other operational problems has proved a tricky task. However, in a recent White Paper – Transforming Corporate Actions Processing – the US Depository Trust & Clearing Corporation notes that industry sources estimate that 10% of the annual cost of processing corporate actions comes from 'write off' funds reserved for losses, which would translate into tens of millions of dollars in annual losses due to operational problems.

ISO 7775 messages for corporate actions had been in place for some time, but these had limited application as they were not deemed sufficiently detailed, or specific, to support the wide variety of corporate actions flows. As a result, the automation benefits engendered by those message types were not as significant as securities firms would have liked.

The advent of ISO 15022 saw these messages redesigned in order to take into account divergent local market practices and the flexibility required to support wider functionality as corporate actions processes evolve. These new messages are seen to be a far more cohesive and satisfactory solution – albeit when they are used in conjunction with strict market practice guidelines. We have seen double-digit growth in message traffic on FIN in this space since ISO 15022 replaced the ISO 7775 messages, as firms that have already automated most elements within their pure transaction flow actively target improvements in corporate actions processing.

Conclusion

Post GSTPA and T+1, it is all too easy to take a bleak view of the securities industry's ongoing STP efforts. While that sense of dejection may be understandable, it is misplaced. The simple fact is that we are significantly further along the road to global Straight Through Processing than we were ten, five, or even three years ago. Real progress is being made. The industry is continuing to focus on STP, its efforts buoyed by ever more potent technologies that facilitate enhanced automation and interconnectivity at a lower cost. We are seeing ever-greater numbers of firms, newly focused on processing efficiency, entering into STP projects during a period of depressed market activity.

As incremental efforts concentrate on specific areas, so the lack of solutions in other areas becomes more obvious. For example, as settlement processing issues diminish following the successful adoption of ISO 15022 and associated market practice, so the focus shifts towards corporate actions processing. As corporate actions flows are analyzed, the necessity of standardized reference data becomes more apparent, and so on. Driven by its users, SWIFT's goal remains to provide business solutions in support of evolving industry issues.

The examples cited earlier in the chapter illustrate how tangible benefits can be generated using the SWIFT model. Based on direction from our user community, SWIFT will continue to establish new business solutions that ultimately encompass and seamlessly link every element within the securities and investment funds transaction lifecycles.

About the Author

Simon Cleary is the head of securities markets and business solutions at SWIFT.

Chapter VII - FIX - Providing the Means to Move to STP [2]

By James T. Leman, Co-Chairman US Business Practices Committee (FIX Americas)

FIX: How It All Started

From the first conceptual discussions about FIX, well before we had adopted that name for it, we wanted to be sure that it was grounded in the spirit of being a collaborative effort bent on inclusiveness. Additionally, there was a strong desire to be neutral to market forces as much as possible and yet responsive to the needs of those who would use it to do business.

FIX began as a collaborative process between Fidelity Management and Research and Salomon Brothers Inc., initiated and nurtured within the Equity trading departments of these firms. From its initial conceptual meetings, it was agreed that groups of clients and brokers needed to be drawn in to commit resources and provide comments on its design and range of messages. After those initial meetings, separate visits were made to a group of clients and brokers inviting them to participate with personnel and resources. Fidelity and Salomon then undertook a pilot to prove the feasibility of the effort on a technical level. Next, the formation of the US based FIX Committee occurred during June 1994, and contained some of Wall Street's major names. Monthly meetings on the range of messages and the details continued with each firm working toward a production version of the protocol.

Finally, in January 1995, FIX version 2.7 was released to the financial community at a meeting held at Salomon Brothers Inc.'s offices in New York. As public interest grew, buy-side, sell-side and vendor firms sought out more information and needed answers to many questions given the newness of the endeavor. To help field these issues and to organize future changes anticipated, the first FIX Technical Committee meeting was held in March 1995. From this point, interest and a surge of changes began to build.

FIX version 3.0 was released in September 1995 to correct and clarify a wide variety of issues that required attention from the first version as well as adding features advanced by the Technical Committee. From this point, the openness of FIX for change became clear. Moving beyond IOIs, orders and executions for US Equities, the desire was voiced to permit changes to accommodate crossing system needs, listed and OTC nuances, as well as special instructions and unique needs for Instinet and ITG's Posit crossing facility.

As FIX's growth increased in the US, the US FIX Committee felt the time was right to include Europe and the UK in the process. This led to the initiation of the European Committee through an introductory conference held in June 1996 for members of the UK and European community. The first European FIX Committee was formed four short months later. Throughout this time the US FIX Committee and the Technical Committee continued to prepare the next

[2] Originally published in *The Journal of Securities Operations*, Fall 2002, The Summit Group Publishing

version of the protocol. FIX version 4.0 was introduced in January 1997. For the remainder of 1997 the use of the FIX protocol continued to grow and efforts to coordinate the US and European Committees went forward through joint meetings and the creation of a Global Steering Committee.

In 1998 FIX was moving to an annual release schedule given the growth of buy-side, sell-side and vendors serving their needs in the US and Europe. FIX version 4.1 was launched in April 1998 including enhancements for initial option trading, ECN features and allocation messaging. During this period, exchanges and crossing systems as well as ECNs expressed strong interest in FIX and its user base continued to grow. With the impending implementation of Year 2000 coding and testing expected to occupy most technology organizations in 1999 the FIX Global Committee decided not to have a new version launched in the first quarter of 1999.

During 1998, the US and European Committees also recommended that the Japanese market was beginning to undertake structural market changes which could benefit from adoption of standards such as FIX. In October 1998, the initial Japanese General FIX Conference was held in Tokyo. The conference was very well received and the various groups making up the financial community acknowledged the benefits of the FIX standard. In March 1999, the Japanese FIX Operating Committee was formalized and initiated vigorous activities to identify and document changes they felt necessary for the Japanese equity marketplace. The FIX Global Steering Committee created the formal entity FIX Protocol Limited in April 1999. The creation of this legal entity would enable FIX to engage service providers and expand the use of the FIX protocol web site, www.fixprotocol.org, which empowered users around the world to learn and participate in FIX.

In 2000, a number of events continued to mark milestones for FIX. In March, FIX version 4.2 was released. This release was quite comprehensive and was accompanied by user and vendor forums conducted in New York, London and Tokyo. The release included program trading elements, New York Stock Exchanges data changes, Japanese allocations, Fixed Income IOIs, initial XML message elements and auto quoting of options as well as a variety of other changes. Also in March, the Global FIX Committee conducted a FIX General Conference in Hong Kong to introduce FIX to the Asia Pacific marketplace. Following on this event the firms in that region formalized the Asia Pacific FIX Committee in August 2000. More recently the initiatives in Fixed Income securities and seeking to move toward XML adoption while honoring "classic" FIX implementations has taken recent focus as well as the broadening of interest to Derivatives and other asset classes.

Those efforts culminated in the FIX organization's reorganization in 2002 where a separate global Fixed Income Committee was established to compliment the work done by regional steering committees and the global technical committee.

While the extensive base of users building on indications of interest (IOIs) and basic order delivery, the protocol has aided in linking the equity buy-side users to all of their key brokers, and later ECNs or order matching services. Equity program trading has more recently blossomed in the US and Europe and promises to do so in the Asian markets. Most recently, the Fixed Income community, especially in the US, has focused on FIX with the futures industry as well as mutual funds developing interest.

These advances, coupled with the adoption of FIX by exchanges around the world, gives recognition to its pervasive adoption by more and more of the participants in the Front Office trading end of the business. While versions of FIX 4.0, 4.1, and 4.2 were being used, FIX 4.3 and 4.4 were worked on aggressively and have been issued to support the firms focused on Fixed Income order routing and post execution processing. FIX Allocations are also receiving attention from clients as a way to smooth their processing activities. These later versions of FIX are expected to be implemented by many firms throughout 2004.

STP or T+1

Straight Through Processing (STP) is very much focused on today and has been used interchangeably with T+1 in the United States by many who have given their opinions on the next stage the markets must move to in adopting efficiencies. The decision to move to T+1 settlement in any country where trading takes place is a very substantial decision. It is especially so in the case of the US market, which is large and broadly used across the world by investors.

In 2002, the Securities Industry Association (SIA) decided not to pursue T+1 in the US market within the timeframes previously laid out and to focus instead on STP. Given market conditions, the events of 9/11 and other economic uncertainties it is questionable whether the SIA and other elements of the securities industry will stay committed to adopting any T+1 timetables.

However, I still feel that while STP can be achieved without moving to T+1 settlement, T+1 in the US, or any other market, cannot be accomplished without STP essentially being in place. The EC and industry later decided T+1 could be refocused to greater efforts to achieve STP. In light of this and the experience to date that shows us that most large brokers and money managers trade in over 40 markets globally, the focus on achieving STP is where our attention needs to be directed as a financial community. STP will become a recognized economic requirement of sustaining profitable positive performance long before it becomes a regulatory imperative in my opinion.

The essence of STP is to capture the elements of a transaction as it starts its life as an order beginning with a portfolio manager or a strategic piece of quantitatively oriented software. STP also, in reality, presupposes that paperless, portfolio and order management systems exist on the buy-side with sufficient integration so that seamless movement of data can be initiated within the buy-side organization.

Similarly, the broker dealers have organized their trading desks to record orders received from clients into a paperless system with linkages to sales traders, listed traders, exchange floors, market making OTC traders, and international personnel around the world. Those systems will eventually feed post-execution processing systems that will see the trade continue on its journey once execution has occurred.

FIX's Contribution

These systems have become absolutely essential since they assist both groups in acting upon increasingly rapid movement of news, price information, and other data about world economic events. However, certain magic occurred after 1992. That was when we first saw FIX used between two parties providing the ability to communicate more and more of this information electronically between parties. FIX enabled this without asking either party to abandon a system they already use or to cease doing business with someone because they couldn't afford to carry out the work necessary to accept the information.

FIX accelerated the information transfer process, cemented in place the necessity of paperless order management and the integration of multiple broker access through existing services used by clients. STP's essential building blocks of buy and sell-side order management were linked together from that point or by mutual advantage.

- Clients could originate, control and communicate orders to their brokers electronically.

- Brokers could receive orders electronically and arrange their systems to pass the smaller ones on directly to the exchanges or market makers located out of house or to in house auto execute software.

As time has passed, the small orders, originally the target of this automation for some, has grown broadly to include all of most large buy-side money managers' flow of large block trades as well as smaller trades. Clerical errors of buy versus sell, wrong tickers, wrong quantities or limit prices or other instructions now in most cases are controlled electronically and errors detected much more quickly.

Over time, the linkage of buy-side and sell-side or liquidity providers was strengthened as FIX was changed to assist new trading venues to be accessed by buy- and sell-side alike. Added to the requests by ECN's, crossing systems and exchanges themselves, we've seen the range of client types and strategies expand. Program Trading using FIX in the US and other markets began in earnest less than 18 months ago and is now accelerating in the US and Europe. In addition, hedge fund clients, a growing powerful force in the market place, are using all of the existing access methods FIX provides for cash markets and now they demand access to listed options and futures markets around the world.

FIX has been adopted in the equity markets globally as the way to communicate IOIs, liquidity information, orders and execution for cross border as well as home market activity. Adopted primarily by the institutional marketplace, the use of FIX in Europe and Asia is also being embraced by brokers attracting retail flow of orders with the intention of routing them to trading counter parties, generally globally capable brokers and dealers, to have them executed in over 40 foreign markets.

FIX for Fixed Income

Most recently the players in the Fixed Income marketplace have seen the need emerge for the buy-side and the sell-side to be able to connect in order to route information including order and execution detail in a wide variety of Fixed Income products. The FIX protocol again adapted to this demand and the Fixed Income Working Group of the FIX Technical Committee developed a comprehensive protocol version included now in FIX version 4.3 that will enable buy-side and sell-side firms to exchange information when connectivity is established.

FIX has shown that combining this watershed event with adoption of FIX by the wide spectrum of buy-side users, whose disciplines range from patient long-term buy and hold managers to quantitative, program oriented, strategists to hedge fund players. FIX has been adopted around the world and has changed to meet the needs of users to reach their critical counterparties or liquidity points in an effective way that promotes STP and anchors FIX at the critical point of communications.

FIX, from its inception, contemplated the messages needed upon completion of the trade to move other information needed to ticket trades effectively. Focus, however, by consensus at that point and on a continuing basis for some time was concentrated on IOIs, order delivery, execution reporting and variations viewed as essential to include all order handling opportunities where liquidity or more automation benefits could be gained. However, in the last nine months with a particular emphasis in Europe and from global buy-side players, a renewed interest in the use of FIX for allocation delivery has emerged.

From the time of FIX's conception, allocation delivery and confirmation generation solutions existed in the market place and were embraced to some degree for both US and international markets. Products such as OASYS and OASYS global, created and introduced by Thompson Financial, as a result of industry collaboration, were used by many buy- and sell-side firms in some markets for some securities.

The last three years have witnessed growing interest in the principles of STP and the arrangement of internal systems on both the clients and brokers sides to adopt more effective post-execution processing. The desire is to eliminate risk of trades not being acknowledged promptly as well as the risk of confirmations not being generated, acknowledged and passed along promptly with the consequential errors resulting in a time of very volatile markets. Cost management remains an issue on both sides as well and is especially so for brokers faced with tighter spreads resulting from the move to decimalized markets in the US.

VMUs Come of Age

With the focus on STP initiated several years ago, a variety of initiatives were undertaken in the community, such as the creation of the Global Straight Through Processing Association (GSTPA), organized to design a matching utility, and now named the Transaction Flow Manager (TFM). Created by buy-side, sell-side and custodian bank players, it hoped to create a virtual matching utility (VMU) that would be used to make STP a reality.

In reaction to this, Thompson Financial assembled several of its predecessor products and combined them with similar products launched by DTCC (the Depository Trust & Clearing Corporation) to form Omgeo. Omgeo has recently announced the launch of its own VMU called Central Trade Manager (CTM). SunGard, another major vendor in the financial technology space has declared it will create its own VMU solution. Clearly, these three solutions expected to emerge for cross border trade matching and were expected to precede the initial or deployed implementation of T+1 in the US. These three VMUs faced the additional burden of demonstrating interoperability to the Securities and Exchange Commission (SEC). Interoperability in essence requires these three and any other VMU purveyors to be able to exchange some level of information with one another so that a buy- or sell-side firm need not support each of these interfaces and methods of operating.

With these three and perhaps several other players offering solutions clients were confused as to which of these three would succeed, which would attain critical mass and which would handle Equities as well as Fixed Income, US and international markets most effectively. Several vendors have offered solutions in line with STP demands that enable FIX messages to be translated into the messages required by each of these vendors thereby enabling clients to use their FIX engines to generate relevant messages that can be directed as requested by the client.

At the same time, a variety of institutional clients are currently either faxing allocations to brokers after trade execution or are doing so verbally. They are now asking for brokers to accept FIX allocations to replace the faxes in a cost effective, efficient solution that employs existing technology currently in place that can accelerate the STP on trade date objective without the expense of transaction fees. With the publishing of FIX 4.4, the ability to move forward with this concept for Equities, corporates and US municipal securities is provided for in the protocol. This version also formalizes many elements necessary for the range of Fixed Income instruments to be portrayed consistently.

Out of this pursuit of efficiency also comes significantly improved management reporting that will allow all users to capture both pre- and post-trade information and the time that data occurred and was transmitted as a report card of performance away from market activity, another dimension of how FIX has made the use of technology and the performance of all parties measurable.

Summary

In summary, you can see how FIX, in its desire to serve the diverse needs of various buy-side users, sell-side brokers, ECNs, ATSs, exchanges, and others has cemented in place through flexibility and openness the essential glue for STP to be born. Further pursuit of standards adoption such as the work FIX and SWIFT have undertaken along with others on XML through Working Group 10 of the ISO organization holds out the hope that a global standard will emerge that enables STP to be a reality. While buy-side, sell-side firms, and the vendor community have considerable work ahead of them to modify processes and systems to achieve STP within their own four walls, the ability to connect and exchange data real time is essential for STP success.

Most recently the FIX organization has conducted a substantial reorganization that saw the:

- Broadening of the membership to include the vendor community
- Creation of global Fixed Income and derivative committees
- Reordering of functional activities within each major product areas by subcommittees focused on business practices
- Education and marketing technology that complements the existing technical global committee
- Formation of a global steering executive committee lead by an elected chairman and the executive director who serves as FIX's first full time dedicated resource

By being responsive in Equities, Fixed Income, and other products for all market participants in home as well as foreign markets, FIX has made its value undeniable. Moreover, its ability to handoff to other technology solutions that will interact with VMUs and other software will extend its value on a global scale in contributing to the achievement of STP.

CHAPTER VIII - HARMONIZING EUROPE'S CAPITAL MARKETS

By Ignace R. Combes, Deputy CEO, Euroclear Bank

Introduction

After decades of relative obscurity, the clearing and settlement business is now the subject of unprecedented scrutiny by policy think tanks, legislators and regulators. Given the complexity and fragmentation of the European clearing and settlement infrastructure, compared to its US equivalent, most of this attention has been focused on Europe. This scrutiny has nothing to do with attractive P/E ratios or blockbuster product pipelines, but more to do with efficiency gains, risk reduction and cost containment.

The most significant of these studies resulted in:

- A series of recommendations from the Committee on Payment and Settlement Systems and the International Organization of Securities Commissions (CPSS-IOSCO)[3]

- Reports from the Centre for European Policy Studies (CEPS)[4], the Giovannini Group[5] and the Group of Thirty (G30)[6]

Most recently, the European System of Central Banks and the Committee of European Securities Regulators (ESCB-CESR) jointly proposed a set of standards[7] for clearing and settlement in the European Union (EU), which is open for market consultation and feedback. The European Commission has also sought to develop policy in the area of clearing and settlement and is expected to publish its views before the end of 2003.

Readers outside Europe may be puzzled by all this activity and may be tempted to think it will have no effect on them. In fact, cross-border trading and settlement has become so widespread that changes in the European markets will affect investors worldwide and may have knock-on effects on the structure of, and interoperability with, clearing and settlement providers in other world markets.

---

[3] *Recommendations for Securities Settlement Systems"* jointly published by CPSS and IOSCO in January 2001, and available at www.iosco.org

[4] The Securities Settlement Industry in the European Union – structure, costs and the way forward" by Karel Lanoo and Matthias Levin, published December 2001, and available at www.ceps.be

[5] The "Giovannini Group" was formed by the European Commission in 1996 to advise on efficiency issues in the EU financial markets. It is chaired by Alberto Giovannini. Its first report: *"Cross-Border Clearing and Settlement Arrangements in the European Union"* was published in November 2001, and its *"Second Report on European Union Clearing & Settlement Arrangements"* was published in April 2003. Both reports are available at www.europa.eu.int

[6] The Group of Thirty (G30) is a group of international financial services professionals that has produced two reports and sets of recommendations: *"Clearance and Settlement Systems in the World's Securities Markets"* published in 1989, and *"Global Clearing and Settlement: A Plan of Action"* published in 2003. Both reports are available at www.group30.org

[7] *"Standards for Securities Clearing and Settlement Systems in the European Union"* published in July 2003 by a working group of the ESCB and the CESR, and available at www.europefesco.org

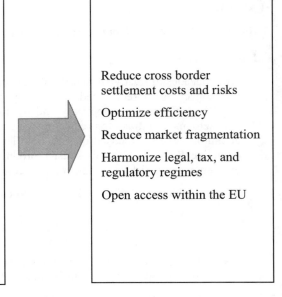

Lamfalussy group of "wise men"

CPSS-IOSCO working group

Group of Thirty

Giovannini group

Centre for European Policy Studies

ESCB-CESR working group

European Commission

European Parliament

Bank for International Settlements

European Securities Forum

Reduce cross border settlement costs and risks

Optimize efficiency

Reduce market fragmentation

Harmonize legal, tax, and regulatory regimes

Open access within the EU

Figure 20 – Drivers of Change in Europe

Going Beyond Interoperability

Broadly speaking, the reports, recommendations and draft standards agree: while domestic clearing and settlement in Europe is cheap and efficient, cross-border clearing and settlement is too expensive and inefficient. The European settlement infrastructure is highly fragmented, with widely differing market rules and practices. Buyers and sellers are obliged to have multiple accounts with multiple providers or to use chains of intermediaries to access the systems required to settle their cross-border transactions. Institutions that regularly need to settle cross-border trades are thus forced to develop highly complex Back Offices with specialized staff trained to handle the idiosyncrasies of each system. Alternatively, they may choose to outsource their Back-Office requirements to a third-party service provider or to purchase the services of an intermediary, such as an agent bank.

Euroclear welcomes these recommendations. We believe the market is best served by continually raising standards in order to reduce the risks and costs of doing business in the international capital markets. The globalization of capital markets is already a reality and this trend has been a key influence on our business development. Clients no longer limit their trading and settlement activities to a single domestic market. Indeed, they have transformed what were once considered purely domestic securities, such as US Treasuries, German Bunds and UK blue-chip Equities, into international securities. We have made major investments in new systems and links with other settlement systems to accommodate our clients' changing needs and to retain a competitive service offering.

We agree that interoperability is essential for the development of a global (cross-border) financial market and Euroclear fully supports efforts to improve interoperability between clearing and settlement service providers around the world. However, in some regions, such as present-day Europe, the number of different service providers is a barrier to interoperability because of the expense involved in building links between them all. In addition, interoperability does not address the fundamental need to harmonize market rules and practices, which will allow Back-Office procedures to be simplified and the associated costs to decline. Our view, in this case, is that infrastructure consolidation in Europe must over-ride interoperability.

In Europe, interoperability per se is insufficient to achieve the kind of savings and efficiencies that the market is demanding, particularly for cross-border settlement. Thus, interoperability can only be viewed as a step on the way towards full consolidation, not as an alternative to it. On the other hand, Euroclear firmly believes that its interaction with settlement systems in markets outside Europe can only be achieved with a relatively high degree of interoperability in order for the global markets to continue their orderly and efficient development.

Strive to Harmonize

Consolidation alone will not overcome all the barriers to the creation of a more efficient cross-border securities market in Europe. Many of the obstacles identified by the Giovannini Group, for example, are due to different market practices and legal and regulatory regimes. Euroclear fully supports the initiatives underway to harmonies these practices and regimes, and is embarking upon a comprehensive harmonization process across the five domestic markets that will ultimately become parts of the Euroclear group, namely Belgium, France, Ireland, the Netherlands and the UK. Indeed, Euroclear's aim is to process cross-border transactions at about the same cost as domestic transactions.

While increased, cheaper and more efficient cross-border activity may well be the major driver behind the harmonization process, we remain aware that cross-market harmonization will have an impact on local practices. It is obvious that the harmonization process will need to be phased and prioritized, based on potential user benefits and the likelihood of success.

At Euroclear, we are playing a very active role in the harmonization process, having been a contributor to both the G30 and the Giovannini Group recommendations. Our unique structure, representing five domestic market CSDs and one ICSD, makes us well placed to work with our clients, market groups and the relevant authorities to achieve a great deal of harmonization and standardization.

For example, we are working closely with Euronext and Clearnet to establish a harmonized settlement environment for their Single Order Book, which will centralize trading and clearing of the 300 to 350 most actively traded securities in the Belgian, Dutch and French Equities markets. We are also working closely with the London Stock Exchange and the London Clearing House to establish a settlement feed to Euroclear Bank, which is expected to be implemented in early 2004. These initiatives will give the market greater choice of settlement location, while broadening the range of trading counterparties.

Our initial efforts will concentrate on those areas most relevant to the successful delivery of our business model. This means that we will focus on resolving the current discrepancies between markets and CSD systems in terms of security data, settlement processing and corporate actions.

Security Data

Securities are referred to in different ways by different markets. For example, in some markets, both ISIN and Euroclear codes are used to identify securities; securities are recorded in both units and in nominal values; different ISIN codes are used to identify securities in registered and bearer form; and different ISIN codes are used to identify the same security in different trading locations.

Settlement Processing

At the moment, in the CSDs and ICSDs in Europe, the operating periods during which transactions are actually processed for settlement are set at different times in each system and rarely overlap.

Market discrepancies also exist in the settlement processing of the securities and cash components of a trade, which leads to different definitions as to when settlement becomes final. For example, some markets settle the securities and cash positions simultaneously with immediate settlement finality, whereas others (e.g. France) settle the cash component separately, at pre-defined times, with finality only achieved at those times.

Corporate Actions

Conventions and practices vary across markets and have major knock-on effects on other processes. For example, different markets apply different record or 'ex-dates' for the same security. Not only are traders faced with different prices in different markets (creating arbitrage opportunities), but custody service providers, including custodians and CSDs, find it extremely difficult to notify clients about a corporate event or to process market claims in a consistent manner.

Euroclear, in partnership with the working groups established by the European Central Securities Depositories Association (ECSDA), the G30, the European Securities Forum (ESF) and others, intends to advance the harmonization process significantly over the next few years. However, the public policy makers will also need to do their part by taking measures to harmonies the tax, legal and regulatory regimes across Europe.

With Special Focus on Europe

Without appreciating how the European capital market infrastructure was created before the introduction of the euro, it is difficult to come to terms with the fragmentation and operational disharmony that exists today in Europe. The main reason that Europe is now needing to address the inefficiencies and high costs of cross-border trading, clearing and settlement is that the infrastructure was designed – rightly so at the time – to meet the needs of each nation. As a result, each country in Europe had its own stock exchange and central securities depository (CSD) infrastructure.

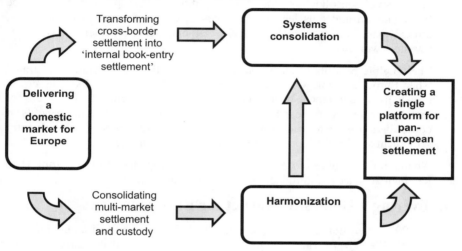

Figure 21 – European Harmonization

The Giovannini Group and the authors of the CEPS report estimate that European cross-border transaction costs are, on average, seven times more costly than domestic transactions. The reports concluded that CSD and international CSD (ICSD) fees represent a relatively insignificant portion (5%) of overall cross-border transaction costs. The reports' authors, as well as the Association Française des Professionnels des Titres, found that the use of intermediaries, such as local agents, represents about 35% of total cross-border transaction costs. The largest cost component (60%) is the Back-Office costs of the users, who are paying dearly for the inefficiencies arising from having to maintain relationships with so many intermediaries and service providers in terms of systems, communications, staff and training. For example, automating an interface with just one settlement system can cost a user up to one million euros in up-front investment.

It is also estimated that the excess costs generated by cross-border inefficiencies in Europe are about EUR 5 billion per year. Major reasons for these high costs are the wide variety of market rules and regulations in each European market and the fragmentation of the settlement infrastructure.

The recently issued ESCB-CESR standards break new ground in defining "systemically important" providers of clearing and settlement services. They propose that their standards be applied to all CSDs, ICSDs, central counterparties and custodians that meet specific market share criteria (5% at EU level or 25% at domestic market level). This risk-based functional approach, without regard to the legal status of the institutions concerned, recognizes the blurring distinction among the providers of clearing and settlement services in Europe today. It will be very interesting to gauge the market's reactions to these proposed standards.

In response to market demand for a less expensive cross-border settlement environment, the European settlement infrastructure is going through a period of massive consolidation and harmonization. This process will reduce fragmentation and thus lead to the types of cost and operational synergies, critical mass and economies of scale that mean lower settlement costs for investors worldwide.

The tangible benefits of such consolidation initiatives were amply illustrated when Euroclear Bank was able to reduce - by 83% - the cost of settling cross-border Irish government bond transactions after in-sourcing the CSD role for these securities. Euroclear Bank was also able to demonstrate the benefits of consolidation by generating savings of up to 90% for users of its book-entry settlement service for French Equities traded on Euronext Paris.

Although the number of CSDs and ICSDs in Europe has declined from 31 to less than 20 since the introduction of the euro, there are still too many.

Delivering a Domestic Market for Europe

In 2002, when Euroclear merged with CRESTCo, we defined a new business model called "Delivering a Domestic Market for Europe" that clearly states our strategy and timetable for delivering the core of a new European settlement infrastructure. Our plan dovetails neatly with the new G30 and Giovannini Group recommendations and confirms that we are already in the process of meeting most of them.

Our business model proposes the creation of a single, multi-jurisdictional settlement platform for the Belgian, Dutch, French, Irish and UK securities for which Euroclear acts as the national CSD, while continuing to offer settlement and custody services for a broad range of other securities, including Eurobonds and domestic securities from 27 other markets, via Euroclear Bank, the group's ICSD. This is a major step in support of a single, integrated capital market for Europe, as it brings together the CSD activities for five of the fifteen EU financial markets with the cross-border expertise of the world's largest ICSD. Over 60% of the Eurotop 300 Equities, more than 50% of the domestic fixed-income securities outstanding in Europe and over 60% of the Eurobonds held in common depositories will be eligible for settlement on this new settlement platform.

By transforming cross-border transactions between the different domestic markets within Euroclear into internal book entries, the settlement costs for high-volume clients will fall from the current €5 to €25 per transaction to domestic levels, typically around € 0.50.

Our objective is to reach the point when there is no duplication of functions within Euroclear, and each standard function is delivered by one integrated process accessed via one common interface. All Euroclear clients will then be able to access all Euroclear-eligible securities through one securities account, with one interface and one payment relationship, while retaining a choice of service levels and tariffs.

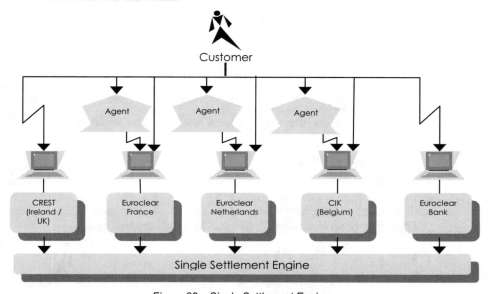

Figure 22 – Single Settlement Engine

A Choice of Service Levels

Euroclear is aware that settlement infrastructure consolidation in Europe will only be successful if the combined entity continues to offer all of the services currently available to all clients in the respective markets, for the same price or less.

Accordingly, Euroclear will offer a choice between two service packages:

- The Domestic Service will consist of the low-cost services provided today by the group's CSDs. Its distinguishing features are:

    - Harmonized CSD services covering local securities

    - Standardized and highly automated settlement and custody services

    - Asset protection governed by the laws of each security's home CSD (e.g. French securities governed by French law and UK securities governed by UK law)

    - Central bank money payment

    - Standardized client support

    - Pricing on an "enhanced cost recovery" basis

- The distinguishing features of the Full Service are:

  - Access to all Euroclear-eligible securities from the five Euroclear domestic markets and 27 other markets, plus a range of international securities, such as Eurobonds

  - Comprehensive DVP settlement, custody and collateral management services

  - Sophisticated client support services, including extensive reporting and pro-active deadline monitoring

  - Credit and securities borrowing facilities

  - Choice of central bank money or commercial bank money payment

  - Asset protection under Belgian law for all Euroclear-eligible securities

  - Competitive prices

By offering a choice of service levels, we are confident that we will be able to address the needs - and concerns - of all our clients. Moreover, clients that want to build value-added intermediary services on top of Euroclear's core CSD settlement services would be free to do so, at very low cost.

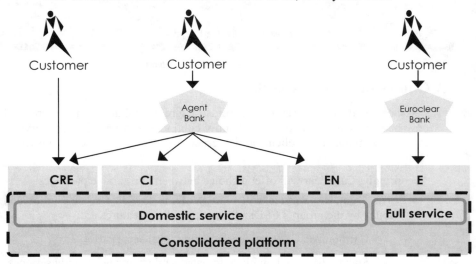

Figure 23 – Consolidated Platform Settlement

While delivery of our consolidated settlement platform does not depend on complete harmonization, without it the Domestic Service package will remain a combination of segregated local packages, preventing users from streamlining their own Back-Office processing chains and to realize significant additional cost savings. Moreover, without a sufficient level of harmonization, the consolidation of systems and the concept of a single access point for users will require more complex and expensive investments in order to realize the potential cost savings.

User Governance is Essential

One of the most important factors in moving towards a more harmonized and consolidated Europe is to insist that the entities created during the consolidation process are owned and governed by their users. This is particularly critical, as consolidation will reduce competition. In this respect, the US system provides a viable model. The DTCC services most of the market and any monopolistic tendencies are kept in check by a strong user presence on its governing board.

The 2003 G30 paper states: "For entities where non-user ownership is significant, the board is likely to focus more or less explicitly on shareholder value objectives..."

The G30 paper also notes that a de facto or de jure monopoly may raise issues of competition policy with market regulators. It suggests that regulatory intervention would be minimized if the service provider can show that "economic rents accrue largely or wholly to market users" and that its board "is balanced among different user interests." In conclusion, it states "...for the majority of situations in which clearing and settlement is through private sector entities, the overall balance of advantage probably lies with a user-ownership structure."

Euroclear is committed to the highest standards of user governance. Our Boards are comprised of experienced non-executive directors representing our users. They reflect the geographical and sectorial spread of our client base. The Boards also include two independent directors not associated with any individual user's interests.

We have also extended the principles of strong user governance to our relationships with our clients. We have set up Market Advisory Committees in each domestic market for which we serve as CSD, as well as a cross-border Market Advisory Committee, to serve as primary channels of market consultation and key sources of feedback. These Committees are empowered under the Articles of Association of Euroclear Bank to address directly the Euroclear Chairman and the Board. We believe that the Market Advisory Committees will provide a highly effective means of ensuring that Euroclear meets the needs of its clients, while greatly assisting us in our efforts to harmonize market rules and practices.

National pride and political arguments aside, settlement is a scale business: a single consolidated settlement platform for all of Europe will achieve the lowest costs. Such a single platform would provide maximum cost reductions in user Back Offices and optimize the use of collateral by having it in only one system. However, we know that this will take time, particularly when we note that it took more than twenty years for the United States – a single market with one currency, one language, one tax regime and uniform regulations – to arrive at two domestic securities settlement systems. Whether in the end there is one or more settlement platforms in Europe is probably immaterial, as long as cross-border settlement costs are minimized. Only then will a single capital market for Europe be internationally competitive and attractive.

About the Author

Ignace R. Combes is Deputy Chief Executive Officer, a member of the Board of Directors and Vice-Chairman of the Management Committee of the Euroclear group and of Euroclear Bank. He is also Chairman of Euroclear Netherlands. He oversees Euroclear's Application Development, Corporate Technology, Fixed-Income and Fund Product Management, and Banking divisions.

Having gained a bachelor's degree in Civil Engineering from the State University of Ghent, and an M.B.A. from the Vlerick School of Management at the State University of Ghent, Mr. Combes started his career in 1976 at J.P. Morgan, working on banking technology and Euroclear-related developments. In 1979, he was appointed Project Leader for the development of a new Euroclear securities settlement system. He became Product Manager for the securities lending and borrowing service in 1982 and was promoted in 1984 to head the New Issues department. Shortly thereafter, he became head of the Services division, with responsibility for day-to-day processing operations.

From 1989 to 1994, Mr. Combes worked in J.P. Morgan's New York office, initially responsible for the worldwide marketing of J.P. Morgan's operational services, then developing a new systems architecture.

Mr. Combes returned to Brussels in 1994, heading Euroclear's Commercial division, then the Corporate Strategy and Product Management division, then the Banking division, before taking on his current role.

CHAPTER IX - EUROPEAN FUND DISTRIBUTION: AN STP OPPORTUNITY

By Craig S. Dudsak, Director Relationship Management Americas, Clearstream

European fund distributors face a double challenge. In the medium term, monetary union and other factors will result in increasing consolidation among funds. In the longer term, the expansion and diversification of investments will provide further opportunities for the business to progress away from the current antiquated market infrastructure and procedures. As most fund distributors are finding out, Straight Through Processing (STP) enables the industry to rise to these challenges and make the most of future opportunities.

The future would not be so challenging if the structure supporting the fund industry were not so outdated. In Europe today, the fund order processing routine remains riddled with inefficiencies. Anybody in their right mind, including the end-investor, would expect in this electronic age that the processing and execution of a fund order would be straightforward. Unfortunately, as the fund distributors and transfer agents only know too well, the process involves an extravagant succession of difficult procedures and actions from a variety of people and systems, this chaos of manual processes gives ample scope for mistakes, failure and risk.

In today's expanding, competitive environment, one, two or more days' performance can be lost on clients' savings because of the fragmented and inefficient market infrastructure. With currently EUR 3,500 billion assets under management, the investment fund market is facing a crisis if it does not address the failing framework. Industry procedures are appalling. Orders are still taken over the telephone, allocations are made by fax and confirmations are sent by telex and or by fax. As specialized staff will recognize, this waste of time and energy is representative of most European fund distributor's Back Offices today. You only need to rehearse the various stages along the typical order chain to identify the current problems faced by institutions involved in investment fund processing.

- A subscription, switch or redemption order arrives in the Back-Office. The staff searches through a directory to find the details of the fund and to identify the relevant transfer agent. They then need to identify yet another agent to find out about the latest net asset value of the fund. Based on this data they convert the lump sum on the order into the right number of fund units or the number of units ordered into the cash price. Before placing an order, the staff may want to check, update, or supplement details and other information about a fund or its agent.

- The next step is transmission. The staff must keep in mind that each of the 1,000 or so transfer agents has its own requirements and standards. An order must be laid out in the specific format prescribed by the relevant transfer agent. Then it must be transmitted through the agent's preferred transmission channel: telephone, fax or even telex.

- By the end of the day, they want to make sure that all the orders went through clearly and safely. It takes rounds of telephone calls, often in foreign languages, to clarify, rectify, modify, complement and, finally, confirm orders with the relevant transfer agents.

This is only the initial stage in the fund order chain. Agents and fund managers confirm that the order has been received. The distributor gives instructions for the settlement of the order, bank account details are provided. Settlement is typically by the 'free of payment' method, which means that payment will take place in a location and timeframe that do not necessarily coincide with the delivery of the relevant fund units. Therefore, this final and crucial stage in the order chain is often uncertain, this in turn triggers another flurry of follow up telephone calls, faxes and telex messages. Finally, settlement reports are relayed back through the same channels. They are reconciled with bank debit/credit reports that typically come through different channels.

Broadband Internet communications are the norm today, where end-investors routinely use computers and the Internet for both personal and professional purposes. In response to this trend the fund industry must realize its inefficiencies and weaknesses, move with the times, and provide a true STP solution for the funds market.

As the European market continues to expand, the front-line salesman's dream could turn out to be the Back Office staff nightmare if the ongoing STP issue is not addressed immediately.

The recent rise of third-party distribution only highlights the European fund industry's swing from a supply-driven to a demand-driven market over the past decade or two. As institutional savings become more popular with new categories of investors, managers must find new ways to stabilize or improve performance, such as 'funds of funds' and 'multiple funds.' These structures are adding yet another layer of intricacy to what is already a complex industry structure.

The most daunting challenge to the European fund industry lies in the double whammy that its structure is about to experience. Overall expansion so far has been going hand in hand with fund proliferation. The assets under management by open-ended funds in Europe are under 50 per cent of the total in the US, but the number of funds is more than three times larger. The populations and living standards are similar on both continents; however, Europe's scope for continuing expansion remains under pressure due to the lack of supporting market infrastructure. In the meantime, a fair amount of consolidation is going on, monetary union, bank restructuring, under performance of some segments and the need for economies of scale combine to rationalize the market and cause more confusion in Back-Offices. This double whammy poses a serious dilemma for fund distributors looking to invest in Back-Office capacity.

These major issues are currently being tackled and as a result, in the last two years we have seen a number of solutions being introduced to the market. Most of these initiatives strive towards providing end-to-end STP solutions for investment fund processing which will allow the investment funds industry face the future with confidence.

As a leading player in the drive for STP, Clearstream Banking has designed Vestima; this is an innovative STP solution for investment fund processing.

Vestima offers a fully integrated order entry, routing, and execution service that is seamlessly linked to the state of the art *Creation* clearing, settlement and custody platform. It is designed to benefit transfer agents, fund distributors and fund managers. It offers complete flexibility in both the level of service offered and choice of connectivity channels. Clients are free to simply route orders through Vestima or combine order routing with Clearstream Banking's clearing, settlement and custody services.

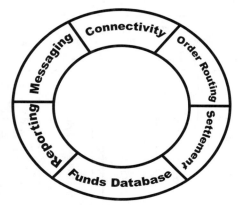

Figure 24 – Vestima (The Product Wheel)

The main benefit to distributors is that the Vestima platform streamlines fund-related operations. It does so through the electronic channels that best suit individual needs. Connectivity options for the Vestima service include web browser, host-to-host file transfer or SWIFT. As a choice of ISO 15022 compliant connectivity options are offered, clients are free to conduct business via one or any combination of these channels. Flexibility of connectivity in Vestima ensures that the method used by one party is independent of that used by the other.

High-volume distributors are more likely to opt for ISO 15022-compliant SWIFT messages (502, 509 and 515) or a host-to-host structure that combines XML and ISO 15022 format messages. Other users will prefer a web-based system that can operate from any PC. Whatever the choice, ease of access, functionalities and standards remain the same.

The Vestima service includes a database that stores details about individual funds and instantly identifies the relevant transfer agent. Constant updating eliminates the scope for confusion as funds consolidate. The platform supports all types of fund orders: subscriptions, redemptions and switches. Whether orders are expressed in terms of value or fund units, the database provides the latest available net asset value (NAV) and historical data allows for comparisons. Order details are entered once and for all in standardized formats that remain valid throughout the chain, including across borders.

With Vestima, the staff can monitor the status and progress of orders. Vestima provides consolidated reporting for orders and can retrieve and list orders according to status. Distributors can make online queries and export the answers. They can display any pre-settlement instructions awaiting confirmation.

The service can also perform auxiliary fund-related functions. These include order-related and fund-related communication, such as investigations, requests for documentation and deadline extensions. Distributors, fund managers and transfer agents can exchange such free-text information between themselves and Clearstream Client Services. Transfer agents can send messages to several distributors regarding specific funds and with range of research criteria.

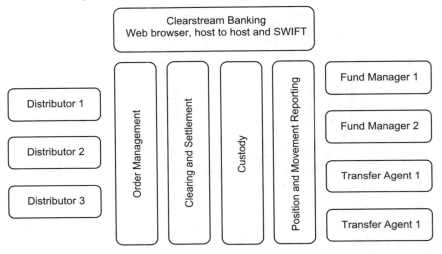

Figure 25 – Vestima (The Concept)

As we are all aware the final and crucial stage of the funds processing chain is settlement. Fund platforms in Europe like Vestima are typically offered by international financial institutions whose main business is often the clearing, settlement and custody of securities transactions.

Vestima gives clients a choice between manual and automated settlement. For the manual procedure, the distributor or transfer agent generates appropriate instructions by themselves. As for automatic settlement, again, advanced STP proves its value. Unlike Vestima, some platforms continue to require unreliable manual intervention or fax messages for settlement, although this is the most crucial process in the whole chain.

Vestima generates settlement instructions without manual intervention. Once the execution order is confirmed, instructions are automatically fed into any designated settlement system. The crucial advantage over error-prone manual and fax intervention is the elimination of settlement risk. With Vestima, settlement is available both on a 'free of payment' (FOP) and 'delivery versus payment' (DVP) basis. This offers transfer agents the flexibility they require to carry out their business.

The practical importance of advanced STP is clear: it enables fund distributors to stick with their current connectivity, clearing and settlement business arrangements. The distributors who are already clients of the ICSD providing the fund platform have the flexibility and option to integrate their fund operations with their other business activities. This brings the benefits of centralized cash and securities management.

Clearstream Banking has sought to meet our users' needs and requirements through the full use of STP techniques. How this can be achieved is not really a secret. You need to listen to market practitioners and become aware of the challenges they face. You need to understand their competing requirements of standardized solutions and flexibility. Finally, you can prove that STP can do for the funds industry what it is doing for securities broker-dealers: streamlining Back-Office standards and procedures and improving service levels.

Vestima is continually evolving with the market. Since its inception 18 months ago it has delivered two new releases, confirming Clearstream Banking's commitment to continue to tailor the service to the changing needs of the clients and the investment fund industry.

The following enhancements have been delivered to all Vestima users.

- ISO 15022 compliance for SWIFT messaging – Vestima has been ISO15022 compliant since launch. This enhancement relates to the enhanced messaging standards that were rolled out by SWIFT on November 17, 2001.

- Improved FMRS (Funds Management Reporting System) – transaction and position reports for fund management companies and transfer agents.

- Free of Payment Settlement – enabling external cash payments in accordance with standing instructions provided by the Fund Company. As an example, this meets the requirements of funds that require advance cash before purchase orders can be processed. This also enables Transfer Agents to work with us without having an account on our books.

- Expanded Funds Order Routing – we have extended the service to include order routing only for all funds not eligible for settlement in Clearstream. This broadens funds coverage for fund distributors.

- One-to-Many Switches – this enables clients to re-invest in several funds of the same family.

- NAV (Net Asset Valuation) database – is now available from Vestima on a historical basis.

- Free-Text Messaging – enables any participant to send text information or queries to one or more other participants on the Vestima system in relation to an order or a fund.

Advanced fund platforms with full STP like Vestima, mark the beginning of a new era for the European funds industry. Instead of wasting their efforts in a fastidious paper chase, Back Office staff can at long last concentrate on the value-added services that clients require.

With STP, 'timely and best execution' turns from a gamble into a serious promise. The Back-Office becomes an integral part of the value chain in today's and tomorrow's competitive markets. European fund distributors can look to continuing market expansion not as a daunting challenge, but as an opportunity.

About the Author

Mr. Craig S. Dudsak joined Clearstream in March 1995, when it was Cedelbank. He is presently an Executive Director responsible for Business Development in the Americas. He previously was in charge of Network Management and the Product Development of Custody and Investment Funds in Luxembourg.

He has over twenty years experience in the securities business. Mr. Dudsak previously worked for Citibank where his last assignment was as Vice President and Regional Operations Manager for the Securities Business in Central and Eastern Europe, the Middle East, Africa, and the Indian Subcontinent. He had also been responsible for Global Custody Operations. He facilitated and qualified various start-up operations and has had experience in operations, technology, and customer service. He is well versed in the legal and regulatory issues impacting the securities business.

Previously, he worked as an independent consultant in various securities related roles. Mr. Dudsak is a graduate of St. Peter's College and did his graduate work at Rutger's University. He was born in the United States, married to a native born Italian and has a 6 year old son.

cdudsak.cb@clearstream.com

PART III - TRANSACTION PROCESSING SOLUTIONS

Many possible existing solutions for transaction processing are presented in this section.

- In Chapter X, Tom McMackin talks about how enhancing front-end systems can improve the firm's potential to attain STP.

- Robert Curtis discusses the opportunities for enhancing Middle-Office processing as a means to STP in Chapter XI.

- Joe Rosen and Ken Scheinblum team up in Chapter XII to describe the relationship between the buy-side and sell-side and identify several ways in which processing can be improved and streamlined.

- Lee Cutrone from Omgeo offers a detailed explanation of its solution in Chapter XIII and describes how central trade matching can be a solution for certain categories of firms.

- In Chapter XIV CheckFree/Heliograph's Gert Reaves presents their solution for using workflow techniques and tools to improve transaction processing.

All of these solutions are currently available and can be used to improve processing for firms that have related problems.

CHAPTER X - STP AND FRONT-END SYSTEMS

By Tom McMackin, CEO & Partner, Open Information Systems

Introduction

Front-end systems for securities processing have been around for over 30 years starting with TTY and "dumb" terminals that offered the user the ability to enter an unedited transaction and retrieve a print image report. These Front-end systems were then, and continue to be, add-on applications to legacy processing applications such as custody, cash management and corporate trust. Rebuilding or replacing these processing applications is expensive and risky both in terms of development and client impact. Alternatively, a Front-end system can provide a make over with minimal expense and risk. There are a number of often competing goals to consider when implementing a Front-end system: flexibility and functionality, performance and maintainability are areas where trade offs often occur. In addition, there are always security and infrastructure constraints that have to be satisfied.

Front-end systems serve two main purposes for the service provider. First, from a marketing perspective, they differentiate the business from the competition. Processing and transaction services evolved from focusing on the capability of the operational staff and how big the data center mainframes were to the product that was provided on the end user's desk. Several generations of Front-end systems have provided varying degrees of client functionality and performance. More recently, Windows and Web based applications have replaced earlier systems and provide new levels of flexibility and user friendliness. Graphics and the ability to manipulate data were differentiating factors that gave sales people something to point at. The current generation of Internet applications has continued to put the marketing focus on the client desktop with new features and a stronger focus on the security of the transaction as it traverses an open communications network.

Second, front systems are used to reduce costs through automation and this has been the driver that has forced service providers toward Straight Through Processing. From the beginning of the delivery of Front-end systems a key objective was to reduce the unit cost of processing a transaction. Prior to Front-end systems every financial transaction required multiple hands to write up and approve the several steps that a transaction moved through. Originate and possibly approve the transaction at the client site; call in or fax to the service provider; rewrite and key into the processing system, file the original; verify, approve and release could be among the many steps a normal transaction moved through. In some cases, certain transactions would require the approval of a third party such as a corporate head office. This would often dramatically increase the likelihood of errors or delays in the processing of a trade.

With the advent of Front-end systems the number of steps began to be reduced and data entry responsibility was often pushed out to the end clients. The first of these systems extended the "dumb terminal" wired directly to a mainframe from a desk in operations to the client desk. This allowed the fax or call in step to be eliminated at the client site and the re-key step at the service provider. The securities industry took its first step toward Straight Through Processing.

There were several problems with these initial efforts. The validation rules for transactions were typically limited and did not force the client to enter a clean transaction. Banks were afraid to push too hard on the client fearing that they would go to another provider for the same service that would allow them to continue to fax or call in. Transaction repair became part of every operations department. Some fields, like CUSIP or ISIN numbers, had to be keyed in from manual tables that were not in the processing applications. Two tiered pricing was used to encourage clean transactions, though this was again tempered by the banks fear of alienating clients.

As the use of PC's became widespread in the business world, dumb terminals eventually were replaced with two generations of "fat" clients. These were software packages that the banks provided that contained a lot of local processing. The first generation of these fat clients was DOS based and the second Windows based. The DOS applications put a local database or file manager on the client's desk for reporting and off line entry of transactions. The distributed approach took work off over burdened mainframes but added a number of client support issues and data management. Communications were over modems and dial up lines that were neither secure nor fast nor dependable. The communications lines often ran straight into the mainframes. This meant that very little could be done in terms of workflow management without major modifications to the processing application. Usually, modifying this application was too risky and/or expensive, so whatever workflow existed before the Front-end application was introduced continued to exist afterwards.

While working at Citibank, we introduced the first Windows based in the securities industry for their domestic custody in 1991 with a product called PConex. It was the first Front-end system that was architected around the idea that the services that the banks were offering in the area of custody, security lending, and cash management had become a commodity. Moving cash or securities in and out of electronic host applications had become something that all the major players did well. PConex put the focus on the client's desk. We felt that the battle for new revenue would come from turning data into information. Delivering management level information in easy to access and graphical formats was key to the success of our strategy. The buyers of the bank's services read the reports we delivered to make the decisions on what the next transaction should be. Clerks then entered trades but were not part of the buying cycle. We developed a reporting engine with a built in report writer and graphics and helped the bank expand the client base.

However, the system was still limited in a number of ways. It looked pretty, but it was still the same direct-wired system into the mainframe. Reporting helped sell clients but we were coming to realize that it was the transaction entry process that kept them around. In the marketing of a commodity product the control of cost was a major success factor and controlling cost would come through the efficient movement of transactions. Lack of a middleware piece limited what could be done.

In 1992 we built a connection between the ISCC and Citibank's global custody branch network that we called Broker Instruction Delivery System (BIDS). Many of the New York broker dealers sent their direct clearing trades through BIDS. The broker/dealers created a file of transactions in a SWIFT like format and after being authenticated by BIDS as an entitled user, sent it over an X.25 line to a PC LAN based application that we built in 90 days. BIDS validated the messages, sent rejects back to the broker/dealer, made a copy of the transaction that was loaded to a Gupta database and then sent a reformatted message to the appropriate Citibank branch over the Citibank network for clearing. Confirmations from the branches were returned to BIDS, matched against the original message in order to create a outstanding/pending file, converted to a SWIFT format and delivered to the broker/dealer.

No capability for repair was built into BIDS. The intent was to receive and deliver messages with no human involvement in order to control our costs. The system was a data switch. We had created a "middleware application" that allowed us to move transactions in a Straight Through Processing environment. While the system did not include a Front-end application it included several new components that served as the basis of middleware architecture:

- Communications
- Client entitlement
- Data mapping & reformatting
- Data validation
- Data loading to a database
- Message formatting
- Message distribution
- Database
- Transaction matching
- Multi-tasking
- Reporting

Later generations of Windows based Front-end systems took advantage of the features of middleware-based architecture and this allowed these systems to operate in a client server environment. Transactions were entered off-line and sent to the middleware application in batches. The middleware system handled connectivity and distribution to one or more host processing systems. Validation on most fields was done on the workstation, though some data, such as limits and available funds, could only be validated on the processing system. Integration with 3rd party applications like rating agencies and exchange rates were done once in the middleware and the data passed off as necessary.

There were still a number of problems that continued to plague this generation of Front-end systems. Transaction workflow was not flexible in terms of decisions being made based on transaction content or other factors. Validation was usually all or nothing and could not be tailored to individual transaction needs. The fat client approach of locally installed software often created a lot of maintenance and client service problems. Communications problems were common, version control and software distribution was often problematic. On the other hand, using local processing power for reporting and transaction entry often provided good performance and added flexibility and functionality.

Early browser / Internet applications often reverted most of the way back to the dumb terminal applications with a few improvements, usually in terms of how attractive the user interface was. Often most, if not all, of the functionality that had been available of the fat Windows systems was removed in favor of centrally served web pages available from a web server. There were also a tremendous number of security issues that had to be addressed and a lot of different solutions were used for this. While the middleware pieces often remained in these systems, the capabilities of these early systems were often dramatically reduced. The Front-end portion of these early web systems often also performed very poorly as larger volumes of data were introduced.

Currently, there are a number of considerations that have to be included in any discussion of Front-end systems for financial services. They are:

- Security and infrastructure
- Functionality and flexibility
- Performance and scalability

Security and Infrastructure

Any Front-end system must able to withstand standard penetration testing, reasonably guarantee the accuracy and confidentiality of the data and be able to work within normal infrastructure. A three (or more) tier architecture using SSL II seems to be becoming the standard where the tiers are:

(1) A web zone where the web servers reside,

(2) An application zone where the middleware applications reside, and

(3) A processing and data zone, where the Back-Office processing applications and the client sensitive data reside, usually in a database

Client data can transit zones 1 and 2 but can only reside in zone 3. In addition, it would clearly be preferable if any data transiting zones 1 and 2 were encrypted before it got to the web servers. In addition, it must be impossible for any connection to be made from zone 1 to zone 3, or the zones are not properly separated. The basic idea behind this strategy is that it is impossible to completely block penetration, but before an intruder can make it to any sensitive system the attack can be detected and blocked. The various zones and their surrounding firewalls become moats intended to trap any intruder.

Several problems immediately become apparent when considering the above configuration. First, the major vendors of web servers and web environments produce products that are not particularly well adapted to the three-tier architecture. At this point, most web systems use web server evaluation of pages for dynamic creation of web pages. ASP (Active Server Pages, Microsoft) or JSP (Java Server Pages, Apache / IBM) pages are the most common examples. This usually means that scripts on the pages directly access the database, immediately breaking the desired three-tier architecture. Second, for disaster recovery and performance purposes, it would be desirable if more than one web server and more than one application server could be run simultaneously. While this is usually possible, often there are restrictions that severely limit its usefulness. True unrestricted parallel processing is an enormous advantage in terms of disaster recovery, performance and scalability.

Finally, in terms of infrastructure, using web-based solutions meant that the client service task changed both in nature and size. Web solutions were provided to run in a browser and it became the end user's problem to have the proper browser available with a connection to the Internet or a VPN. Client service no longer had to deal with modem problems, installation problems, etc. due to the lack of software at the client's site.

Functionality and Flexibility

In terms of functionality and flexibility, purely web-based front end systems often suffer in comparison with their fat Windows based predecessors. On the transaction entry side, there is often much less processing performed in the browser than in a program using a database so the client has to wait for validation to be performed at the server. Often this involves several submissions to the server, taking far longer than previous data entry. There are also tasks that are more difficult to perform using a browser, such as reference table lookups, that impede rapid data entry and transaction processing strictly using a browser interface.

On the reporting side the problems are often much worse. HTML is ill-suited to presenting large amounts of data and as a pretty dumb terminal, provides almost no utility in terms of being able to modify reports. HTML is designed around single page presentation and a 200 or more page report is extremely cumbersome to print, difficult to navigate and is very inefficiently transported to the user's browser. In addition, every time a report is run, the entire report must be downloaded to the end client, often an excessively time consuming task. Using standard tools, such as Adobe's PDF viewer, can help alleviate some of these problems, such as being able to print the entire report. Using Java can allow some functionality, but this is often blocked at the end client's browser.

Since these front-end systems often depend on a database that is kept on the server that is an extract of the host application, there can be additional complications if the server database is not synchronized on a real time basis to the host for both reporting and transaction entry. On the reporting side the information may not be up to date. More importantly, if the data is not up to date on transaction entry a transaction could get through that should in fact be rejected.

On the positive side, the ability to do a change once on the server and have it immediately in use for all clients is an enormous advantage. Fat client applications had to be updated individually on a workstation-by-workstation basis. This normally meant that a bank client service representative had to visit each client and install a new release of a system. Often this created support problems where clients were on different releases during a rollout. In the thin client versions of these systems this is eliminated since the application code is kept centrally and when it is updated all users are impacted immediately.

Performance and Scalability

Many of the front systems were created to relieve the workload on the host applications. Large volumes of reporting data and reporting requests from that host data could bring these systems to a stand still during critical timeframes during the day when transactions had to get through. To some degree this problem was solved with the fat clients in that reporting data was distributed to the local user database once a day and reporting was done locally. Transaction entry did not compete with data down loads and report execution because of the distributed nature of the applications.

With the advent of thin client Front-end applications the problem of a centralized monolithic database reappeared that often stored from 18 months to several years of data. Transaction entry again competed with large reporting requests and instead of the power of a mainframe supporting the database the bottlenecks were often much smaller servers.

The bottlenecks of performance and the fat client architecture impacted the ability to deliver Straight Through Processing. Distributed processing made it difficult to manage the different states of a transaction when the next state may require a user in a different location or from a different institution. There was not a hub or centralized server that was the keeper of every transaction independent of the status it was in. Performance impacted Straight Through Processing by potentially tying up the transaction and jeopardizing its movement through a process that could be time sensitive.

Product Alternatives

Front-end systems were typically built by financial institutions as ground up development or by assembling components offered by various vendors. Crystal Reports and Actuate became the reporting standards the banks incorporated in their systems. Their products were pretty slow and difficult to use. But often pretty was a key factor in the sales cycle so they sold. Financial Science and others sold a securities data model that was really geared for host processing and included too much information to be practical for a Front-end system. Yet it was used by several institutions. Transaction entry was not available off the shelf so it was often built internally to the banks requirements. The development efforts that did yield a product produced products that were inflexible and could not meet evolving market and product requirements like Straight Through Processing.

Netik, a British company, offered an integrated solution for both reporting when they combined an internally built transaction entry application with a reporting application, acquired through an acquisition, based on Crystal Reports and the Financial Sciences' data model. The monolithic nature of the data structure the tool set used did not deliver performance. While the system worked for several small institutions it was unable to meet the needs of global institutions and the company has suffered financial and management turnover issues in recent months.

Open Information System addressed these issues that have plagued others building Front-end applications for the securities industry in its Information Manager product by starting with a fresh look at the problems from the ground up. Because of our experience at Citibank we knew we had to build an architecture that would:

- Deliver the highest levels of performance,
- Provide the flexibility needed for Straight Through Processing with manual entry or import,
- Adapt to changing product and market requirements,
- Integrate Reporting, Transaction Entry, Administration and Security and meet the needs of both end client users and operations.

We started by building separate logical databases within a single physical database to eliminate performance issues. Our analysis showed that about 95% of the data and report requests were for today's information. This week and this month constituted another 4% with the remaining 1% going against historical data. By structuring our databases to line up with the behavior of the users we were able to dramatically impact performance. We are going against less than 0.5% of the data to answer 95% of the inquiries. We additionally set priorities within the database to insure that transactions would always take the highest priority and could flow through our system without being impacted by the reporting application.

With this approach we have been able to handle several gigabyte data downloads to the database with accumulated data reaching over two terabytes and not see any deterioration in response time for reports and maintaining instantaneous response for transaction entry. Some of our clients integrate data from several global systems including custody, securities lending, cash management, commercial paper and medium term notes.

Straight Through Processing requirements stretched the limits of what was possible on fat client systems. Some systems offered what was often called "third party approval" which meant that a user could enter a transaction in one location and it could be approved by a user in another. This served the needs of head office needing to approve branch-entered transactions but it was not really STP. But in more complex transactions like the issuing of Commercial Paper where a broker might initiate a trade that needs to be verified internally and then moved to the actual issuer of the commercial paper, potentially modified and returned to the dealer before it is sent to the operations department of the bank acting as the Issuing and Paying agent and then released to the DTCC for settlement. The several states that a transaction had to move through and the notification of the users involved were well beyond the capability of fat client server applications. The Internet and thin clients changed all this.

Impact of the Internet on Front-Ends & STP

Thin client applications changed the potential for STP within Front-end systems and had a dramatic effect on the way host applications could be designed. A properly designed Front-end application could move the transaction straight through every state of its process and hand off to the host only good transactions that could be released. The role of the host could be reduced to an accounting engine and the books of the organization.

OIS incorporated a table driven Work Flow Manager into its transaction entry initial thin client basted Front-end. The approach allowed us to move a transaction through a complex set of states with any attribute of the transaction dictating the behavior or movement to the next state. Coupled with that, we incorporated the ability to notify the party or parties who were responsible for the next state if it required manual intervention. This allowed us to move standard transactions straight through a complex process of several states while pulling out exception transactions that might exceed a certain financial limit, be in a certain currency involve a certain client for example.

The Internet coupled with an application server that is the keeper of all transaction as they move through their various states, provides a single point where all in process transactions are stored. In the fat client model a failure of a workstation currently responsible for the transaction could terminate the flow. In the thin client model and authorized user can pick up the transaction and move it to its next state. The notification module can send e-mails or faxes to responsible parties when their attention is required.

In addition to the Work Flow Manager and Notification modules we developed a series of Transaction Monitors and incorporated them into the transaction entry system to insure visibility of every transaction that entered the system would be guaranteed. Transactions that flowed straight through would only show up on a monitor with a completed status. However, in-process transactions are updated in the monitors on a real time basis. This allows a manager to monitor workloads in an operations center down to an individual client, user or operations clerk. In a global environment workloads from one location such as London can be reassigned to another operations center in a different geographical region in the event of excessive volume or a systems failure. A manager in a department can similarly assign work within the department depending on individual backlogs, a sickness within the group or a Fed deadline.

Conclusion

The combination of a flexible and thin client design, Work Flow Manager, Notification, and Transaction Monitors imbedded within a Front-end application allows an On-line Transaction Processing system to be architected in such a manner as to maximize Straight Through Processing.   Any transaction can be allowed to flow straight through based on passing stringent criteria for that specific transaction. The fact that transaction criteria can be based on any combination of attributes allows operations to be assured that they will only work with exceptions to those rules.   Modules like Notification and Transaction Monitors guarantee that when an exception occurs the appropriate party who is responsible for its resolution will be made aware of its existence it will be instantly visible to that individual and any others, such as managers responsible for load leveling.

The Internet and thin client architecture has made it possible to build Front-end applications that in fact strip much of the responsibility from host applications and allow them to focus on core accounting functions.

While most Front-end applications implemented within financial institutions are implemented on top of legacy applications and compete with them in processing transaction flows, as these systems are re-architected their nature can and should be limited to allow the Front-end to work flows of both financial and administrative transactions.   The size and complexity of host applications has caused their evolution to be a much slower pace than the Front-ends but in order to maximize STP they must surrender transaction entry to Front-end systems.

About the Author

After graduating from Columbia's MBA program in 1972, Mr. McMackin and an associate founded Computer Facilities Inc. This start up company sold time-sharing and in-house computer systems to community banks in the northeast. Computer Facilities grew to over six million in revenues before it was sold to Itel in 1976. At Itel, Mr. McMackin managed development, customer service and operations. He also played a major role in Itel's acquisition of three other suppliers of data processing to community banks.

Mr. McMackin joined Citibank in 1980 as the business manager of a division that sold turn-key systems to money center banks and later transferred into the Securities Services division. He was tasked with revamping the business with respect to electronic delivery of information to its customers, and re-positioning Citibank as a market leader in electronic banking.

Mr. McMackin created an internal working group of business and technology managers, representing the Cash, Securities and Trade Finance divisions from around the world. From this initiative, a global electronic banking system was built that allowed customers to view information and enter transaction from any location to any Citibank wholesale application. He was also responsible for the team that designed and built the ISCC link for Citibank.

Mr. McMackin left Citibank in 1993 and founded Open Information Systems (OIS) with Mr. Groshans. OIS products include Information Manager an Internet based electronic banking system used to web enable legacy applications and Money Market Manager, a Back and Front Office system for the processing of Commercial Paper and Medium Term Notes. OIS' products are used by most of the global banks and their customers including Citigroup, JPMorgan/Chase, HSBC, ABN Amro, Bank of Tokyo and US Bank. They deliver a high degree of STP to their client base. OIS was recently awarded Institutional Investor's award for the "Best Use of the Internet for Operations" for one of its customer's installation.

Mr. McMackin holds an undergraduate degree from Boston College and an MBA from Columbia with a major in Operations Research.

tcm@openinfo.com

CHAPTER XI - STRATEGIC USE OF THE MIDDLE OFFICE FOR STP

By Robert M. Curtis, Director of Product, CSS Q Middle

Introduction

The conflicting demands of the current trading environment - to cut costs while simultaneously improving regulatory compliance and risk management – make Straight Through Processing (STP) an imperative for survival, not merely an initiative for future consideration. Still, without money to burn, STP initiatives must be highly focused on those areas with the greatest potential return on investment. As this chapter will demonstrate, the Middle Office is the best candidate for full automation and Straight Through Processing initiatives in the brokerage industry.

Benefits and Challenges of STP

The benefits of STP have been heralded for years and are well known: reduced transaction costs as human intervention and human errors are eliminated; minimized exposure and risk as faster processing leads to faster problem resolution; enhanced communications with trading partners through better, more standardized interfaces; and better compliance oversight as electronic data capture brings greater transparency. According to an industry survey on STP, conducted jointly by GartnerG2 analysts and the Securities Industry Association (SIA), although STP is becoming an industry priority, manual processes are still commonplace. Nearly half of all transactions are still paper-based.[8] Within the securities market, more financial service providers are beginning to recognize the effectiveness of STP implementation. Not only does STP reduce the cost, risk and complexity associated with trade processing, but it also speeds the flow of standardized information to all parties involved.

According to David Furlonger, vice president and research director for GarnterG2, "STP makes sense for the industry and should be made a priority. STP is much larger than just an IT issue. It directly impacts the bottom line of a financial services firm and ultimately defines its competitive positioning. Firms that pursue STP more aggressively will achieve a competitive advantage over firms that put implementation lower on the priority list."

Although full integration has proven to be a slow process, the survey showed that investment in STP will continue. "Some organizations plan to spend one-quarter of their total IT budgets on STP this year, and a majority of respondents anticipate STP related spending will increase by 21% in 2002."[9]

Yet, why has the quest for efficient processing to date gone largely unrealized? The answer is simple. It is because the challenges of true STP, just like the benefits, are varied and great.

---

[8] "Financial Services need straight-through-processing, say analysts", OUT-LAW.com, August 8, 2003. Full article can be viewed online at: http://www.out-law.com, under "legal news and business guides".
[9] ibid

The first hurdle that must be cleared when striving for STP is the electronic capture of data at the point of client contact, or more simply, at the point of sale. While there are a multitude of software packages that facilitate this frontline data capture, simply capturing the data is not enough. The data must be vetted for integrity not just for the Front Office system that is capturing it, but more important for all the subsequent processes downstream that must handle the same data if STP is to be achieved. This is the first hurdle and often the first misstep made by firms striving to achieve STP. Early on, in their enthusiasm to embrace STP, many firms purchased contact management, order entry, and other packages that bring electronic data capture to their frontlines, but which are not integrated with existing processes or existing databases. Rather than moving these firms toward their STP objectives, ill-considered Front Office software typically exacerbates their problems by adding complexity and new data repositories, and failing to integrate with existing components.

If the first challenge of STP is to validate data properly at the point of initial capture, the next challenge is to consolidate data into a single database. Transparency, or the ability to see across all of a firm's data at once, is absolutely key to managing risk and exposure, as well as to compliance oversight and reporting. Without consolidated data, the key benefits of STP are lost. But just as the proliferation of narrowly focused Front Office software has moved firms away from the single-data store, other factors also make this goal difficult to attain. Most significantly, there has been a tendency in the past for different product lines within a firm (e.g. Fixed Income, Equities, Derivatives, etc.) to be supported by their own software applications and, just as frequently, by their own databases. The existence of data in silos within different product lines adds to the complexity and difficulty of implementing one database for an entire enterprise. This problem not only compromises STP initiatives, but also causes firms to miss out on other benefits that a single, transparent database would bring, such as improved client service and enhanced cross-selling opportunities.

The next critical challenge to be overcome if STP is to be achieved is integration. Integration is the key to STP success. Some necessary points of integration are obvious. The varied applications rolled out in Front Office initiatives must be integrated or they must be replaced with more comprehensive solutions. The applications used across different product lines must also be integrated with each other and with downstream processing. Yet some of the integration needed for STP is less obvious. For example, integration with real-time market data is a crucial component that is sometimes overlooked. Real-time market data is vital when validating incoming transactions for appropriateness and preventing errors at the point of sale. With integrated real-time market data, the best systems can validate prices against the quote, ensure that margin requirements are being met, and prevent other such errors that are the bane of STP.

Just as real-time market data is a necessary component of STP, real-time processing in general is another STP challenge that many firms face. While this may seem obvious ("Straight Through Processing" and "real-time processing" are essentially synonymous) to firms using legacy, batch-oriented systems, the problems are real, substantial and often insurmountable. Without real-time information coming from the Back Office, the entire STP food chain breaks down. This is to say that it becomes impossible to validate transactions properly at the point of sale, to manage exposure and risk, or to ensure compliance. Without real-time, end-to-end transactions, proper vetting upfront becomes impossible. Without this validation, the trade exceptions quickly become unmanageable.

The final significant obstacle to achieving STP is connectivity. The ability to connect easily and efficiently to the outside world using industry-standard protocols and formats is essential to STP success. As the trading landscape continues to change at an accelerated pace, the ability to connect to trading partners, exchanges, alternative trading systems, FIX networks, ECN's, the many evolving pools of liquidity in the marketplace today, and to all the existing clearance, settlement and matching services becomes ever more important. Of course, a crucial problem with external connectivity is the lack of a single industry standard, but proficiency with FIX, XML and some ISO standards will allow a firm's STP solutions to connect to the most vital institutions on the street. Still, STP solutions that can quickly adapt to and connect with the remaining external proprietary systems have a significant advantage over those that cannot. Perfect any-to-any connectivity might be as unattainable as the Holy Grail, but it is a worthwhile goal for STP and beyond. Additionally, when integrating internal systems, the more open and standardized the messaging employed, the easier integration becomes. (XML is most likely one of the best choices for internal messaging, as it can also be used externally with a fair amount of success.)

Why the Middle Office is Vital to the Success of STP

A fairly narrow, but often employed, definition of the Middle Office consists of the trading room and all ancillary functions that prepare trades for the Back Office. Broadening this definition to include all processes and data that can benefit from centralization and consolidation properly positions the Middle Office as the hub for virtually all STP initiatives within a firm. Just as the trading room is the inevitable point of convergence for disparate business processes, applications and product lines, the Middle Office is uniquely situated to meet the challenges, and reap the rewards, of STP. By the very virtue of being "in the middle," a firm's Middle Office components are either at the heart of its STP successes or integral to its STP failures.

A powerful, open and flexible Middle Office platform answers the single greatest need in brokerage processing: the need for freedom without compromise. A Middle Office platform with the right attributes allows firms complete freedom to choose the Front Office systems that they want to use without sacrificing STP to the Back Office, without sacrificing real-time transactions and information, and without compromising on the critical areas of compliance and risk management. All the disparate systems capturing data on the front lines of financial services firms - client account data, order entry transactions, etc. – intersect in the Middle Office, as do the various systems supporting different product lines. If the Middle Office platform is properly designed and implemented, this deluge of information can be brought together and funneled toward the Back Office. If not, the Middle Office becomes a swamp that must be drained and pumped at great effort and expense. The manual intervention, redundant data capture, and human errors that plague many Middle Offices drive transaction costs up, but also make this area a prime target for STP reform. The various problems in a disjointed Middle Office promise great returns on investment when solved.

Unless the Front Office systems, and the varied, product-specific trading systems, are to be abandoned (which end-user resistance usually precludes), the Middle Office has to become the focal point for the eradication of STP challenges. The Middle Office must first enforce the rules that will validate data and transactions on behalf of all downstream processes. Enforcement must be in real-time and must reference live market data in order to protect the Back Office from trades that should never have been accepted. Otherwise, exception-based processing becomes too unwieldy to support. To achieve this real-time editing, the business logic of the entire enterprise must be embedded in the Middle Office platform, which in turn, must make that logic readily accessible to any calling programs connected to it. The old IT adage of "garbage in, garbage out" could not be more germane to STP initiatives. Ensuring the integrity of the transactions feeding the process in real-time must be a firm's first priority.

The Middle Office is also uniquely positioned as the first site within the stream where a single, consolidated database is feasible. The importance of this cannot be overstated. When the Middle Office provides a financial services company with a transparent view of its data, the benefits are felt throughout the organization. Only when the data from the plethora of systems converging on the trading room is consolidated can risk and exposure be holistically evaluated. Anything less than a holistic view is inaccurate.

When all the data is in one location, compliance can move from rudimentary and often unacceptable after-the-fact reporting, to aggressive and proactive oversight and enforcement. By offering a single, consistent view to all client-facing personnel, service is improved and costly errors are averted. Opportunities to cross-sell and up-sell multiply; and for STP, having one version of information is vital. For example, many systems in use today will have more than one database defining the attributes of the securities traded by the firm. The effort to keep this information synchronized is costly and wasteful, but more importantly, when the information inevitably goes out of synch, trade-exceptions skyrocket and STP breaks down. By consolidating security master information in the single most effective place, the Middle Office, cost savings are immediately seen and STP is facilitated.

Just as the Middle Office is the obvious, and perhaps only, place where all of a firm's data can be consolidated, it is also the most logical place for integration to occur. Over time, trading room and Front Office users have selected the systems that best suit their needs. Even though these systems are disjointed from the enterprise as a whole, users are unwilling to abandon these systems and the features they deem necessary, in favor of more STP-friendly solutions. Therefore, the best Middle Office solutions are powerful integration platforms that allow firms the freedom to continue using disparate systems without sacrificing STP. Predicated on industry standard messaging and protocols and employing open programming and architecture standards, a strong Middle Office suite gracefully melds Front and Back Office components together. By communicating internally and externally in XML, FIX, and other standard ways, and by fluently mapping one method to another as needed, the Middle Office translates good communication skills into potent and necessary integration skills.

Only by focusing on the Middle Office and the platforms deployed there will the brokerage industry ever achieve truly functional Straight Through Processing. It can be done and the Middle Office holds the key.

About the Author

Currently, Robert M. Curtis is Director of Product for CSS Q Middle. Mr. Curtis has 15 years in the Brokerage Software Industry, working almost exclusively with Middle Office order management and trading systems.

CHAPTER XII - STP AND THE BUY-SIDE

By Joe Rosen and Ken Scheinblum

How Sell-Side Firms that can sell crazy investments to otherwise smart people have failed to sell something that really makes sense ...

The Sell-Side

We admit there are times when we are awed by the sell-side firms – investment bankers, brokers, and dealers - the people and firms that provide financial products that are carefully crafted, engineered, and marketed to institutional investors. These institutional investors collectively known as the buy-side are the mutual funds, insurance companies, pension fund money managers, hedge fund managers, and so forth that eagerly and aggressively look for opportunities to turn cash into investments that provide superior returns and therefore make them more attractive to potential investors than the tens of thousands of other buy-side firms doing the same exact thing. Many of the sell-side firms that inhabit "Wall Street" are financially immense and carry great clout economically, politically, and socially. They are run and staffed by some of the greatest minds that money can buy.

These firms with their nearly unimaginable resources have generated profound and lasting changes to financial markets worldwide. It seems as though in the blink of an eye, investors went from a choice between stocks and "bonds" to an endless stream of variations on old themes and entirely new instruments. Ken once worked for an insurance company that (many year prior to his arrival) had purchased bonds issued by railroads with one hundred year maturities and coupon rates around three and one half percent. Those investments look like brilliant investments once upon a time; they were matched against life insurance policies with guaranteed interest rates of one and one half percent to two and one half percent. We are not sure if investment professionals gave each other "high fives" in the mid to late 1800's, but we are reasonably sure the insurance companies who were the primary buyers of these bonds thought they had created a money machine generating spreads of one hundred to two hundred basis points – and had locked those profits in for one hundred years!

Who could have guessed that railroads would have financial difficulties? Who could have gazed into their crystal balls and foreseen the advent of competition from the airline industry (airplanes?) and the trucking industry? Even more importantly the notions that new insurance products, tax law changes, and various macro economic events would change the insurance business to such a degree that we would laugh at the people that made those investments was beyond comprehension. Railroads needed money. Insurance companies needed the investments for the premiums they collected in order to pay claims and make a profit. The sell-side meets the need. Anybody want to buy some one hundred year maturity, low coupon railroad bonds today?

Today both buyers and sellers are more sophisticated. Very bright people with powerful computers create trading and hedging strategies that were incomprehensible even a few decades ago. The sell-side is just like any manufacturing firm: find out what the buyer needs or wants and build it. If that fails, build what you can and convince the buyer that it is what they need and must have. These are the folks that have given us mortgaged backed securities (and later every flavor of asset backed securities one can dream up: CARS, CARDS, CMO's, PAC's, TAC's, IO's PO's and residuals – and just what is an "inverse floating IO strip" anyway) and Derivatives, both standard (products such as exchange trade futures and options) and custom-on-the-spot instruments (OTC Derivatives in combinations that boggle the mind).

The sell-side has an incredible knack of selling the wildest, most esoteric instruments. This goes way beyond the so-called "story" stocks and bonds. Single handedly they invented the notion of risk management as we have come to know it today. And surprise, surprise they have the instruments to help us manage our risks. How are they able to do this? We already mentioned that they have the resources to attract the best minds. They also have the resources to invest in technology, both hardware and software, that the vast majority of buy-side firms do not even know exist. They also have the resources to pay "salespeople" exceptionally well, which, in turn, attracts great marketing people. Frankly, this is the only reason Ken can imagine why a portfolio manager with whom he once worked purchased a large quantity of Inverse IO Floating MBS strips. We are not sure there are many people alive that can model the cash flows on these instruments, let alone calculate what, if any, value, they add to a portfolio. And how can one possibly value these genetically altered financial instruments? No problem. The broker that sold them to you will be happy to give you a price quote for accounting purposes – for a fee either directly or indirectly.

We tell these tales to draw a picture in the reader's mind. The sell-side is sharp. The sell-side has a huge advantage over many of their clients. The sell-side can flat out sell. (We have friends on the sell-side – really.) So we are left with the questions: why couldn't the sell-side get the buy-side to see what the advantages of STP would be to everyone that participates in the financial markets? How could they let a truly good concept get trashed, brushed aside, and generally ignored by the buy-side? How could something so good go so bad?

T+1 and STP

As mentioned above, the sell-side gave birth to modern financial risk management utilizing the tremendous resources they have at their disposal. During the maturation process of analyzing risks, the scope and granularity of the factors that can be measured and thereby controlled have exponentially increased. Notionally, the industry always knew that the period between when a trade was executed (Trade Date) and when cash and securities changed hands (Settlement Date) represented a degree of risk. Specifically, there was always the potential for counter party failure, either the failure to deliver or the failure to pay. The technology and procedures in the past allowed for a five-day settlement period generally referred to as T+5. That is, the exchange of securities and cash would take place five business days after the trade was agreed upon. This preceded the days of the Depository Trust Company (DTC) and electronic transfers of positions, not to mention paperless securities. There are still many among us that remember the armed guards accompanying the vault personnel to the armored cars in the morning to pick up securities for delivery to the correct settlement bank for that day. Then in the afternoon the cycle was reversed, as the armored cars would arrive with the physical securities of purchases that had settled that day and the guards would travel with the vault staff until the transfer bags were safely behind the great steel doors.

To help reduce the period of exposure, the United States moved from a five day settlement period to a three day settlement period, better known as T+3. This is our current practice. Around the same time, DTC merged with the National Securities Clearing Corp. (NSCC) to become the DTCC (Depository Trust & Clearing Corp.). During the intervening years there were fewer and fewer armored car trips as most stocks were placed physically at DTCC and security movements could be conducted through "book entry." It took a little longer for bonds, both corporate and government, to make the move into a central depository, but slowly it occurred. Technologically and procedurally, very little changed in the Back Offices of most investment firms. There was this new confirmation/affirmation process through DTCC designed to identify and correct errors before actual settlement date. But the real truth was not much had changed. People were using the same systems and procedures, but they were just doing everything a little faster. Some people claim the process became more efficient, while many others claim Back Office costs just increased, representing a lack of tangible increases in productivity.

The sell-side firms, partially in reaction to what was happening in other markets and principally because of a desire to further reduce the perceived risk between trade and settlement dates, instigated a new push – the move from T+3 to T+1, or next day settlements. The really good news is that the people behind the T+1 push understood this transition would be far more challenging than going from T+5 to T+3. As a practical matter, people and systems were incapable of simply speeding up, what they did (or staffing up) as occurred in the Eighties to meet the new T+3 deadlines. There was a clear recognition that significant structural changes in the industry, its procedures, and systems would be necessary to make next date settlements a reality. Hence, the concept of Straight Through Processing (STP) was given life, sort of like the monster in Mary Shelley's book Frankenstein. Great idea; really bad execution.

The sell-side started to do what it did best – sell. This time they were pushing T+1, not a financial product for some real or imagined problem that the buy-side could recognize or, even if they could, really care about. This time the sell-side was either extremely slow to hear the message, or they did not want to hear the message that the buy-side sent back: T+1 versus T+3 was a "street" problem. The sell-side failed to do what it had done successfully for so long, turn a problem into an opportunity. The continuously inextricable linking of T+1 and STP compounded this failure. It got to the point, and still is to a degree today, that T+1 and STP are synonymous in certain people's minds. The sell-side was pushing to reduce their exposure (risk), but they never pointed out (or did so extremely poorly) that there were tangible benefits to the buy-side. There is an old saying in marketing: "Don't sell the steak. Sell the sizzle." Well our friends on the sell-side were so preoccupied with risk reduction; all they were selling was the fire under the grill, and they spent most of their time selling the regulators, not to their clients. To their shock and amazement, they did not find any takers on the buy-side. They were even more stunned when the buy-side pushed back on the regulators - in essence forcing a delay in the previously mandated move to T+1. Today, in an effort to rescue T+1, the sell-side (along with a host of consulting firms and software vendors that bet the proverbial ranch on the rush to T+1), are desperately trying to decouple STP from T+1, the move they should have made in the first place.

Gives and Gets

In 2002 we started to see the early signs of an attempt to get the buy-side to (forgive the expression) buy into the STP concept. At a roundtable discussion titled "The future returns: The asset management industry must reduce operational cost to survive" during a Sibos conference, some interesting points were made. Donald Brydon, chairman of AXA Investment Managers, in his remarks to the delegates, said in part: "The asset management industry faces major challenges, made significantly more acute by the performance of the markets." He also said, "that there are still grounds for optimism in his industry, but only the fittest will benefit from the opportunities that lie ahead." He continued that the industry would have to pay far greater attention to both operational cost and risk. "The consequence of the current operating background for large parts of the asset management industry … is that it will no longer be managed for growth but for profit." He added that, "We stand more chance of lowering our costs if we can get common standards of messaging." [10]

So the sell-side was finally started to realize T+1 was not the way to the hearts of the buy-side. That is the good news. So they changed the tune: it is not about risk, it is about profits. John Bogle of Vanguard probably felt his heart go pitter-patter. A long time advocate that reducing costs ultimately produces better returns for investors, Bogle, and disciples of his thinking, started to see that just maybe there was something to this STP concept. The bad news is they did not have a well-conceived concept of how STP would work in actual practice. The investment industry could not even agree to a standard for trade matching.

- Should the Omgeo model become the standard?
- Should the GSTPA TME (Global Straight Through Processing Association Trade Matching Engine) be the standard?
- Was there room for two potentially competing standards?
- What about all the firms that wanted to act as "middlemen" for matching, essentially aggregators for smaller buy-side firms that would not or could not technologically participate in either standard?

---

[10] Sibos Issues on-site, Tuesday 1 October 2002 edition, Copyright © SWIFT SCRL ("SWIFT"), Avenue Adèle 1, B-1310 La Hulpe, Belgium

While these very public battles (and they were pretty ugly at times) raged on, the buy-side only became more confused and more certain that STP was a myth. Later in this chapter we will discuss the specific impediments to STP, but the basic reality is the sell-side still had not crafted the right message. Most business people look at transactions (and business relationships in general) as a series of gives and gets. The buy-side clearly understood what the sell-side wanted. What the buy-side would get in return was murky at best.

Conceptually, the sell-side was on the right track. To borrow and slightly mangle a phrase created by the campaign manager of a former US President who has his office in New York City: "It's the costs, stupid." Of course this realization took hold as the equity markets were dropping like stones tossed in a pond. The mantra of every CTO and CIO was, "ROI, ROI, ROI, ..." Unfortunately, no one had a solid handle on operational costs and only guesses at the true costs of failed trades. The bottom line was the buy-side comprehended the gives, but they only understood the gets on some ethereal level. With decades of consulting experience between us, we can tell you "ethereal benefits" are really hard to put into an ROI calculation. No hard ROI. No sale. No investment in technology that might support somebody's notion of STP.

Buy-Side Costs

So far we have cast the sell-side in the role of the bad guys, unintentionally of course. The reality is not that simple. The buy-side has been, and maybe always will be, focused on Front Office issues and concerns. The Middle Office and the Back Office are business necessities that hurt profits and distract from the business of managing money. Time and effort have been lavished on real-time market data to feed sophisticated trading systems and trade order management systems. Studies are done to determine the effectiveness of the Front Office. (With apologies to Mr. Rogers, can you say Plexus Group?) Who has done research that is universally recognized as accurate (or at least reasonable) with respect to post execution costs and more specifically the cost of an unmatched trade or a failed trade? There is a lot a research and a lot of data. But it all relies on the investment firms that participate. Personal experience tells us most firms do not have a detailed grasp on these fundamental costs of doing business. All the buy-side cares about is keeping the gross identifiable number as low as possible. (Anecdotally, Ken worked with a "Big 6" firm in the late 1980's to help establish some benchmarks for the components of Back Office costs. The variation in the responses, especially from companies with similar profiles, ultimately led to the demise of the study because no one associated with the project had confidence in the data.)

Let us consider some of the work that has been attempted to quantify operational costs. In a Wall Street & Technology Article in late 2002, the author stated:

"The most costly part of a trade is the cost of intermediating the trade. The Plexus Group estimates that an average of 100-200 basis points may be lost through inefficiencies in the trading process. 'A significant number of today's trades involve manual processes for at least some phase of the transaction,' explains Mark Volker, senior vice president for business development at SunGard Financial Networks. 'Even though a decision on T+1 was postponed until 2004, firms can gain immediate benefits with STP solutions that are available today, and that can improve throughput, capacity, and accuracy.'"[11]

Portfolio managers and traders would kill for an extra 10 basis point in their returns, and the Plexus Group estimated in 2002 that 100 to 200 basis points were lost because of "inefficiencies." Yet, the buy-side continues to focus on alpha or some other Greek as significant when there is a huge leak in the next room. In that same story, a SunGard case study was cited:

"Navellier, a quantitative/fundamental analysis and fund firm based in Reno, NV, uses Post-Trade Services to automate the confirmation and trade affirmation processes, as well as trade allocations for its sponsored WRAP program management. Navellier was able to reduce its 19-hour trade matching and affirmation process, to only 2 hours with Post-Trade Services. Employees no longer work late hours and are able to process information automatically via advanced scripting. SunGard was also able to significantly reduce Navellier's trade-confirm download time from a nearly day-long process to only 2.5 minutes. In addition, SunGard automated Navellier's WRAP program's trade allocation process, which previously included 20-30 page faxes of detailed allocation data. Navellier and SunGard worked cooperatively to automate the process of communicating block-trade allocation instructions that spanned hundreds of individual accounts."

We guess we were the only ones that read the story. Or at least we were the only ones that took it seriously and tried to learn from it. We think we may have been the only ones that saw the following story that came out of the 2002 Sibos meeting produced by Omgeo and Fulcrum Research. Or we were the only people that believed there was a hint of truth in the story.

---

[11] Achieving STP Today, By Wall Street & Technology Online, Oct 2, 2002 (1:41 PM)

Recent Research Amongst European Institutions Estimates the Cost of Failed Trades at Record Levels

SIBOS, Geneva - 30 September 2002 -

Omgeo, the leading provider of global trade management services, announced today the results of a commissioned survey carried out by leading research house, Fulcrum Research, on European institutional views surrounding trade processing issues.

Cost of Failed Trades

One of the key findings of the research was the high estimate of the cost impact of failed trades. The average figures provided were €388 for the cost of failed cross border trades, compared to €182 for domestic failed trades. This is the first research study of this type to ever be conducted amongst the European investment management community and these estimates are significantly higher than previously believed.

Causes of Failed Trades

By an overwhelming consensus, the main reason cited for failed trades was human error, supporting the notion that true efficiency can only be achieved through Straight Through Processing, where trades are processed electronically with minimal human intervention.

13% of Front Office respondents were unable to provide answers as to the causes of failed trades, but did display an awareness that failed trades are a widespread market phenomenon with serious impact on costs. The second most likely reason for failed trades, according to the research, was the provision of incorrect data, which although second, had half as many points as human error further emphasizing the significance of human error as a reason for failed trades.

Commenting on the study, Adam Bryan, CEO, Omgeo, said, "This research is highly significant for the fund management industry. Failed trades are costing firms and their investors an excessive amount of money because of the lack of efficiency in trade processing. The answer to reducing the rate of failed trades and therefore trading costs is through the implementation of Straight Through Processing where manual intervention is kept to a minimum".

"STP delivers money back to a firm's bottom line as it reduces the rate of failed trades, thereby enabling them to maintain their competitive edge. The research shows us that while European institutions are beginning to feel the heat on operational efficiency issues and transaction costs, they do not realize to what extent they are failing to achieve it; exemplified through their answers on the SDA Rates."

An Important STP Indicator - Same Day Affirmation (SDA) Rates

There was an alarming set of responses regarding an important STP indicator: same day affirmation rates (affirmation of a trade before midnight on Trade

Date). SDA rates are key to the achievement of STP as it means that both parties to a trade have agreed the trade details within a day, allowing more time to focus on dealing with exceptions and thus preventing trades from failing. In the survey - 100% of European institutions grossly misestimated their SDA rates, with the average gap between perceived and actual rates of 37%1. Italy had the widest perceptions gap between actual and perceived rates, with respondents estimating that SDA rates were at 92%, whereas in actual fact they are only at 41%. In the UK, the perception gap between actuality and reality was narrowest: SDA rates were estimated at 76%, whereas in actual fact, they are at only 60%.

Figure 26 – Omgeo Article

Operational Efficiency and Transaction Costs

Despite this disappointing level of knowledge about actual figures, there does seem to be consensus on the importance of achieving greater efficiency and reducing transaction costs. Results from the research clearly underscore that operational efficiency is of increasing importance.

Over 79% of UK, French, German and Italian institutions identified it as their top concern along with the issue of transaction costs. Among the results, the UK stood out as the country where both the front and Back Office saw operational efficiency and transaction costs as a prime concern, with over 90% of UK respondents stating these as the two issues they were most concerned about. There was also consensus regarding the measures required to increase operational efficiency and reduce transaction costs. 69% of all respondents stated that the main measure to introduce was STP or process automation.

The main drivers cited for achieving greater operational efficiency and lowering transaction costs amongst European institutions were maintaining competitive advantage and reacting to client pressure. Understandably, the top reason provided by 38% of Front Office respondents was client pressure, while 35% of Back Office respondents gave the reason as a means of achieving competitive advantage amongst their peer group. These responses are attributable to an increasingly competitive marketplace as a result of the current challenging economic environment.[12]

May we remind the readers of this chapter, both of the above two quoted stories came out in 2002. Clearly there is a disconnect between the available research and the actions (or inaction) of the buy-side as a whole. If one thinks that is shocking, here is what Bloomberg was telling anyone who would listen in 2001 based upon a 1999 TowerGroup Study:

---

[12] Bold and underlined portion are for emphasis and not original to the publication of the story.

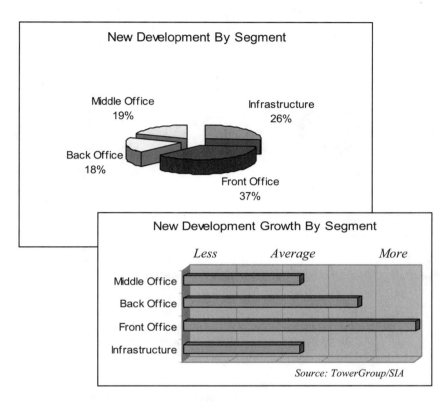

Figure 27 – Technology Spending by Segment

Basically, the TowerGroup via Bloomberg was pointing out that money was pouring into the Front Office; the sum of the money spent on the Back Offices and Middle Office combine still did not reach the spending for the Front Office. Not much has changed since this study. Bloomberg then pointed out a SWIFT study that indicated one third of failed trades were a direct result of a lack of STP:

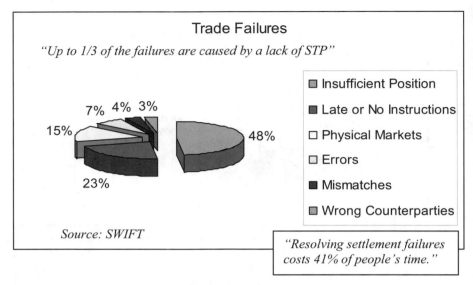

Figure 28 – Impact of Trade Failures

Just in case you missed it, the box at the bottom right says, "Resolving settlement failure costs 41% of people's time." One would think building the case for the ROI on STP would be easy. To make it even easier, Bloomberg said that slightly more than half of settlement costs are due to a lack of STP.

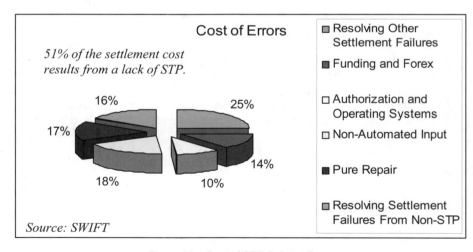

Figure 29 – Cost of STP-Related Errors

Then to make absolutely clear the magnitude of the problem, Bloomberg cited these SWIFT statistics:

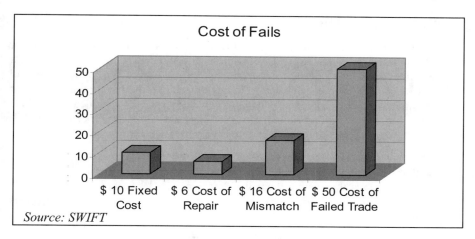

Figure 30 – Cost of Fails

Let us see, SWIFT says there is an industry cost of $12 billion in 2001 dollars and that the cost per trade problem ranged from $6.00 to $50.00 and that is on top of the fixed costs of actually doing a trade. We are guessing we were the only buy-side folks in the room when this news was delivered. How else can one logically explain the failure of the buy-side to fully embrace the STP concept? So as not to be labeled cynical, there are in fact a few firms that "got it." (It is not "real STP," but let's not burst their bubble and let's give them credit for trying.) Here is an excerpt from a July 2003 press release[13]:

A London-based investment bank reaps the rewards of a Straight Through Processing initiative broken into manageable steps.

In a bear market, there's only one route to expansion for equity brokerage businesses: Make processes more cost-efficient.

With an eye to increasing its share of the Japanese market, Tokyo Mitsubishi International (TMI), the investment banking arm of Bank of Tokyo Mitsubishi, has come to view technology as a key competitive weapon.

"For now, the only way to get new business is to take it from other people," says Don Simpson, managing director of operations and technology at TMI. "And to do that, you have to be able to do business faster, better, and cheaper than anyone else."

...

Figure 31 - Press Release

---

[13] Copyright 2003 Sun Microsystems, Inc

Volume Going Up

Japan's deregulatory Big Bang in the late 1990s created opportunities for London-based TMI to expand its business. But the bank quickly found that its existing Back Office system was stretched to the limit. "We found we would not be able to handle increased volumes or achieve the turnaround times our clients required," Simpson says. Accordingly, TMI upgraded its server platform and set in motion a series of Straight Through Processing (STP) initiatives, reaping the rewards progressively along the way.

The most dramatic advances have come from the introduction of a new settlement system to handle the firm's Japanese and international equity business. Since the system went live last year, TMI has moved from an STP rate of zero to 95 percent for cash Equities and reduced processing costs substantially.

TMI's Straight Through Processing gains are a result of an alliance with the British independent software vendor Coexis, whose Java technology-based Syn~ solution replaced TMI's Gloss Equity settlements system.

At the heart of Syn~ is an engine that allows banks to handle everyday processes ranging from how they send confirmations and SWIFT instructions to calculating the interest on a specific deal. On top of that, Coexis provides a series of banking solution templates. These contain the business rules and standard processes for handling reference data, routing and managing orders, and settling transactions-and they can be tailored to suit the requirements of a particular bank.

Reference Check

TMI's initial STP project centered on reference data, one of the key causes of trade-processing errors. In a survey by TowerGroup, almost 80 percent of respondents cited inaccurate, inconsistent, and incomplete reference data as a major cause of their failure to achieve STP within their organizations. Where firms do have automated processes, almost half the exceptions that occur are related to reference data.

Coexis worked with TMI to develop a system for the central control, management, and storage of reference data, particularly counterparty reference data (names and account details belonging to the participants in a trade).

Syn~ReferenceData manages static data right across the business from Equities to credit approvals. It provides the "golden copy" of all data relating to counterparties, which is used by Front Office, compliance, credit, operations, and risk systems across the company.

"TMI were our first client, so we added to our library of components, because there were things they wanted to do that we hadn't included," explains Andy Moorley, product manager for Coexis Syn~. "We then worked with them to implement our rules for their specific circumstances. That enriched our understanding of what would be needed particularly for handling reference data, which was quite a new area."

With Syn~ReferenceData successfully installed, the bank moved on to activate additional Syn~Settlements functionality. In addition to achieving a 95 percent STP rate, the firm has become noticeably more competitive on a cost-per-ticket basis. It is now looking to triple its volume of business over the next two years, without significantly increasing spending on staff.

Benefits to the Buy-Side

What are the benefits to the buy-side if they roll up their collective sleeves and put in the effort to make STP a reality? The answer is simple: money. That money may be in the form of increased profits dropping to the bottom line of the income statement or in significantly improved investment performance by virtue of huge cost savings. STP would make mid-tier and smaller companies more competitive with larger firms because they could benefit from the work the larger firms must do to remain relevant.

Donald Brydon, chairman of AXA Investment Managers, also told the 2002 Sibos conference attendees that the asset management industry must reduce operational cost to survive. He further stated that the industry would have to pay far greater attention to both operational cost and risk. "The consequence of the current operating background for large parts of the asset management industry … is that it will no longer be managed for growth but for profit." He went on to say that to maximize revenue, therefore, the industry would have to exercise tight control over all costs and undertake "a ceaseless search for more efficient ways of carrying out our activities." The events of the recent past have damaged self-confidence in the asset management industry, Brydon acknowledged. "It is important that we work not only at reducing the costs and increasing the focus of our businesses but that we remember to put clients first." He reminded delegates of the words of Sigmund Warburg, whose birth centenary had just been celebrated: "Go and ask the client what he wants and then try to give it to him." This maxim, he suggested, "Ought to be ringing in the ears of all those leading the asset management business today." [14]

If the benefits of STP (more money) are clear, what is the hold up? Brydon basically warned the Sibos delegates to become part of the solution or their very survival was questionable. Yet not much has happened in the intervening period. The next section deals with the very real impediments and details that made STP a myth in the minds of many, or at least an exercise in futility.

The Impediments

In 2001, there was widespread recognition that reference data would be a major roadblock to successfully implementing STP. Here is a news release from Finextra.com:

> *London* – Four out of five financial institutions see badly managed reference data as a major cause of internal Straight Through Processing (STP) failure,

---

[14] Copyright © SWIFT

according to a report published today by TowerGroup, Reuters and Capco.

STP is the automation of the entire lifecycle of a financial trade and depends upon consistent data about the client, the instrument, the deal and settlement. The research surveyed 131 financial markets industry professionals around the globe and found that on average, 30 per cent of failed trades are caused as a direct result of poor data management. The leading cause of these failed trades was identified as the inaccurate identification of settlement counter-parties, reducing STP in the post-trade and settlement arena.

Despite the impact of poorly managed data, 37 per cent of respondents stated that their organization did not have a reference data strategy. In addition, 55 per cent said they did not have, or were unaware, of the existence of defined data reference standards within their organization. These findings highlight that by failing to implement the necessary controls and strategies to manage the quality and consistency of their reference data, banks are exposing themselves to undue risk, inefficiency, costs and failed trades.

The research highlights the industry's reliance on manual entry and maintenance of reference data, even though human intervention increases overheads and the risk of errors. A third of respondents indicate that 90 per cent of their data is updated manually. Only four per cent of respondents have automated maintenance for over 90 per cent of their data. This lack of automation is reflected in the resources financial institutions are using to maintain data, with 10 per cent of organisations employing over 200 staff to re-key information.

With T+1 deadlines looming and STP as a pressing business requirement, the research also indicates the enormous task at hand for the majority of financial institutions. The average number of client records and instruments held is over two million. This volume of information is made harder to manage because it is also widely distributed, with 48 per cent of respondents indicating that this data is held in 10 or more systems across their organization. In eight per cent of cases the data is held in more than 150 systems.

Tim Lind, Senior Analyst, TowerGroup, said: "Reliable reference data is fundamental to all aspects of the investment process, but as the research shows, its management will be one of the biggest challenges facing financial institutions going forward to T+1. What we found through this study and our own extensive STP and T+1 research is that although the industry is aware of the inadequacies of their data management practices, the issue is only just being given the attention or the level of priority it deserves. The message is clear – to achieve true STP, financial services institutions need to consider how to effectively define, manage and augment their reference data."

Martin Cole, Managing Director, Reuters Consulting, commented: "Achieving true STP in an environment full of disparate and unconnected

---

[15] "Financial Institutions View Poor Data Management as a Major Obstacle to Achieving STP and T+1" 15 October 2001, For a copy of the report please visit www.finextra.com/datamanagment.asp

systems is a huge challenge, and one which TowerGroup predicts the global securities industry will spend an estimated $19bn on over the next four years alone. This report has confirmed that data management has a crucial role to play in achieving the goals of STP and T+1. By drawing on many years of managing and distributing the data produced by 263 of the worlds exchanges, Reuters is well positioned to offer a complete data management solution."

Roger Preece, Partner, Capco, says: "This research shows that data management is still being largely ignored at the institutional level. Accurate, consistent and timely reference data is one of the key foundation blocks for achieving STP, managing risk and performing effective client relationship management. It does not exist at the moment and therefore must be one of the major priorities for industry participants. Costs, control and client service must be the focus and our recently announced joint venture with Reuters has been established to provide solutions which enable financial institutions to solve this issue."[15]

Figure 32 – Press Release from Finextra.com

Earlier in this book the topic of reference data is discussed in detail. What this news release so clearly and succinctly points out is that as early as 2001 the notion of STP, driven by a T+1 mandate, would not succeed.

Wall Street & Technology magazine in a March 2003 story highlighted some of the issues surrounding reference data:

"Investment data is the lifeblood of securities operations. Most large institutions not only maintain multiple repositories supporting individual applications, but each of these is likely to have its own vendor data feeds, staffs of analysts and unique cleansing protocols. The resulting data inconsistencies stall transactions and workflows until analysts can reconcile them. Because of complicated infrastructure, most institutions face some or all of the following data-related issues:

- Lack of data transparency creating difficulties in restructuring business processes and automation to improve Straight Through Processing

- Basel II requirements and potential penalties for operational risk related to quality, control and auditability of investment data

- Capacity bottlenecks caused by highly manual data management in some areas

- Mounting volume of investment data managed and new automation (such as corporate actions processing) that creates new types of data consumption

- The need to bridge unrelated systems to upgrade risk management, research, new product development or application development

- The dilemma of how to address burgeoning data management requirements while cutting costs of overhead

Though the facing problems at any given moment may appear to be tactical, such as overcoming obstacles to STP or meeting regulatory requirement for operational risk oversight, the overriding issue is strategic and central. At base, the data infrastructure is either functional in terms of efficiency, economy and capacity, or it is not. Two measures of the quality of the data infrastructure are the costs associated with internal reconciliation among systems (including the projected losses associated with delayed or failed transactions) and the costs of redundancy among independently managed data silos."[16]

The reality of the data problem will be difficult to attack because in the end it is all about money. In today's world the providers of reference and other market data have a financial incentive to keep their data proprietary and in a form unique to the provider. To do otherwise would make their data a commodity and prevent the suppliers from getting paid premium prices. There are no simple answers as to how to address this problem. But without a solution, STP simply will not achieve its potential.

Along with the problem of data integrity, the industry does not have any standards. Or is it that the industry has too many "standards?" Progress is slowing being made by FIX with the release of the XML schema for version 4.4, which recognizes that not all trades are made with equity securities. Finally, Fixed Income securities will have some support. But there are still too many holes especially with regards to foreign exchange and trade corrections. SWIFT has made significant strides in supporting investment settlement data, but the biggest change could be their recent decision to change their pricing model. With this change it is hoped that all banks can afford and will join the SWIFT network.

Adopting an XML format and allowing IP messaging clearly goes a long way to democratizing a significant part of the STP equation. While various flavors of XML appear as tantalizing solutions to standardization of communication protocols, the truth is there are more versions of XML than flavors of ice cream at Baskin Robins. Without rationalization and wide acceptance of standards, the prospects of reaching the STP pinnacle are remote.

Finally, and most significantly, it is going to take a lot of capital – both from the buy-side and the sell-side - to fund the work necessary to find solutions to the impediments. That is easily stated but still hard to get solid commitments of funds and participation. Tied to the effort of working through or around the details, the solution vendors must be partners with both the buy-side and sell-side. Unfortunately, technology vendors and software firms are typically not held in the highest regard by the management of investment firms. Joe vividly remembers from his days as a global Hedge Fund's CIO when two major vendors flat out lied about a phantom interface between their respective 'industry leading' applications. However, without the active participation of ISV's (Independent Software Vendors) and other technology vendors, from where will the tools and infrastructure come? In the near term, this will mean

---

[16] The Challenge of Establishing Enterprise Data Consistency, Wall Street & Technology Online, Mar 12, 2003 (10:51 AM), by Ger Rosenkamp, the CEO of Asset Control

more money. Vendors will either require capital injections to meet the new standards or companies will have to be willing to pay higher costs. The mentality of squeezing your vendors for the "best deal" will only serve to cost firms money in the long run. Remember the phrase: they are your partners in achieving success.

What Will It Take to Make STP a Reality?

In March of 2003 at a Data Management Conference produced by Wall Street and Technology, Michael Atkin from the Financial Information Services Division of SIIA made the following observations:

- STP is not an event, it's a business requirement
- Only bad things can happen between trade and settlement
- Goal is to reduce errors, eliminate manual processes and reduce risk

To that list we would add scalability. As the global economy improves, and it will improve, volumes will go up. STP is critical to increasing transaction volumes. The industry can no longer just throw bodies at problems, and it really does not matter if the bodies are in New York City or Bangalore, India. People cost money, and people make mistakes.

Right now several groups are trying mightily to help get the industry to a true STP environment. Clearly, the FIX organization, SWIFT, and DTCC (and certain other global central clearing facilities) are making strides. We are not sure they are always in sync and always are sharing the identical vision. The reality is that to achieve there either has to be a tremendous "push" or a tremendous "pull" within the industry. The sell-side had their shot at pushing STP, and they blew it. Recovery to a position of power sufficient to force the STP issue will be challenging now and in the foreseeable future. The buy-side is simply too fragmented to demand an STP solution, so the prospect for "pulling" a solution out of the key players is hard to imagine.

As we gaze into our crystal ball with Atkin's words in our heads (STP is not an event, it's a business requirement), we see three possible outcomes:

In probably the worst-case scenario, the government (the SEC, Eliot Spitzer, or some foreign agency) will wake up and realize how much money is being wasted on inefficient practices. They will realize the impact on pension funds, owners of mutual funds, and the "average investor." Then they will demand action. Those demands will come in the form of new laws and regulations. We have seen what happens when the government, even with the best of intentions, gets involved in these matters (e.g., US Patriot Act, Sarbanes-Oxley, and others).

A leader will emerge who, through sheer force of will, charisma, and keen business acumen, will serve to unite both sides of the street. That leader will make the players see the light and cause them to recognize that the clock is ticking. That leader will have the vision, have the ability to communicate the vision, and create the sense of urgency vital to make STP a reality. Yes, there will be some winners and some losers, but the leader will champion what is ultimately best for the entire industry. Unfortunately, we have been told through our sources that Santa is busy, and the job does not pay enough for Joe and Ken to consider it.

The road to STP will be an evolution. Change will not be radical; it will come slowly, piece by piece. The powerful hand of market forces on both sides of the street will find common ground and grind through the details one by one. However, we fear that a rapid rise in the markets may cause the industry to put STP on the back burner because, just as in the bubble years, everybody is making a ton of money – who cares about the inner workings that keep things moving? The same, of course, is true in a market collapse. People and firms will be fighting for their lives, not what is in the best long-term best interest of the industry.

We know the benefits of STP, especially for the buy-side and those that rely on buy-side firms. We understand, at least at the conceptual level, why the sell-side desperately wants T+1 (which will by quickly followed by T+0 in our humble opinion – a topic that clearly merits its own article[17]). We started this chapter with a simple question: where is the buy-side on STP? Clearly they, as a group, are confused and lack a clear vision and leadership. They do not truly appreciate the benefits that will accrue to them if STP were a fact of life because many firms do not have a handle on their costs. And even if they did, they do not know how they compare with others in the business or if the costs are reasonable. They certainly do not have a sure fire recipe for effectively increasing productivity and reducing costs. (If there was such a methodology, you can be sure some consulting firm would be cleaning up implementing everywhere they could.)

How did the buy-side get so hopelessly lost in the woods? Our friends on the sell-side certainly did provide the right road map. They failed to sell the right concept. We know that STP must become a reality or the entire industry is in peril. Now go put on your cape and make it happen!

About the Authors

Joe Rosen

Mr. Rosen is an authority on the strategic use of information technology for competitive advantage in financial services, and was a partner for nine years at a financial software consultancy. He has worked with financial technology for over twenty years, as both developer and user of advanced trading, analytic and investment software, with a focus on the securities and investments industry. His work has encompassed major analysis and development projects across all functional and product areas of the industry. As a management consultant, Mr. Rosen advised the executive management of a leading institutional brokerage firm on strategic technology planning and implementation issues related to the firm's move toward electronic trading. As part of this assignment, he conducted a

---

[17] "T+5, T+3, T+1, ... T+0: The STP Imperative ", by Joseph Rosen and Michael Rosen. *The Journal of Securities Operation* (Fall 2002), pp. 51-55.

comprehensive survey of buy-side and sell-side firms on institutional Equities trading and technology trends.

As founding Chief Information Officer and Director of Quantitative Research for Dubin & Swieca and Highbridge Capital, he was responsible for developing and implementing a plan for the IT and operational support structure of a new hedge fund. During the course of this project he researched, analyzed and negotiated contracts with vendors in seven primary functional areas; built a trading room and installed/integrated the various vendor technologies. For the same firm, he was responsible for the design and development of the integrated risk management, performance measurement and asset allocation/optimization functions of the Manager Analysis and Research System (MARS).

Previously, Mr. Rosen was founding partner of financial technology consultancy Rosen Kupperman Associates, where he advised executives of leading technology users and suppliers on three continents and also worked with the U.S. Congress Office of Technology Assessment (OTA) on their studies of technology in the global securities market. Mr. Rosen also served in a senior management position with a pioneering software company providing on-line trading systems to Wall Street firms, where he helped develop one of the first automatic execution systems for trading Equities.

Mr. Rosen has been widely published around the world on financial technology and risk management topics. His commentary has appeared in numerous international financial and technology publications, including, among others, Computer World, Euromoney, Financial Times, Global Investment Technology, Pensions & Investments, Wall Street Journal and Wall Street & Technology. He co-authored Advanced Computer Applications for Investment Managers (Elsevier), Using Technology for Risk Management (Simon & Schuster) and The Global Directory of Financial Information Vendors (Irwin).

His most recent books are The Handbook of Investment Technology (McGraw-Hill), and The Handbook of Fixed Income Technology: Management Issues for Today and Tomorrow (Summit). Mr. Rosen is a frequent speaker globally, having chaired, moderated and spoken at dozens of industry events, from Paris to Singapore to Israel, and including the 7th Annual Computers In The City Conference in London, where he organized a full-day session on "International Contrasts in IT Management Style: What Makes Financial Technology Pay?" He has also been interviewed on national television on the subject of program trading. An alumnus of Columbia University with MBA degrees in Finance, International Business, and Marketing, Mr. Rosen also holds MA and ABD degrees in International Politics and Quantitative Methods from the State University of New York at Stony Brook, where he lectured in Political Science. He was an Adjunct Professor of Business Policy at Manhattan College, and has lectured at NYU Stern Graduate School of

Business. In addition, Mr. Rosen served as an infantryman in the Israeli Army in the mid-70s.

Ken Scheinblum

Mr. Scheinblum has over 20 years of senior level experience in the institutional buy-side arena. He is the Founder and CEO of ii Solutions, LLC, a business transformation outsourcing firm specializing in mid-tier institutional investment advisors. Previously, he was the Managing Partner and Founder of Pragma Group, LLC, an investment consulting firm for the top 200 buy-side firms.

Ken has considerable experience and knowledge of the challenges of the buy-side as well as the software, tools, and other solutions available. He has been involved in both buy and build solutions for his clients and employers. He has a deep understanding of what works in the real world based upon his hands-on approach to problem solving.

Prior to becoming a consultant, Ken ran an operations group for a large, global financial services firm. He was the head of investment accounting for a firm with over $25 billion in assets. His last stop in the corporate world was as a senior member, specializing in alternative investments, of a portfolio management team that oversaw $18 billion.

kscheinblum@iiSolutionsLLC.com

CHAPTER XIII - STP IS HERE TO STAY

By Lee Cutrone, Managing Director of Industry Relations, Omgeo

Setting the Scene: Firms Have Increasing Pressures

The underperformance of investment funds during recent years has become a truly global issue and the bear market has exasperated the matter even further. Reports suggest that in the US alone more than $7 trillion of assets have been lost due to the lack of performance of funds. The pressure on European fund managers is steadily mounting and governments as well as regulators are looking at structural reforms and stricter, regulatory guidelines as an effective means to get this issue under control and funds (back) "into shape". The Asian markets are equally affected and although regulatory action has somewhat lagged behind Europe and the US, market participants have recognized that in order to wet international investment appetite, reforms to increase operational efficiency and lower risk and cost are long overdue.

A positive move has been seen with financial institutions and regulatory agencies taking the needed steps and examining business processes and capital risk management a lot more carefully. However, the reality is that markets are still down, IT funding is sparse and the users of technology, especially investment managers, are a naturally conservative community with a tendency to take an "after you" approach to progress. To add more complexity to the challenge of moving firms and the industry up the automation curve, the global financial services industry remains highly fragmented, despite several waves of consolidation since the stock market bubble burst in March of 2000.

In the U.S. there are as many as 7,000 asset managers with more than $23 trillion under management.[18] Several thousand of these firms are hedge funds or "alternative asset managers" that didn't even exist less than a decade ago. The situation is similar in Europe and Asia, where global players co-exist with an impressive number of smaller, mostly non-automated, firms, bringing the number of asset managers in these markets to an estimated 2,500 with around $13 billion of assets under management.[19]

This market fragmentation, combined with a notable lack of funding for technology projects, has completely transformed the landscape for industry wide Straight Through Processing (STP) since the heady days back in 1998 when the GSTPA initiative emerged. Two consequences of these changes:

- The one-size-fits-all solution devised by GSTPA – the TFM – was dead on arrival when it finally rolled out the door towards the end of 2002
- The pressure on firms' bottom lines is steadily increasing and regulators as well as market participants are calling for greater cost transparency

This second issue was specifically addressed in the recent Myners Report, which stated that fund managers need to keep the costs charged to investors

---

[18] Source: Omgeo Proprietary Data, August 2003
[19] Source: Omgeo Proprietary Data, August 2003

down, while maintaining greater transparency and unbundling their fee structures.[20]

As shown above, the market is extremely fragmented. As a result, any professional marketer would equate this challenge with not just one solution for the market but with multiple solutions directed at specific market niches – all aimed at improving operational efficiency with a return on investment tailored to the individual firm. More specifically and among the asset managers in particular, there is wide variation in the levels of technological sophistication, to the point that broker/dealers and custodians still have to deal with unacceptably high levels of cost and risk directly related to (mostly) smaller, non-automated investment managers' inefficient ways of sending allocations and processing trades.

- There are firms that have fully automated their trade processing and there are firms that still rely completely on phone and fax.

- Many of the newer hedge funds in particular are smaller organizations with little infrastructure that depend entirely on their brokers to get their trades processed and settled. Many small investment advisors do the same thing.

- Other somewhat larger players outsource to their custodians. Outsourcing middle and Back Office operations and focusing on core competencies is still at an early stage, individuals within firms are sometimes reluctant to hand their spheres of influence over to third parties.

In such a complex environment, a solutions provider must be able to bring flexible solutions as well as a wide range of offerings to market in order to be successful. These flexible solutions should provide the user with the ability to operate with their entire community of counterparties while staying a step ahead of the competition and moving further up the STP chain. For trade management solutions the most efficient way to move up the automation line is through central matching. Central matching provides participants with a central or common "meeting place" to match all of the various and needed information when moving a trade to settlement. Industry organizations such as the Securities Industry Association (SIA) in the United States have openly supported such processing moves. However, history tells us that not all participants are able to leap to a completely new way of securities processing and instead are more likely (and able) to move gradually towards a central matching model, especially if they are offered a clear and easy migration path.

One experienced solutions provider that can offer the industry the needed range of services noted above is Omgeo. Its solutions span straightforward trade confirmation offerings and centralized databases of settlement instructions to complete central matching solutions. It makes these services available through a choice of interfaces ranging from Web-based FIX-compliant software to highly secure direct host-to-host connections. And it provides customized solutions that are tailored to the practices and sophistication level of each local

---

[20] Source: Myners Review of Institutional Investment, March 2001

market and takes into account the quick ROI (return on investment) firms are looking for today: 12-18 months. The pages that follow will expand on the STP solutions offered by Omgeo.

Making STP Happen: a Broad Range of Solutions

"Achievement of Straight Through Processing will significantly reduce costs of settlement, including the growing costs of resolving error in the documentation and processing of trades, and it should create scalability that can meet future increases in trading volumes…STP will remove many, if not all, of the obstacles to realization of what should be the ultimate goal – settlement in T+0." Alan Greenspan, Chairman of the Federal Reserve Board

It's very encouraging to see economists like Mr. Greenspan recognize the value STP will bring to our industry. His quote is as valid as ever, even after the SIA (Securities Industry Association) postponed a US move to T+1.[21] Many have since commented that T+1 was only an accelerator of change, of improving processes – the drivers for increasing STP levels remain cost mitigation, risk management, regulation, revenue growth and increased client service.[22] Those were also the drivers at the heart of the industry's move to ETC (electronic trade confirmation) back in the early nineties. ETC was based on a simple concept: instead of drowning in the tide of paper that flowed back and forth between trade counterparties after a deal was struck, they electronically swapped and confirmed all the vital details in standard message formats, which helped to streamline the confirmation process tremendously.

To help reduce the onslaught of paper flow and reduce the number of failed trades, The Depository Trust Company (DTC) launched the first version of its Institutional Delivery (ID) System in 1973 to handle electronic communications between the investment manager, the broker/dealer and custodian banks.[23] The solution unfortunately only handled a piece of the ETC flow, leaving allocations out of the mix. This was remedied with the launch of Omgeo OASYS[SM] in 1991.

Today, OASYS is the industry-standard service for the automated communication of U.S.-domestic Fixed Income and equity trade allocation breakdowns, a critical step toward achieving end-to-end STP. To support STP, OASYS provides users – investment managers and broker/dealers – with a reduction of both costs and risks by eliminating the need for any manual intervention when processing their trades. By not having to deal with repetitive and time-consuming manual processes, Back Office staff within the securities industry is able to focus on providing better quality services to clients.

---

[21] July 18, 2002

[22] Source: Gartner Group, May 2003 – survey of 184 global investment managers

[23] The ID system, now part of the *Omgeo TradeSuite*[SM] solution, was updated in 1994 to include additional interactive options allowing for same-day trade confirmations, affirmations and settlement instructions.

Conseco Capital Management

One OASYS Fixed Income user, Conseco Capital Management (CCM), has achieved a variety of benefits from using the service. The Indiana based organization is a Fixed Income investment advisor with over $26.2 billion in both taxable and tax-exempt assets under management. CCM serves a wide variety of market segments including: Taft-Hartley plans, foundations & endowments, insurance companies, public funds, corporate pensions and mutual funds to name a few. Before adopting Omgeo's solutions, CCM's operations and information systems management teams sought to reduce inefficiencies associated with their reliance on manual trade processing methods. Their employees were verbally communicating Fixed Income and equity trade allocation details to brokers over the phone, and then dealing with subsequent communications inaccuracies. As a result of the company's reliance on these manual processes, CCM's operating costs were significant. Back Office employees were spending too much time processing trades, resolving errors and dealing with failed trades.

In the autumn of 1998, as a part of its ongoing STP initiative, CCM eliminated its reliance on time consuming, manual processes and adopted OASYS. 'OASYS has given us a huge increase in our level of efficiency," says John Huybers, Assistant Vice President, Information Systems at CCM. Today, nearly all of CCM's trades processed via OASYS are for Fixed Income instruments. The company is reaping economic benefits because its Back Office employees can communicate Fixed Income trade allocations in an automated manner. Before processing trades in an electronic environment, CCM required six full-time equivalents to process its trades. Today, only four are needed and the other two have been redeployed to others areas of the company, including investment research and portfolio analytics. This is a reduction of trade processing labor costs by approximately 33%. Huybers states that CCM has been able to "significantly reduce operating expenses and increase the productivity of our employees."

In addition to reducing manual processes, CCM aimed to decrease the number of problematic trades. After implementing the new operating environment, CCM achieved a 65% reduction in the number of trade exceptions and a 50% reduction in the number of trade failures. CCM officials also state that, "A decline in the number of failed trades is good for the overall health of our business. When trades fail, investment-return opportunities can be lost or reduced." Neither of which are easily recouped easily in today's economic environment.

As seen with CCM, using OASYS and Omgeo TradeSuite^{SM} separately provides many improved operational efficiencies, but only provides the first step of achieving STP. When using Omgeo OASYS-TradeMatch^{SM}, the combination of OASYS and Omgeo TradeMatch^{SM} (the U.S. central trade matching service for investment managers and broker/dealers[24]), Omgeo clients are able to transition to a true central matching environment. In the end, users are moving further and further up the efficiency meter in a sensible and planned manner.

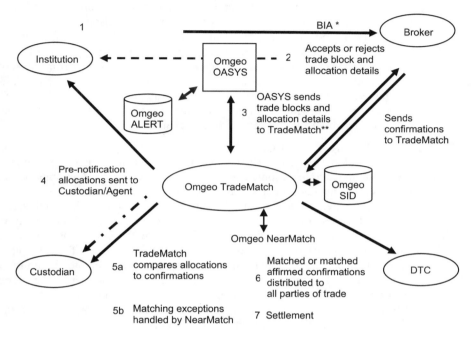

Figure 33 - Omgeo OASYS - TradeMatch[SM]

*   Broker Internal Account numbers appended from ALERT if using both products.

**   For existing accounts, TradeMatch calculates Principal Amount, SEC Fees and Net Settlement Amount and determines Settlement Location for the OASYS message for matching purposes. SEC calculation and rounding rules conform with the new Investor and Capital Markets Relief Act recently passed by Congress.

LSV Asset Management

LSV Asset Management (LSV) has reported the benefits it obtained by processing trades through OASYS-TradeMatch.

LSV Asset Management, a user of OASYS-TradeMatch, provides active equity management services for a range of institutional investors. Using proprietary investment techniques and a value style of investing, the firm has generated strong relative returns over the past several years. Largely as a result of its investment performance, LSV has grown its assets under management from $2.5 billion to nearly $10 billion over the past four years.

---

[24] Omgeo TradeMatch is a part of the Omgeo TradeSuite STP solution

As is most common with firms relying on manual processes, LSV was communicating trade details with its counterparties through a combination of fax, emails and the telephone. "For us, adopting OASYS-TradeMatch was a no-brainer. Now we have a single point of entry, so that our allocations can be input once and routed to brokers, and then automatically on to settlement," said Tremaine Atkinson, chief operating officer of LSV. Today, the institution processes trades so quickly and efficiently that with the exceptions that do occur virtually none of them turn into trade failures due to human error. The company affirms 90% of its trades on T+0 – or on the same day – and less than 1% of its U.S.-domestic trades result in exceptions. Investment managers, such as LSV, are provided with a simple solution to improve their operational efficiency by using this service free of charge.

Historically, OASYS and OASYS-TradeMatch have appealed to investment managers that have a substantial amount of assets under management, are actively trading, and have some existing Front and Back Office automation. In most cases this includes an order management system. For smaller investment managers, however, investing in STP projects can be a daunting challenge - time as well as money. "While large firms have the burden of complexity in implementing the T+1 initiative, small firms have the burden of building a solid business case for technology and automation," states TowerGroup[25]. Slim IT budgets have forced smaller investment managers to continue to process their allocations manually, causing many problems for their broker/dealer counterparties who continue to receive thousands of faxes and phone calls every day. This is clearly not a very efficient way of processing trades and is a painful cost for many broker/dealers.

To eliminate these pain-points, many of the larger brokers have created their own Web-based solutions for their investment managers to utilize. The intent is that the investment managers would upload their allocations to the broker's site, which in turn are sent electronically to the broker's trade processing system. This scenario creates a more efficient environment for the broker/dealer, but for the investment manager it means that they need to visit every single broker's Web site - not an ideal and easy way of processing trades. As a result, many of these sites are not utilized as much as they could be by the investment managers.

To address the challenges outlined above, Omgeo launched a new service in March 2003 with four major broker/dealers called Omgeo Allocation Manager[SM].

---

[25] Source: TowerGroup report, 2002

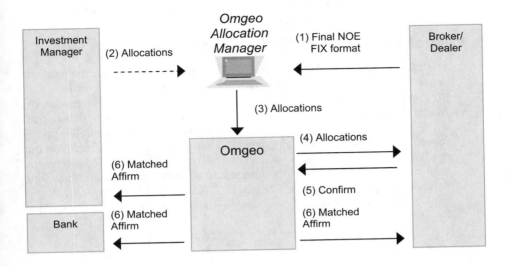

Figure 34 - Omgeo Allocation Manager SM

The solution, a multi-broker portal accessible via a secure Web-based connection, is free for the investment manager, simplifies allocation submission, minimizes cost and has the potential to improve operational efficiencies inherent with the estimated 3,000 investment managers still manually processing trades in the U.S. The "founding brokers," Credit Suisse First Boston, JPMorgan, Morgan Stanley, and UBS Securities LLC, all helped in the development of the service, and are able to make use of their existing technology investments – i.e. the Omgeo Allocation Manager feeds all of the allocation information to their existing connections to OASYS, OASYS-TradeMatch and in the future to Omgeo Central Trade Manager[SM]. The new solution also embraces the FIX (financial information exchange) format, a global industry protocol that many broker/dealers are already using.

The service went live in July 2003 with a six beta investment managers and numerous others have since signed up and are also beginning to use the service. Industry organizations, such as the SIA and the ICAA (Investment Council Association of America), have publicly applauded the efforts made by Omgeo and the brokers to automate this part of the business. For example, John Panchery, Vice President and Managing Director of Systems & Technology at the SIA said, "I want to thank Omgeo for the really vast work they did on developing the Web-based Allocation Manager. When you really think about it there's only one choice in this day and age and that's the Internet, so kudos to Omgeo and the broker-dealers that helped support them."[26] Others have also vocalized feedback including Chase Investment Council, a user of the service: "Our firm is able to focus more time on

---

[26] Source: SIA STP/Central Matching Roundtable Event, August 5, 2003

servicing clients rather than processing trades." Efforts are already in progress in Europe and Asia with broker/dealers to create a similar solution.

Central Matching – the Future Today

Central matching has been the focus of much industry debate over the past few years. Once just an idea in the minds of many, matching utilities have lost their vaporware stigma and become a reality for an industry of thousands. Market conditions may have dictated that the take-up has been slower than many had anticipated, however central matching is slowly but surely proving its value in the marketplace, one firm at a time. Later in this chapter, you can read the first-hand experience of one firm, Royal London Asset Management, who has implemented Omgeo's domestic and cross border central matching solution, Omgeo Central Trade Manager[SM] (Omgeo CTM). However, let us explore exactly why central matching is the model the industry is striving towards.

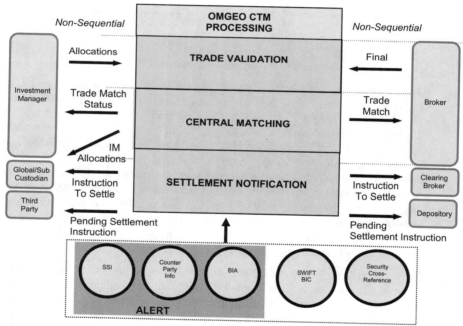

Figure 35 – Omgeo Central Matching

Local matching provides the industry considerable increases in efficiencies, and reduces cost and risk across the board. However, local matching must be considered as an interim step towards full STP. Unlike local matching, central matching provides all counterparties (investment managers, broker/dealers and custodian banks) with the ability to have a proactive role in the trade process. As a result, the trade moves along the processing chain right through to settlement at a much faster and more efficient rate. The elimination of sequential steps results in fewer unmatched trades – all parties can enter data when it is convenient rather than waiting for their counterparty to fill in information. Exception-only processing results in a significant reduction in the time spent managing trades - matched trades go straight through to settlement.

Critical with Omgeo's solutions, investment managers have instant access to a global community of 950+ broker/dealers via a single platform for both domestic and cross-border trading. This is because Omgeo has developed a "bridge" to handle data flow and message format translations between investment managers using Omgeo CTM and their broker/dealers using Omgeo OASYS Global^{SM}, Omgeo's global electronic trade confirmation service. In a fragmented industry, as described in the introductory section to this chapter, it is even more important to unite a community of counterparties on a single platform and using the same standards to gain industry-wide STP. The best application in the world is useless if you have no one to trade with.

Unlike previous central matching models, Omgeo CTM does not offer a "one-size-fits-all" model. It is flexible enough to adapt to current (and future) market conditions and to meet all trade counterparty requirements. Its "follow-the-sun" processing capabilities allow firms to be more productive (and therefore competitive) by trading around the clock, and its stable platform enables firms to cope with volume peaks and surges.

It is true to say that the cost and length of implementation was once a barrier to implementing central matching. However, simplified implementation options minimize the time, effort and resources required to implement Omgeo CTM and reduce overall project lifecycle to just 4 - 6 weeks. This means that firms can benefit from an extremely quick and clear return on investment – critical in tough economic climates when every IT spend is carefully evaluated. To further help eliminate any additional barriers, firms are also able to utilize existing technology investments made in their Front Office/Middle Office solutions (e.g. trade order management solutions) by leveraging partnerships Omgeo has made with such vendors.[27] By doing so, firms rely on the same vendor to build a connection to Omgeo CTM (or Omgeo's other STP solutions) on their behalf to their solutions.

Unlike some firms, who are adopting a "wait and see" approach when it comes to central matching, Royal London Asset Management was the pioneer in this field. As the first investment manager in the world to centrally match trades using Omgeo CTM, they describe their positive experiences.

---

[27] The Omgeo STP Partner Program^{SM} has nearly 50 partners with over 50 available interfaces.

Julian Baines, Investment Servicing Manager, talks about how Royal London Asset Management (RLAM) quantified the success of Omgeo Central Trade Manager[SM]

The Challenge

"I had been looking at automating our Back Office operations for many years, but one of the main challenges I was up against was internal skepticism: "How do we need to re-engineer our processes? This might turn into a huge undertaking. There are a number of other projects that are far more important at this point in time, such as Year 2K and the introduction of the Euro." It was not until RLAM merged with United Assurance and Scottish Life in 2001 and the size of our business quadrupled, that it became apparent that we would not be able to handle effectively our increased trade volumes with inefficient, manual processes in place. At that time, we still printed trade confirmation messages from Omgeo OASYS Global[SM 28] and matched them manually to our portfolio accounting system and we still communicated 100% of our Equities and Fixed Income trade allocations to our broker/dealers over the phone. The process was slow and prone to human error, people were shifting paper backwards and forwards and meeting the custodian cut off times was difficult. By further automating our Back Office operations we would be able to reduce our operational risk and trade failure rates dramatically, we would be able to easily handle much higher trade volumes and increase our SDA (same day affirmation) rates. In December 2001 I was finally given the go ahead to sign up for an STP solution as the time was now right to address a long ignored and constantly postponed issue."

Why Omgeo?

"I spent years researching the market to find "the right" automated trade processing system for RLAM. The decision to go with Omgeo and to implement Omgeo Central Trade Manager[SM] (Omgeo CTM) was a straightforward one: Omgeo is a commercially aware and client focused organization. It understands global market trends and has a proven track record of providing a broad range of STP services – including OASYS Global[29], Omgeo ALERT[30], Omgeo Benchmarks for OASYS Global[31] - to its clients around the globe; I felt very comfortable that it would advise us well in terms of our IT investments and longer term strategy. In addition, we

---

[28] RLAM was using *Omgeo OASYS Global*, an electronic trade confirmation system, to process trades. The problem was that RLAM's portfolio accounting system was not linked to *OASYS Global*, which meant that data had to be transferred from Front Office to Back Office system manually.

[29] *Omgeo OASYS Global* is a worldwide electronic trade allocation and confirmation service supporting T+0 affirmation.

[30] *Omgeo ALERT* is a global database and standard for the communication of settlement and account instructions.

[31] *Omgeo Benchmarks* is an online performance measurement tool designed to enable investment managers and broker/dealers to measure their own and their counterparties' operational efficiency.

already had a good, long-term working relationship and were encouraged that Omgeo would partner with its sister company Thomson Financial, who owned our Back Office system "Icon"[32], to implement a fully automated link to Omgeo CTM. For us that meant that we would not have to manage multiple relationships with vendors, which would make our life a lot easier. Omgeo had done another smart thing: it had built a link between its ETC service OASYS Global, used by 950 brokers and 350 investment managers worldwide, and its new matching solution Omgeo CTM. This bridge made sure that we would be able to communicate with all our brokers from day one."

Positive ROI for implementing Omgeo CTM?

"The relationship between IT spend and revenues is a complex one as it is difficult to determine the exact impact of a successful IT project on a firm's overall business process. At RLAM we do have a formal cost/benefit process in place: it is looking at how much we are planning to spend prior to kicking off a project, it measures how we are doing in terms of spend throughout the course of the project and it measures the final spend. If we overspend at any time, the amount needs to be signed off by the project sponsor and our finance director. Traditionally, we have been looking at a 4-year payback, but seeing the current economic climate, more and more projects require a much quicker turn around, such as 12 – 18 months. Nowadays, you have to be able to prove some early pay back to get a project signed off in the first place. When I did my research to determine how much it would cost to automate our Back Office processes, I estimated to spend approximately £250,000. But as an early adopter of Omgeo CTM we ended up paying a lot less, so if you are thinking of positive ROI in terms of "getting your STP investment back", we were more than highly satisfied.

I also look at positive ROI in a much broader sense: after having implemented Omgeo CTM our custodian scorecards showed that our trade failure rates had dropped by 50%. I view this as a massive achievement, especially considering how much money is lost when a trade fails.

We also dramatically reduced our operational risk, or "the risk of not being able to deliver stock that we committed ourselves to delivering on time, due to the trade not matching". An unexpected and positive side effect was that by automating our allocations and becoming more operationally efficient, the relationship with our brokers has greatly improved. We are now known in the market for our forward thinking and commitment to efficiency and STP. Operational performance is without doubt becoming a key method to evaluate trading counterparties: we evaluate our brokers along those lines, and they evaluate us using the same parameters.

Since implementing Omgeo CTM, the number of trades we process has increased by 30%, which in the current economic climate is a very encouraging figure. The robustness of Omgeo CTM was put to test this

---

[32] Thomson Financial Icon is a real-time investment management, administration and portfolio valuation solution.

February, when we experienced the biggest day of trading in RLAM history: 900 trades across 15 markets in Europe, the US and Japan. If we had had to process that amount of trades manually, we would have been swamped and, on average, only one in two trades would have matched the first time. Omgeo CTM allowed us to increase our first time trade-matching rate to 75%, which left us with a much smaller percentage of exceptions to sort out. That day we really tested the water and Omgeo CTM lived up to our expectations. Even the last resistance at RLAM was overcome as this day really changed people's attitudes. We significantly cut the man-hours it would have taken to handle these volumes manually and our staff's time was used more productively to support our additional business.

Omgeo CTM also allowed us to increase our (same day affirmation) SDA rates. Prior to implementing Omgeo CTM it took us on average 20 hours to affirm a trade; now we are down to 9 hours; my target is to affirm within 3 hours. To achieve this goal, our brokers will need to increase their operational efficiency as well. The fax is still used too frequently and, as a result, it is very difficult to deal with trade exceptions swiftly. You might wonder why this is so important to me and what economic value I see in it? Increasing SDA rates means that trades match earlier, which gives us more time to find and sort out problems. Historically, the Back Office has dealt with problems the next day; I would like to come to a stage where we are dealing with today's problems today. This means that reconciliation can be done on a real time basis, which will allow our fund managers to obtain information on how they are performing much earlier on. The Myners Report is a good example of how attitudes are changing: pension fund trustees are much more cautious nowadays with respect to whom they are giving their money. In times like these, when markets are down, you have to be a lot smarter as it is a very competitive world. The benefits your firm is bringing need to be transparent, you need to show how well your firm is doing compared to its competitors, and operational efficiency, high SDA rates, low trade failure rates etc. are all key differentiators.

I have a competitive element in me (maybe from my former football days!) and I like to climb league tables. I am committed to making sure that in the UK RLAM is amongst the top in terms of operational efficiency. Omgeo CTM has certainly increased our competitive edge and I will continue to strive to stay ahead of the game."

Figure 36 - Royal London Asset Management Case Study

Effective Data Management: Devil in the Details

It is said that only three things matter when it comes to property: location, location, and location. Similarly, one could say that three things matter when it comes to trade settlement: data, data, and data. As discussed in previous sections of this chapter, there is a broad array of STP solutions available to the industry, but without proper management of the data, the trade is destined for failure and trade processing becomes not so straight through.

If one looks at the specifics of a trade, it is apparent that it is merely a collection of data. The challenge is to manage this data properly to create accurate information. The efficient management of this data and information is a key element to achieving global STP. This is not to say that managing the transaction processing efficiently through innovations like matching is not important; far from it. It is only to say that unless the matching engine is fed the right stuff, i.e., good data, trades will have much in common with that proverbial investment property nightmare, the white elephant, incurring great care and expense to maintain while yielding little profit.

How do we know this is so? The answer, of course, is in the data. Recently Omgeo undertook an analysis of 24,000 trades in 25 markets to see why some trades fail to settle on time. The results were illuminating. It turned out that workflow efficiency issues are the primary cause of trade processing exceptions only 9 percent of the time. A much bigger problem was late, incomplete or inaccurate data, which led to more than half of all out-trades, or "exceptions."[33] As important as central matching is, the results indicate that focusing only on matching as a means to improve workflow efficiency misses the point. In fact, other industry research has shown that 30% of trade failures are caused by poor data and the same research also indicated that 79% of clients agreed that inconsistent, inaccurate and incomplete data is a major cause for STP failure.[34]

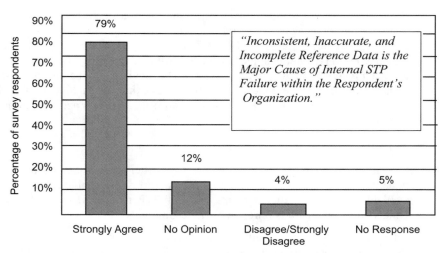

Source: Reference Data: The Key to Quality STP and T+1, October 15, 2001; a joint Reuters / TowerGroup / Capco survey of various financial institutions

Figure 37 – Reference Data as a Cause of Trade Exceptions

How expensive are all of these trade exceptions? As a part of the same research, Omgeo asked a cross-section of its global client base that and other

---

[33] Source: Survey conducted by Omgeo regarding fees and taxes data, settlement information and costs of trades and exceptions. (2001)

[34] Source: Reuters, Capco, TowerGroup Survey, September 2001

related questions. According to the survey, firms spend approximately $15-$30 to process a trade exception, versus the $3-$7 for a clean trade. This number increases to $100 - $150 for a failed trade, without including market movement or interest costs. Clearly, not small change given the number of trades involved.

Interestingly enough, over 90 percent of Omgeo's clients surveyed for the research cited fees and taxes data, as well as settlement cycle information as the types of data that caused the most problems. Moreover, clients indicated that the number of exceptions related to fees and taxes information can run as high as US$750 per month, while the number of exceptions from settlement information can run as high as $1,500 per month. Some quick math shows that the cost of trade exceptions in each of these data areas averages approximately US$3,600 per month, or more than US$80,000 per year for the two areas combined.

How can the industry fix this problem? In addition to offering a broad array of ETC and matching solutions, Omgeo has developed an initiative called Omgeo Quality Data Initiative, or QDI. Through the QDI, Omgeo will be able to push clients toward consistent data population, improve data quality on Omgeo ALERT^{SM}, Omgeo's global database and standard for the communication of settlement and account instructions, and educate clients on populating "quality" SSI's or standing settlement instructions.

Based on research completed by Omgeo and the industry it becomes apparent that the proper management of trade data throughout the trade process is a key element to achieving global STP. Without effective data management tools imbedded in STP solutions, the latest and greatest technology will only get end users halfway down the road to STP. The devil is in the details and as mentioned above, if the trade data is not accurate, than the trade will fail and as noted, it costs a lot more to fix the trade than if the data was accurate from the beginning.

Summary

STP is an attainable goal for all industry participants, but a major barrier remains – the realization that there is a broad array of flexible STP solutions available today no matter a firm's level of STP readiness – as outlined by Omgeo and demonstrated through client testimonials.

There are still some significant hurdles for all industry participants to overcome, particularly cost issues associated with IT spending, but as Omgeo also highlighted the ROI and eventual cost savings, especially for institutions and brokers implementing central matching solutions and achieving high SDA rates, is well worth the investment today to prepare for what will ultimately be in the not so distant future.[35]

---

[35] Omgeo is a leading provider of post-trade pre-settlement trade management solutions, processing over one million trades per day and serving 6,000 investment managers, broker/dealers and custodians in more than 40 countries. We partner closely with service providers, infrastructure suppliers, industry standards organizations, and our clients to increase operational efficiency and reduce risk for the world's investment management community through STP solutions. With 27 combined years of experience, Omgeo is the

About the Author

Lee J. Cutrone was named managing director, Industry Relations of Omgeo in early 2001 after serving in a similar capacity at Thomson Financial ESG since 1998. Prior to that role, Mr. Cutrone was the managing director for the Americas region at Thomson Financial ESG since 1995.

In his current role, Mr. Cutrone acts as liaison between Omgeo and its constituents and "stakeholders," including clients, global advisory boards and working parties, regulators, vendors, depositories and industry groups, ensuring that clients and other industry participants have a direct point of contact for interacting with Omgeo on a strategic business level. Mr. Cutrone is also involved in establishing the strategic direction of Omgeo's services, and for structuring key business relationships to deliver appropriate industry-driven solutions. Mr. Cutrone is currently serving as an advisor to the SIA's STP Steering Committee and Cross-Border Committee and previously served on the Institutional Transaction Processing Committee (ITPC), as well as the T+1 Business Case RFP sub-committee.

Prior to his employment at Thomson Financial ESG, Mr. Cutrone was senior vice president of the Securities Division at the American Stock Exchange (AMEX), having held several executive positions there since 1975. Mr. Cutrone has also held positions at Stone & Webster Securities Corporation from 1973 to 1974, and Merrill Lynch, Pierce, Fenner & Smith, Inc. from 1971 to 1973. He holds a B.A. in Economics from St. Francis College, Brooklyn, NY, and a MBA in Finance from Pace University, New York, NY.

lee.cutrone@omgeo.com

result of a global joint venture between The Depository Trust & Clearing Corporation (DTCC), the securities industry's respected utility and Thomson Financial, a leading provider of financial workflow solutions. Omgeo's Board of Managers includes recognized global experts who provide industry oversight and help shape the vision of Omgeo.

CHAPTER XIV - STP AND WORKFLOW

By Gert Raeves, Business Development Director, HelioGraph

Introduction

Management Game A:

Transaction Process Management: Straight-To-Profits?

This is your mission, should you choose to accept it. To develop, market, and sell a software-based solution to one of the few remaining areas of low-automation in the civilized world. You will face market indifference, inertia, and hostility.

The promise: your product will be purchased by the thousands of banks, asset managers, brokers and investment banks that have yet to invest strategically in this area. Mission impossible or potential money-spinner?

Imagine you are doing a business studies course and the inevitable management game beckons. Here is the challenge: you are the CEO of a software company that has identified an interesting market niche. Legend has it there exists today, in 2004, an entire market segment where business critical processes involve paper-based processing, and where the automated systems that exist cannot easily exchange information. It is the software entrepreneur's equivalent to discovering a lost valley where dinosaurs roam free. Welcome to the world of opportunity that is securities Straight–Through Processing (STP).

Historical Definitions – STP

STP has suffered from being an ill-defined catchphrase that has appealed to marketers from a very wide spectrum of software providers. Telco networks, portfolio management systems, order management systems, middleware, production workflow, data warehousing, service connection gateways, standards bodies: they will all happily claim to "give you STP." The phrase "straight-through" is in many ways unfortunate: operational excellence may very well mean high-volume, low-latency, zero-intervention data being transported in-and-out of systems, but may in may other cases require time, reflection, visibility and intervention. Where a business-critical step of the process necessarily involves a human decision, the very notion of "straight-through" will increase operational risk.

And yet the ability to assume automated operations and straightforward integration between disparate systems should be the starting point of any useful answer to the question "what is STP?" Where possible and desirable, there should be no technological constraints to the free flow of data, and there is immense value in a robust, high-throughput "processing factory" for anyone who needs to offer a wide range of products to lots of clients over different channels.

This is also where the initial technology offerings for the STP-hungry were focusing: the providers of industry standard middleware and data transport tools that have effectively made low-level integration a commodity.

But to limit STP-technology to a mechanical "single integration layer" would be to deny the granular nature of operational risk. Putting in place the facility for systems to communicate is pointless if the receiving application has no use for the type of data that it can now receive. What use is the ability to send a notification of a pre-settlement match from a SWIFT gateway to a portfolio accounting system that does not have any concept of settlement monitoring? As the industry is moving beyond simple connectivity and integration solutions, suppliers are forced to recognize how their products and services are constantly suffering from value-erosion, unless they can articulate a compelling vision of new and more value-add functions.

The emphases moves from simple "enabling" technology (integration and connectivity) to "empowering" technology (process monitoring. metrics, MIS, analytics).

It is in these instances that the technology needed is one that draws attention risk-bearing stages of a transaction, and provides an exception management and business intelligence environment for process-oriented activities. The most widely used label for this type of functionality is Workflow, or Business Process Management (BPM) software.

Again, workflow and BPM in isolation have an inherent tendency to promote "the process is the purpose" thinking. As any head of Operations knows, drawing a pretty flowchart of a process is useful analysis, but cannot make the process any more efficient without addressing essential integration bottlenecks. In other words, the application of BPM disciplines to the problem of securities STP inevitably leads to integration requirements.

As elements of EAI and BPM technologies become in isolation ever more commoditized, their combined application to the area of STP offers a compelling business case, and promises to resolve the old "workflow or integration" dilemma.

Recently, industry experts have started to use the phrase Transaction Process Management (TPM) in order to characterize this approach, where the focus on transaction allows the concept to bridge both business and technical considerations, and is very effective at combining both tactical and strategic instances of a TPM project.

Transaction Process Management – an Attempt to Define

Why is TPM such a powerful concept?

In our view, it is the first example of an integrated STP framework that has the potential to satisfy both operational and management objectives, and is flexible enough to be applied to a short tactical project with near-immediate ROI, but also to enterprise wide information management strategies. TPM combines workflow, process modeling, messaging, Web services, and enterprise application integration, but is in itself not a product: it is a mindset that needs to be adopted by an organization in order to realize the full benefits.

This vision allows TPM providers to align themselves with the business goals of their clients, and not just with a departmental objective. It allows the transformation of straightforward task-based automation into process-oriented, continuous monitoring of business-critical activity. This in turn allows TPM solutions to be positioned as a key contributor in attaining organizational goals. The often-quoted distinction made by Michael Tracy and Fred Wiersema in "The Discipline of Market Leaders" between the three types of market leadership that organizations aspire to is useful in the TPM debate as well: whether the ultimate corporate goal is operational excellence, product leadership, or client intimacy, TPM can help firms achieve it.

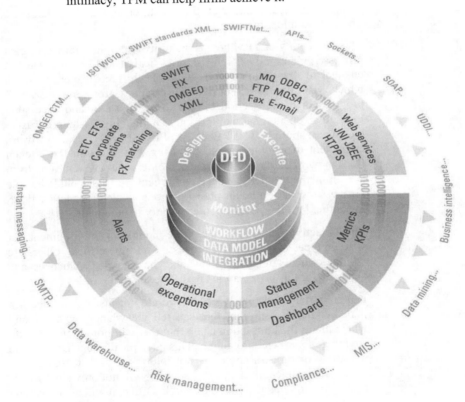

Figure 38 – Trade Flow TPM

A tentative definition of TPM should therefore include the following:

Transaction Process Management helps organizations to achieve their corporate goals by providing the tools:

- To manage, monitor, and measure transactional business activity
- Across disparate systems and protocols
- Identifying and reducing operational risk
- Through a single user interface
- Using trusted data, integrated systems, and harmonized processes

Let's look at each of these in more detail.

Manage, Monitor and Measure Business Activity

We are not in a design phase here, i.e., we are not talking about re-engineering a process. TPM is transactional, runtime, and practical. While business process re-engineering may well lead to an implementation of TPM, this is not what TPM seeks to deliver. TPM will take an existing process, analyze the make-up in terms of integration, data and workflow requirements and implement a practical solution.

The key quality of TPM here is visibility and transparency: when a process is identified as high-risk or critical, it will find the relevant channel to draw attention to itself. There are different ways in which visibility is achieved. This ranges from the measured progression of transaction through a set of states and accessible through an operational workstation to a great big flashing intrusive message shouting THERE IS A PROBLEM! This software equivalent of a two-year old throwing a tantrum on the kitchen floor is particularly useful for stakeholders that are removed from the immediate operational environment. This could be the business owner of a repair process who is located on another floor, in another building, even another country or continent.

The objective is to offer the right monitoring environment for specific types of risk. Some processes are time-critical, others are volume-critical, or cost-critical, and the intended audiences and channels for this information are different.

It is important however to ensure we are not just talking about a pure monitoring solution, that can tell me what is going wrong where along the transaction chain, but that will not allow me to do anything about the problem. This is typically the case if the workflow or process engine is not interfaced to/ integrated with processing applications. A TPM solution will not only alert you of a confirmation mismatch in the Middle Office, it will also give you an opportunity to remedy the situation by making changes in the content or status of a specific transaction context. The notion of transaction consciousness is crucial: a message is just a message, and there is no point in intervening in a message exchange without understanding that message B is a confirmation of message A, which is subsequently cancelled by message C.

The transaction context and business process awareness is where the securities industry comes into its own. There are a number of well-defined "units of process" where a standard practice exits, such as Electronic Trade Confirmation, and Electronic Trade Settlement. A standard way of exchanging information exists, along with a set of rules that govern interaction and collaboration. This is a specialized world with its own protocols (SWIFT, FIX, OMGEO, etc.) and typically an area where TPM solutions start to look most like applications in their own right.

Across Disparate Systems and Protocols

The securities industry does not do process-oriented thinking well. Success or failure in automating an operational process very often depends on the ability of staff to understand the detail of a particular product, rather than understanding the mechanics of the Middle and Back Office process. The operative question is very often "what is the product," and not "what is the process." In most of the larger and internationally diversified environments there is perceived value in knowing what the factor on a mortgage-backed is.

To move from that situation to one where the nature of the asset is irrelevant, but there is a common procedure/system in place to execute/confirm/settle/reconcile whatever the product, takes a mental leap as well as a technological one.

Historically, every Middle and Back Office process has been driven by Front Office requirements. Trading a new product, signing a new client, connecting to a new execution platform, they are all instances of events that will create a silo of downstream processing as soon as they are instigated. It is only with the benefit of hindsight that the efficient IT director will realize that all the functions of the Fixed Income department are very similar to those of the equity, cash, FX, and Derivatives desk.

This blind spot for what matters operationally has dogged progress in industry-wide STP for many years, and is unlikely to disappear anytime soon. There are some very powerful forces maintaining that particular status quo, and it is a tangled mess of business prejudice and technological blind alleys. Operational departments are typically understaffed and overworked, and it is very common to find people in management positions who are too engrossed in day-to-day fire fighting to take a step back and think about improving the process.

The first step when trying to analyze similarities between these operational silos is not too difficult – yes conceptually it is clear that most "things" that pass through a Back Office need to be booked, reconciled, confirmed, settled, etc, and there is interaction with the same or similar internal and external systems. An equity trade executed on SETS, confirmed over OMGEO, and settled using SWIFT messaging to a custodian, is still very similar to a Fixed Income trade even is it is executed on a different exchange or ECN, confirmed over TRAX, and settled using a Euroclear EUCLID link.

Identifying and Reducing Operational Risk

There is such a thing as too much information – and no more so than in securities operations. A lot goes on even in a medium-sized Back Office, and from up close everything is urgent, important, and needs to be acted on within aggressive deadlines.

When traditionally manual areas are first automated, the appetite for online or real-time information is great, but the thrill of seeing a transaction go straight-through wears off very soon, as management is inundated with reports and applications that will show them quite literally everything that goes on in the business.

Turning operational information into useful business intelligence is the raison d'etre of Transaction Process Management. The need to know about different risk scenarios differs greatly depending on a user's role. The same operational data store needs to tell production support of invalid SWIFT messages, the ETC clerk about unmatched trade confirmations, and middle management about the performance benchmarks of individuals, departments, and counterparties.

It is the transformation of raw operational data to business intelligence that will allow a TPM project to address the strategic corporate goals. If that goal is operational excellence, TPM will pinpoint the bottlenecks that exist within the organization and outside. It will allow you to maximize the efficiency of your trading counterparties and suppliers, telling you which brokers send high-quality settlement information, and which do not. If you are aiming for product leadership, TPM will allow you to treat operational processes with the contempt they deserve (in that view) and get away with it. If an investment manager feels he should be focusing on investing money, an operational TPM infrastructure will offer acceptable operational performance with minimal management attention (maybe maintained by a third party). If client intimacy is your goal, TPM will allow you to answer client's question fast, and resolve potentially embarrassing client issues before they happen. An efficient TPM implementation will immediately raise service levels, keeping clients happy. It will also provide the management intelligence to know who are your "premium" clients, and which ones may be costing you money.

Using a Single User Interface

Information in a typical Middle and Back Office environment is sourced from dozens of disparate systems. These all have their own user Front-end, which makes it difficult to find the information you need when you need it. TPM creates a highly visible self-aware intermediate layer of transaction processing and the user interface should be flexible enough to satisfy very different information requirements. That user may be creating a new SWIFT message, resolving an ETC mismatch, monitoring SWIFT NAKs, establishing a FIX session, viewing a real-time dashboard of KPIs, or managing an invalid corporate actions notification.

Again different channels need to be available, and web deployment is a key consideration. In today's multi-site, multi-region, multi-time zone environments, it is of vital importance that users can log in from anywhere (including hotel rooms and home offices) and have access to the same operational and business intelligence.

Using Trusted Data, Integrated Systems, and Harmonized Processes

There is very little value to be derived from a sophisticated business intelligence solution, if you cannot be sure the data is there in the first place. The ubiquitous nature of message queuing and other middleware technologies has largely solved this problem, so TPM should re-use and not duplicate existing investments in this area.

Integration is the first step, and a TPM solution needs to capitalize on decades of investment in this area, without introducing new or bespoke queuing or database technologies. This in turn enables technical interoperability, and is crucial in a single-window strategy. Integration is such a difficult task that you really want to have to do it only once.

Robustness and scalability of the core integration and rules engines are obvious complements to the type of 'light' deployment that is available using application server technology.

Conclusion

The concept of Transaction Process Management is the most powerful articulation yet of the mix-and-match approach to solving the dilemmas of securities STP. With a history of niche development, the STP arena will find in TPM the potential to combine the best of expertise-heavy, site-specific back-end processing, with today's requirement to access all data anytime anywhere over any channel. Pure EAI solutions have failed to deliver STP, while the BPM concept if reduced to pure workflow cannot claim to offer a true end-to-end STP solution. It is in the delivery of BPM through an EAI infrastructure that TPM is now uniquely positioned. TPM combines operational functions with advanced status and process monitoring. The scalability and portability of a web delivery platform opens up the possibility of pervasive STP across all functions and regions.

About the Author

Gert Raeves is currently business development director at HelioGraph Ltd. With a background in securities processing and standardization bodies, Gert is interested in exploring new ways of defining and solving familiar problems. HelioGraph 's latest version of its TradeFlow TPM product is used by buy- and sell-side firms to simplify Middle and Back Office processing.

gert.raeves@heliograph-global.com

SECTION IV - SUPPORT PROCESSING SOLUTIONS

Most of the STP focus is on transaction processing, but true STP should cover the support functions as well. In this section we present several alternatives for improving processing for other activities.

- Scott Vey discusses how SunGard's solutions for Corporate Actions can be used to support post-trade processing of corporate actions.

- In Chapter XVI, Peter Patch describes the results of another proprietary TSG survey. This survey talks about Corporate Actions, and STP provides some guidance for firms seeking to improve their processing of Corporate Actions.

- Joe Rosen and Ken Scheinblum review the problems with current accounting practices and discuss some different approaches that could improve overall processing.

- Larry Wentz offers a view of how FX processing can be improved in Chapter XVIII.

- In Chapter XIX David Flinders talks about how City Networks' product helps firms automate their reconcilement activities.

CHAPTER XV - STP AND CORPORATE ACTIONS

By Scott E. Vey, Chief Architect, SunGard Asset Management Systems

The Missing Pieces to Corporate Actions STP

In my experience observing the operations departments of banks, from the smallest community banks to the largest of the super-regionals and global custodians, the most overworked and least appreciated groups are those that service capital changes and / or corporate actions. These groups are responsible for the oversight of the payment, collection and reconciliation of dividends, splits, tenders, calls and the vast majority of other action types whose terms are growing more and more creative all the time. In their daily routines they are fraught with worry over the prospect of a "break" or a miss, where an action is handled incorrectly, or overlooked altogether. The result of a mistake or an omission on the wrong action could lead to hundreds of thousands, if not millions of dollars in liability to the institutions that they represent.

I have attended financial industry seminars that have dealt exclusively with the issues of corporate action processing and the industry's continuing efforts to achieve Straight Through Processing (STP). The financial industry has been pursuing STP through the notion that consistently formatted financial data could be delivered and processed by disparate systems and platforms without human intervention. This concept has been the primary topic of the speakers from many different aspects of the industry - from data collection businesses to pricing data vendors, to middleware data massagers, to banking and brokerage end-users. The clear theme was the ongoing effort to realize some sort of standardization of the information that comprises the corporate action notification, and the standardization of the delivery of that information across the industry. Organizations such as the Securities Industry Association (SIA), Depository Trust & Clearing Corporation (DTCC), SWIFT and ISITC-IOA are all working hard to negotiate standards and propose solutions that could be adopted by the securities industry. All of these efforts are aimed at achieving Straight Through Processing through the development of standard information layouts and delivery mechanisms.

Consider the Source

But when the financial industry is viewed as a whole, millions are spent by financial institutions and data vendors in staffing departments whose principal function is to gather, verify and correct corporate action information. The same function is repeated over and over again from one organization to the next. If a complex corporate action is on the horizon, it is a given that the asset servicing departments of literally thousands of financial institutions across the country, and the globe, are simultaneously wrestling with the exact same problem. Every institution must struggle to verify the terms of the action – the important dates, the payment rates, the basis allocations that pertain to the issuer, and the basis allocations that pertain to any payable securities. It would be difficult to quantify just how much money is spent by the industry in chasing down this information, but the dollar amount, when aggregated, would be staggering. And the initial tally would probably have to exclude the overtime logged due to reversals and second-tries related to the delayed publication of terms, or incomplete terms altogether.

When examined closely, the crux of the expense lies in the poor information coming from the issuer of the action itself. Because corporate action information is initially published in a haphazard, non-standard manner, the domestic and global securities processing industry is forced to play a reactionary role for the life of the action and beyond. Data vendors who sell this information to the financial industry are forced to staff research departments around the globe whose sole task is to "discover" corporate action announcements through any means possible. It is common to gather announcements through newspapers and other publications, press releases and even word of mouth in some parts of the world. Many in the financial processing industry fault these data gatherers and data vendors when the information passed along is less than robust, but this would be misguided animosity. The methods used for the initial capture of the details of an action vary so greatly that true standardization is defeated at the outset.

Turn the Tables

Given the expanding complexity of the corporate actions themselves, and the huge expense incurred by the industry in attempting to service these actions, it would seem that it is now time to place the onus on the originators of these actions. The financial industry should collectively mandate that the issuers of any corporate action do so through a controlled entry point to the marketplace, and pay a fee to have the action properly registered by the industry itself. Which organization should be the registrar, public or private, is not the point. Rather the point is to realize STP and drastically cut the overhead required to service corporate actions. And the best possible way to achieve this processing goal is to require that issuers provide the industry with accurate, reliable information that meets a set of minimum criteria, or the action does not get published, serviced, or enacted.

This relatively simple mandate would garner immediate compliance from the issuers. After all, the mandate would be coming from the banking and securities industry itself; the very same industry that provides the financial backing to make these actions possible for the issuers. And this would apply to both the equity and debt markets.

The expense to the individual issuers would be minimal. Since any particular issuer might be involved in a small number of actions within a given year, the fees charged to the issuers would have little or no impact. Any fee associated with the registration of an action would not be intended to discourage such actions, but to defray the cost of broadcasting complete information to the industry in a standardized format via multiple protocols.

The economics realized by the banking and financial industry would be enormous.

Daily electronic delivery of the universe of registered actions would be provided to the industry by the registering organization. There are a number of standardized formats in use around the world, so the efforts of the securities processing industry to bring further consistency to this matter will continue to present a challenge.

But as a by-product of the registering organization, the next biggest stepping stone to STP would be realized by the assignment of a single unique identifier to each registered action. Just as unique identifiers exist for the securities underlying the actions, there should be a corresponding identifier for the corporate actions involving these instruments.

Currently, in the absence of a unique identifier, all financial organizations, from data vendors to financial institutions, are forced to make an educated guess when receiving updates for, or responses to, a corporate action. The educated guess usually involves a set of matching criteria used to try to pinpoint the action being updated or referenced. Data elements like security identifier, effective dates, rates, and number of options are common pieces of information used to try to identify the action being referenced. This is an inexact science to say the least and has more pitfalls than can be easily summarized. STP will never be realized as long as the securities industry must rely on home-grown matching hierarchies to identify an action.

A replication or derivation of the existing convention used for repetitive contracts could be used as a template for a unique identifier. If adopted with such a convention, the identifier would be a permanent tag for the action, able to be referenced and interpreted in the future without confusion. One of the primary functions of the registering organization should be the issuance of this standard, unique identifier for the action.

The financial industry could then use this identifier to quickly reference any corresponding corporate action by incorporating the identifier into standardized delivery formats and databases across all applications. The addition of this primary reference number to all industry applications and formats would initially require capital investment, but this expense would be defrayed in short order considering the economies that would be realized.

It has been frustrating that the industry has been unable to arrive at a simpler and more direct approach to resolving Straight Through Processing, domestically and globally. Countless resources have been dedicated to improving the flow of information from the issuers of the actions to the beneficiaries of the actions. Those in the banking, securities, and data vendor industries who are caught along the way have sacrificed hours, weekends and holidays in the attempt to offer reliable sound information to their clients, whoever they may be – each other in some cases. Perhaps a new tack is in order; an approach that removes the initial inconsistencies from the data capture process and provides a universally accepted, persistent identifier as a reference for the action.

Sometimes the simpler approach can be lost. The adoption of a simpler approach could go far in realizing the industry-wide goals of accurate, timely, and Straight Through Processing, improved profit margins and even well adjusted operations staffs.

By Peter Patch, Director of Market Research, The Summit Group

The world of corporate actions remains in a state of dynamic tension, as users search for more complete solutions to an ever-growing challenge. The challenge grows with the increasing scope of issues, the expanding array of transaction types, the complexity of data requirements, and increasing risk of loss from failure of (un-) timely, (in-)accurate and (in-)complete communications.

The demand, above all, is for something that may never exist: a solution which addresses the full spectrum of needs, from debt to equity, from dividends and interest payments to discretionary and non-discretionary corporate actions, for North American and international securities, provided both online and through bulk delivery. The system must be at once economic in processing corporate actions today and responsive to the needs of the market tomorrow.

Market participants display a degree of schizophrenia in their assessment of corporate actions: "Yes, to no-small degree, they are satisfied with the accuracy and timeliness of data, and the scope of instruments and actions covered," but "No, to no-small degree, they are frustrated that accuracy and timeliness are not greater and that no provider covers the full scope of their information requirements."

With regard to software "solutions" the same ambivalence prevails: the existing platforms go a long way, but not nearly far enough. Making progress will require a certain amount of pain. Pain for the user will arise from the need to invest in automation at a time when funds for investment are still exceedingly scarce. This is true both for those firms - typically larger firms - with proprietary systems and those firms - typically somewhat smaller - using third-party solutions.

Pain for the software platform provider will arise from the consolidation of the users of data and the reluctance of the users to pay for what they claim they need. Pain also arises, inevitably, in the industry committees exploring standardization of communications and message types, which offers the data provider the opportunity to address an expanded set of needs - through investments which, by virtue of standardization, support automation - but which raise the specter of commoditization of their basic product.

An industry utility, such as DTCC, can be a partial solution to the notification problem. The Global Corporate Action Validation Service, launched by DTCC, provides financial institutions with a standardized source of corporate action information. The service handles instruments traded in the Americas, Europe, and Asia.

Methodology and Response

The corporate actions survey was conducted online, inviting an identified group of securities industry professionals to report on the market environment, as experienced within their firm.

Respondents were evenly distributed across brokerage firms, bank custody and trust operations, and asset managers. Total responses exceeded 120, of which the large majority completed the entire survey. Respondents were heavily weighted towards operations managers with responsibility for the corporate actions activities within their respective firm. Smaller proportions of respondents were in information technology, financial control, portfolio management, marketing, and general management. The survey was conducted over the Internet using a proprietary electronic survey methodology developed by The Summit Group.

Data Requirements

The challenge of the corporate actions data provider stems to a large degree from the diversity of requirements and the ever-changing, ever-expanding nature of those requirements. Particularly vexing are discretionary corporate actions, such as tender offers, which require a response from the owner of the securities on a specified timeline, and for which, failure to adequately notify and capture that response can represent a substantial financial risk.

The needs hierarchy for the data user is clear enough: It all starts with identifying the specific data that is required.

- First, if the data is not accurate, when it arrives is of little importance.

- Second, if the data is not timely, the scope of coverage is irrelevant.

- Third, if the scope of coverage leaves gaps, as it almost inevitably does—at least to this point—then the user has no choice but to look to a second or third provider to plug those gaps.

Next, once the kinds of data required are identified, the user must think about how the data will be processed. How the data as transmitted interact with the user's system is critical. Without standardized message types, the data cannot be processed in an automated fashion. The system must also be able to send and receive voluntary corporate action communications on an automated basis to the degree possible.

The economics of the system in operation represent the next challenge. The out-of-pocket cost for data must be addressed along with the cost of implementing systems modifications and upgrades. During the recent downturn, the economic equation has defined the constraints on operations, and the pressure toward industry consolidation.

The economic catch-22 can be stated concisely: for this complex system that continues to evolve rapidly, it is always hard to allocate the staff time and capital to address system deficiencies. However, the proverbial dilemma is that it will always cost more on the back end if there is an unwillingness to invest up front.

Finally, as each of the above issues is addressed—the data, the processing, the economics—the user organization must continue to assess the risks associated with inaccuracies and incompleteness in any stage of the process. There is little credit given to those who get everything right, but there is plenty of downside to allocate when any part of the process goes seriously wrong, even if only for a single corporate action.

Vendor Selection Criteria: Corporate Actions and Tax Lot Information

Market respondents also expressed interest in tax lot information for securities. However, the level of importance of this data was consistently markedly lower than for general corporate actions data. In both cases, however, data accuracy was rated somewhat more important than timely delivery, and timely delivery was rated somewhat more important than data coverage.[37]

	CORPORATE ACTIONS	**TAX LOT**
Accuracy	4.85	4.2
Delivery	4.8	4.0
Coverage	4.5	3.8

Figure 39 - Vendor Selection Criteria: Corporate Actions vs. Tax Lot Information

Sources of Market Satisfaction and Dissatisfaction

Given the essential requirements of corporate actions processing, it is perhaps inevitable that the sources of satisfaction and dissatisfaction are the same. The data are largely accurate, but not accurate enough - as long as any errors arise in the data. Errors arise both through the missing of corporate actions events and the failure to update information as new information becomes available.

The timing and availability of data has improved, but has not improved enough - as long as any data is delivered with insufficient time to ensure timely processing. It remains a simple fact that in some cases, corporate action events are processed late.

The scope of data coverage remains a problem, although by using an essential set of vendors, all but the most obscure instruments can be largely covered. Still, coverage remains uneven and incomplete.

A fundamental problem is that human error is still a concern. Occasionally, although with gradually decreasing frequency, users will still catch (or be caught by) human errors in the data provided. It is not acceptable that data providers continue to excuse such errors as clerical oversight.

Ease of use remains an issue in corporate actions data. The data vendor's system should be user friendly, and messages sent should always be formatted. Ease of communication flow is important—basic corporate actions data should feed directly into the accounting system for the user. Errors over time will be minimized through the comparison and scrubbing of data from multiple sources, which will directly reduce the cost of operations.

---

[37] These data were recorded on a 5 point scale, where 5 = very important, 4 = somewhat important, 3 = neither important nor unimportant, 2 = somewhat unimportant, and 1 = very unimportant.

Market Satisfaction by Market Segment

In quantitative terms, the market respondents express much greater satisfaction with data for North American securities, as distinguished from international securities. To a lesser degree, the market reports greater satisfaction with Equities data relative to Fixed Income data. There is also some evidence that supports the proposition that the market is more satisfied with bulk data than with online delivery of data. (An exception to this latter pattern is Fixed Income for North America, where satisfaction with bulk data and online delivery is essentially equal at 3.90).

	NORTH AMERICA	INTERNATIONAL
Bulk Equity	4.10	3.30
Bulk Fixed Income	3.89	3.06
Online Equity	4.00	3.19
Online Fixed Income	3.90	2.97

Figure 40 - Market Satisfaction with Corporate Actions Data (By Market and Type of Data)[38]

Data Vendor Switching Spectre

Given the continuing issues with regard to accuracy, timeliness, coverage, ease of use, economics, and risk, providers must acknowledge that the competitive game is far from over. The market always wants more: higher standards of accuracy, more timely reporting, more complete coverage of markets and instruments—but the market may never be completely satisfied

The cost pressures and the risks are too large for the user community to rest or become complacent. The pressures flow upstream from the users to the data providers, and on to the system developers.

As a consequence, more than half the market reports that there is an even chance or better that it will add or switch corporate action data vendors within the next three years. The question remains open as to which vendor will win the race for data accuracy and reliability from a single source.

The turning point may occur as one or more industry leaders take partial ownership of the cost of errors, by combining standards of accuracy with economic consideration for the cost impacts of data errors on their user base.

---

[38] These data were recorded on a 5 point scale, where 5 = very satisfied, 4 = somewhat satisfied, 3 = neither satisfied nor dissatisfied, 2 = somewhat dissatisfied, and 1 = very dissatisfied.

Data Vendor Switching by Market Segment

The market data indicate that corporate action remains a contested market. The majority of market respondents indicate they are (at least) as likely as not to add or change data providers for dividend and interest data, where 57% (North America) and 58% (International) report they are likely to add or switch data vendors.   For Fixed Income, 54% (North America) and 62% (International) report they are likely to add or switch data vendors.   For Equities, the proportions are somewhat lower, with 42% (North America) and 57% (International) reporting they are likely to add or switch data vendors.

	NORTH AMERICA	**INTERNATIONAL**
Dividend & Interest	57%	58%
Fixed Income	54%	62%
Equities	42%	57%

Figure 41 - Corporate Actions % of Respondents Reporting Likelihood of Adding or Switching Data Vendors > 50% [39]

Corporate Actions Systems: The Quest for Automation and the Cost Equation

Achieving higher levels of automation – as well as accuracy and certainty of performance - are perpetual objectives at each stage of the process: from the acquisition of data, to the scrubbing and verification of data, to the calculation of entitlements, to the notification and response to elective actions, and to the final distribution of any resulting economic proceeds - in cash or securities. Squeezing costs out of this system is an ongoing preoccupation.

One way to reduce costs, risk, and to improve control, is through systems integration. Improving control through integrated systems is a complex and cumbersome process, but the controls are still worth the price. The payoff can be attractive: upgrade once, information forever. At the same time, given the financial constraints in the marketplace, firms continue to struggle to get value for their corporate actions dollars.

For many firms, spending on securities infrastructure remains capped. Corporate actions are not necessarily an exception. For others, the freeze on spending is beginning to thaw: there is a subset of firms who are beginning to accelerate their investment in corporate actions systems.

Corporate Action System Selection: Buying Criteria

With regard to system selection, there are a series of factors that buyers typically apply to their decision. These factors include:

---

[39] Indicates the likelihood of adding or switching vendors over the next 2 years.

Completeness

Completeness of functions reduces the number of vendor products users require.

Flexibility

The vendor needs to be flexible enough to provide alternative solutions to internal problems. An off-the-shelf product is never going to have all the features needed. Ease of connectivity is a related requirement.

Workflow

Workflow flexibility is required as corporate actions take on many different varieties, and must adapt to the workflow in different organizations.

Operation

The ability to see the system implemented in an operations setting allows the buyer greater confidence regarding its ability to support buyer requirements.

Credibility

The buyers must have confidence they can believe in what the sales person tells them.

Cost-Value

The system must be cost-effective in terms of savings potential.

Corporate Action System Selection: Implementation Process and Vendor Support

A variety of issues with regard to system implementation play into the system selection process. These may include:

Ease

Ease and cost of implementation is critical. What is the cost of implementing new technology? This plays a key role in the evaluation of a new product.

Follow Through

Do the individuals who participate in the sale follow through to the implementation process, so there is no loss of knowledge from the vendor perspective?

Project Management

What is the time to market for the system, and does it have clearly defined implementation plan, providing a healthy return on investment?

Features/Documentation

Are missing features or enhancements properly documented, with deadlines/ownership assigned to the vendor as to when additional or missing functionality will be delivered?

Data Transfer

What is the capacity of the system to import/export data to a legacy mainframe environment?

Corporate Actions System Vendor Selection: System Functionality

A defining characteristic of a corporate actions system is the degree to which it interfaces with multiple components of the corporate (broker, bank or asset manager) computer system, while performing multiple functions within the corporate actions domain, while simultaneously maintaining the consistency and integrity of an array of interdependent data sets. As a consequence, there are several areas of functionality, each of which is at once interdependent and essential to the proper functioning of the system.

There are multiple areas of functionality all of which are viewed as being important to the overall system. High on the list are such issues as data cleansing and voluntary corporate actions notification and response capture. These are among the critical areas of focus at present, along with reporting capabilities, data vendor links, and the completeness of overall functionality. Audit trail and security, as well as exception management, are likewise areas of focus. The responses of capturing standard and non-standard details of corporate actions, and the calculation of entitlements round out the list. (Responses were recorded on a five point scale, with 5 = very important.)

SYSTEM ATTRIBUTES	IMPORTANCE
Data Cleansing	4.7
Notification & Response Capture	4.7
Complete Functionality	4.6
Reporting Capability	4.6
Data Vendor Links	4.6
Audit Trail & Security	4.5
Exception Management	4.5
Capture Standard Details (ISO)	4.4
Entitlements Calculation	4.3
Capture Non-Standard Details	4.1

Figure 42 - Corporate Actions: Vendor Selection Criteria

Corporate Actions System Vendor Selection: Buying Process

In many ways, the ability of the vendor to support the user during buying and implementation process is as important as the functional capabilities of the corporate action system. Vendor support capabilities determine to no small degree the "value in use" of the corporate action system, as opposed to the objective attributes of the system on a stand-alone basis.

There are several notable features of these facets of the buying process:

- Flexibility and adaptability are at least as important as value for price. If the system cannot be tailored to function effectively within the work environment of the user, the system will never realize its potential value in operation.

- Ease and speed of implementation and integration are almost equally important. System implementation can be seriously disruptive to ongoing operations, so that the cost of implementation associated with these disruptions are high in relation to system value.

- Pre-sales support and financing/payment considerations are of lesser importance to the user. The challenge is on the operating side—getting the system installed and fully operational. Pre-sales issues and financing issues pale in comparison to becoming operational.

BUYING FACTORS	IMPORTANCE [40]
Flexible/adaptable	4.9
Value for Price	4.8
Ease & Speed of Implementation	4.7
Ease of Integration	4.7
Pre-Sales Support	3.9
Flexible Payment	3.8

Figure 43 - Corporate Actions: Buying Process

Corporate Actions Systems Spending: An Array of Objectives

System spending plans are far from uniform across the marketplace. Rather, spending plans reflect the "pressing priorities" for the individual firm, as it tries to balance the pressure to fix a system generally under strain, and to limit expenditures to defined budget constraints.

Among the priorities expressed by firms were the need to improve data management, to automate the process by which information (in formatted messages) update corporate databases, and to improve efficiency and control through integration and automation.

Within data management, firms are focusing on activities as scrubbing data from multiple sources, posting and reconciling new data to existing internal records, and integrated reporting across consolidated systems.

With regard to communications, new message types are being implemented, and the tracking of new messages improved, including ensuring consistency across multiple legacy databases.

Perhaps the broadest array of projects aimed at automating selected sub-processes and integrating systems across activities. These efforts encompass centralizing overall corporate actions processing, including custody and fund accounting, and automating custody and broker reconciliation for settled, on loan and pending positions, as well as SWIFT enhancements.

Corporate Actions Data and Systems: Spending Plans

Market respondents were asked to quantify their spending plans in terms of rate of growth of spending, comparing the average spend over the past two years to the next two years. The average growth in data spending (past two years vs. next two years) ranged from 2.5% to 5.5% for corporate actions data, depending on the category of data. Growth in

---

[40] Importance was rated on a 5 point scale, with 5 = Very important.

spending was higher for Fixed Income than for Equities and higher for international securities than for domestic securities.

Within the market, a significant segment reported plans to increase spending by at least 20%. For international securities, at least one-fifth of the market respondents indicated growth in data spending of 20% or more. For domestic securities, roughly one eighth of the market indicated data spending growth of 20% or more. Thus, for each category of data, there is a market segment that is planning to accelerate spending.

For corporate actions software and system spending, the average rate of growth (past two vs. next two years) was 4.0%, with 17% of the respondents indicating a growth in spending of at least 20% over the two-year periods.

	AVERAGE SPENDING GROWTH	GROWTH IN SPENDING > 20%
Domestic Fixed Income	4.7%	13%
Domestic Equities	2.5%	12%
International Fixed Income	5.5%	23%
International Equities	4.2%	20%
System Spending (Overall)	4.0%	17%

Figure 44 - Corporate Actions: Spending Plans

Corporate Actions: Leaders and Challengers

In the survey, respondents rated the data vendors with regard to their strength in different segments of the market for corporate actions data. In this section, the market leaders and market challengers are identified for each market segment. Typically, the market leaders were close in rating. However, there was a significant difference between the ratings for market leaders as distinguished from market challengers. (The survey results are reported on a 5 point scale, where 5 = very good, 4 = good, 3 = adequate, 2 = poor, and 1 = very poor.)

Bulk Data: North American Securities

For bulk delivery of North American Securities data, Bloomberg was a market leader across the board. Xcitek showed strength with regard to bond and equity data, while FT Interactive took a leading position with regard to dividend and interest information.

BULK DATA: NA GROUP	DIVIDEND & INTEREST		BONDS		EQUITIES	
Market Leaders	FT Interactive	4.43	Xcitek	4.58	Xcitek	4.71
	Bloomberg	4.39	Bloomberg	4.30	Bloomberg	4.29
Market Challengers	S&P	4.22	JJ Kinney/ S&P	4.20	FT Interactive	4.24
	Reuters	3.83	FT Interactive	4.15	S&P	3.75
			Financial Info	4.10	Financial Info	3.44

Figure 45 - Bulk Data: North America

Online Data: North American Securities

For online delivery of North American Securities data delivery, Bloomberg was again a market leader across the board. Xcitek again showed strength with regard to bond and equity data, while FT Interactive remained a leader with regard to dividend and interest information.

ONLINE DATA: NA GROUP	DIVIDEND & INTEREST		BONDS		EQUITIES	
Market Leaders	Bloomberg	4.50	Xcitek	4.63	Xcitek	4.78
	FT Interactive	4.36	Bloomberg	4.48	Bloomberg	4.59
Market Challengers	Reuters	3.85	FT Interactive	4.04	FT Interactive	4.00
	S&P	3.72	Financial Info	3.86	Financial Info	4.00

Figure 46 - Online Data: North America

Bulk Data: International Securities

For bulk delivery of International securities data, FT Interactive was a market leader across the board including dividend and interest information, bond data and equity data. Telekurs/S&P was a leader in both Equities and bond data. Bloomberg was a market leader with regard to dividend and interest information, and showed strength in both bond and Equities data. Xcitek showed strength with regard to bond and Equities data.

BULK: INTERNATIONAL GROUP	DIVIDEND & INTEREST		BONDS		EQUITIES	
Market Leaders	FT Interactive	4.44	FT Interactive	4.00	Telekurs/ S&P	4.67
	Bloomberg	4.35	Telekurs/ S&P	3.90	FT Interactive	4.50
Market Challengers	Telekurs/ S&P	4.04	Xcitek	3.67	Xcitek	4.33
	Reuters	3.57	Bloomberg	3.50	Bloomberg	4.13

Figure 47 - Bulk Data: International

Online Data: International Securities

For online delivery of International securities data, Bloomberg was a market leader with regard to dividend and interest information, and showed strength in both bond and equity data. Xcitek was a market leader with regard to bond and equity data. FT Interactive took a leading position with regard to dividend and interest information, and showed strength in both bond and equity data. Telekurs/S&P was a leader in both bond and equity data, and showed strength in dividend and interest information.

ONLINE: INTERNATIONAL GROUP	DIVIDEND & INTEREST	BONDS	EQUITIES
Market Leaders	Bloomberg 4.40 FT Interactive 4.33	Xcitek 4.33 Telekurs/ S&P 4.20	Telekurs/ S&P 4.50 Xcitek 4.33
Market Challengers	Telekurs/ S&P 3.86 Reuters 3.86	FT Interactive 4.00 Bloomberg' 3.85	Bloomberg 4.27 FT Interactive 4.25

Figure 48 - Online Data: International

Market Leaders: A Historical Perspective

With regard to the coverage of bulk data, Xcitek retained its leadership position for Fixed Income and equity corporate actions for North America. FT Interactive took the top position with regard to dividend and interest notifications for North America as well as for international securities. FT Interactive was also the coverage leader for bulk delivery of international Fixed Income corporate actions. Telekurs/ S&P was the coverage leader for bulk data delivery of international equity corporate actions.

BULK DATA: COVERAGE	2000	2002	2003
North America			
-Dividend & Interest	Bloomberg 4.5	Bloomberg 4.3	FT Interactive 4.5
-Fixed Income C/A	Xcitek 4.6	Xcitek 4.3	Xcitek 4.6
-Equity C/A	Xcitek 4.4	Xcitek 4.4	Xcitek 4.7
International			
-Dividend & Interest	Telekurs/ S&P 4.3	Bloomberg 4.1	FT Interactive 4.4
-Fixed Income C/A	Xcitek 5.0	Xcitek,/Telekurs 5.0	FT Interactive 4.0
-Equity C/A	Xcitek 5.0	Xcitek 3.8	Telekurs/ S&P 4.7

Figure 49 - Bulk Data: Coverage

With regard to the accuracy of bulk data, Xcitek once again retained its leading position with regard to North America for both Fixed Income and equity corporate actions. FT Interactive took the top position for accuracy with regard to dividend and interest notifications for both the North American and international markets. FT Interactive was also the accuracy leader for international Fixed Income corporate actions. Telekurs/ S&P was top-rated for bulk data accuracy for international equity corporate actions.

BULK DATA: ACCURACY	2000	2002	2003
North America			
-Dividend & Interest	Merrill Lynch 4.5	FT Interactive 4.1	FT Interactive 4.4
-Fixed Income C/A	Xcitek 4.4	Xcitek 4.3	Xcitek 4.6
-Equity C/A	Xcitek 4.5	Xcitek 4.4	Xcitek 4.7
International			
-Dividend & Interest	Telekurs/ S&P 3.7	Telekurs/ S&P 3.7	FT Interactive 4.4
-Fixed Income C/A	Xcitek 5.0	Xcitek 4.3	FT Interactive 4.0
-Equity C/A	Xcitek 5.0	Xcitek 4.3	Telekurs/ S&P 4.7

Figure 50 - Bulk Data: Accuracy

With regard to reliability of delivery for bulk data, Xcitek was in the top position for both Fixed Income and equity corporate actions in North America. FT Interactive took the top position for reliable delivery of bulk data for dividend and interest notifications in both the North American and international markets. FT Interactive was the leader for reliable bulk delivery for international Fixed Income corporate actions. Telekurs/ S&P was top-rated for reliable bulk delivery of international equity corporate actions.

BULK DATA: RELIABLE DELIVERY	2000	2002	2003
North America			
-Dividend & Interest	Interactive Data 4.1	Std & Poors 4.3	FT Interactive 4.4
-Fixed Income C/A	Xcitek 4.5	Xcitek 4.4	Xcitek 4.6
-Equity C/A	Bloomberg 4.5	Xcitek 4.3	Xcitek 4.7
International			
-Dividend & Interest	Interactive Data 3.8	FT Interactive 4.1	FT Interactive 4.4
-Fixed Income C/A	Xcitek 5.0	Xcitek 4.3	FT Interactive 4.0
-Equity C/A	Xcitek 5.0	Xcitek 4.7	Telekurs/ S&P 4.7

Figure 51 - Bulk Data: Reliable Delivery

With regard to coverage for online data, Bloomberg retained its leading position with regard to both North American and international dividend and interest notifications. Xcitek was in the top position for online coverage for both Fixed Income and equity corporate actions in North America. For international securities, Xcitek took the top position for online coverage for Fixed Income corporate actions, while Telekurs/ S&P captured the top ranking for online coverage of equity corporate actions.

ONLINE DATA: COVERAGE	2000		2002		2003	
North America						
-Dividend & Interest	Bloomberg	4.8	Bloomberg	4.5	Bloomberg	4.6
-Fixed Income C/A	Xcitek	4.8	Xcitek	4.6	Xcitek	4.6
-Equity C/A	Blmbrg,Int Data	4.9	Xcitek	4.4	Xcitek	4.8
International						
-Dividend & Interest	Telekurs/ S&P	4.5	Telekurs/ S&P	4.5	Bloomberg	4.5
-Fixed Income C/A	Valinform	5.0	Xcitek	4.5	Xcitek	4.3
-Equity C/A	Telekurs/ S&P	4.3	Xcitek	4.0	Telekurs/ S&P	4.5

Figure 52 - Online Data: Coverage

With regard to the accuracy of online data, Bloomberg captured the leading position with regard to North America for dividend and interest notifications. Xcitek retained its dominant position for online accuracy of both Fixed Income and equity corporate actions in North America.

For international securities, FT Interactive captured the top spot for dividend and interest notification. Xcitek took the top position for online accuracy of international Fixed Income corporate actions, while Telekurs/ S&P captured the top ranking for online accuracy of international equity corporate actions.

ONLINE DATA: ACCURACY	2000		2002		2003	
North America						
-Dividend & Interest	Standard & Poor's	4.7	Telekurs/ S&P	5.0	Bloomberg	4.5
-Fixed Income C/A	Xcitek	4.6	Xcitek	4.5	Xcitek	4.6
-Equity C/A	Bloomberg	4.4	Xcitek	4.3	Xcitek	4.8
International						
-Dividend & Interest	Bloomberg	4.1	Telekurs/ S&P	4.3	FT Interactive	4.4
-Fixed Income C/A	Xcitek	4.5	Xcitek	4.5	Xcitek	4.3
-Equity C/A	Xcitek / Telekurs	4.0	Bloomberg	3.7	Telekurs/ S&P	4.5

Figure 53 - Online Data: Accuracy

With regard to reliable delivery of online data, Bloomberg retained its leading position for North American dividend and interest notifications, and captured the top ranking for reliable online delivery of dividend and interest notifications for international securities as well. Xcitek retained the top position for reliable online delivery of both Fixed Income and equity corporate actions in North America, as well as for reliable online delivery of international Fixed Income corporate actions. Telekurs / S&P captured the top ranking for reliable online delivery of equity corporate actions.

ONLINE DATA: RELIABLE DELIVERY	2000	2002	2003
North America			
-Dividend & Interest	Standard & Poor's 4.7	Telekurs/ S&P 4.3	Bloomberg 4.5
-Fixed Income C/A	Xcitek 4.6	Xcitek 4.6	Xcitek 4.6
-Equity C/A	Xcitek 4.5	Xcitek 4.7	Xcitek 4.8
International			
-Dividend & Interest	Bloomberg 4.4	Telekurs/ S&P 4.3	Bloomberg 4.4
-Fixed Income C/A	Xcitek 5.0	Xcitek 5.0	Xcitek 4.3
-Equity C/A	Bloomberg 4.1	FT Interactive 4.2	Telekurs/ S&P 4.5

Figure 54 - Online Data: Reliable Delivery

Corporate Actions: Conclusions

For the users of corporate actions data, the perpetual quest for more complete solutions continues. The growth in volume and in financial risk associated with processing corporate actions shows no sign of abating. The sources of data and the systems providers are moving gradually but inconsistently towards the more complete solutions that would address those needs. Conditions are not getting easier, and what help is available to address this unnerving terrain falls short of the market's full requirements.

There is no alternative but to continue to press ahead with partial fixes. In the near term, as market conditions hopefully improve, improved economics for brokers and banks, along with the trend towards market consolidation will provide some (probably modest) degree of relief.

A combination of diligence and patience is required to address the corporate actions challenge, with industry participants taking limited steps in the near term towards the longer-term solution.

For the corporate actions department, this will mean a combination of actions to address the most pressing needs. These actions may focus on any of the activities from data delivery, to data scrubbing, to improved system integration, to automating pieces of the overall process.

For the corporate actions provider of data and/or systems, moving towards the broader solution takes on a greater degree of urgency. Those who fall behind in this quest are likely to facing an accelerating hemorrhaging of their client base. Reclaiming a leadership position, once lost, will not be easy. Increasing vulnerability and accelerating losses of share are the more likely result.

At the industry level, the sustained effort to create utilities and to expand the role of standardization with regard to message types and formats represents the surest route to increased automation, more effective control, and reduced exposure to risk for market participants. The efforts by the DTCC, as well as the SIA committee process, represent important steps in this direction.

Nevertheless, the challenge of achieving the more complete solution will remain for the indefinite future. There will be no clear winners, only painful losers. Complacency is not an option. The penalty for any relaxation of focus will be severe. The market for corporate actions is unforgiving, at every stage of the process.

About the Author

The author's biography was included in Chapter II.

CHAPTER XVII - STP AND ACCOUNTING

By Joe Rosen and Ken Scheinblum

STP and Accounting - Should they be spoken in the same sentence?

The classic definition of STP in securities industry: trading and operations focused.

Sun Microsystems has defined STP as an effort to become more efficient and cost effective with the ability to manage the trade process throughout the entire lifecycle. Another vendor, Digelet, says: "STP can be defined as a process in which the flow of information between systems and counterparties moves in a seamless flow without requiring manual intervention. STP is primarily achieved through continuous enrichment of the messages flowing through these systems. Along with these message-based systems, the core to achieving STP is managing the reference data. The goal of Straight Through Processing is to achieve operational efficiency and that is continually being driven by a global push for reduced settlement periods and better management of risks."[41]

Bloomberg has produced what we consider to be one of the best graphical representations of what STP means, in reality, to the investment community:

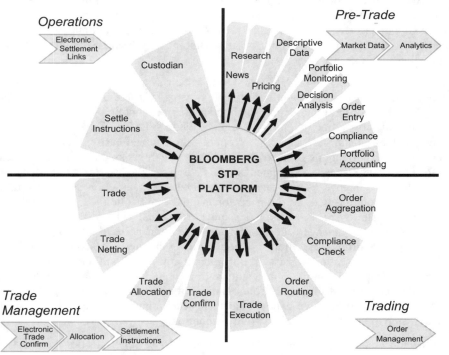

Figure 55 – Bloomberg STP Description

[41] Copyright © 2002 - Digilet Corporation

This chart, although Bloomberg centric, is a fair high-level representation of the life of a trade. The Bloomberg model is a derivative of the typical depiction of STP that attempts to represent STP as a "value chain:"

The Market as a Value Chain

Figure 56 – Integrating the Process

If one pays close attention to the Value Chain model, the word accounting never even appears. There might be an implied link via the box that proclaims, "Focus on Back Office automation" although the chart itself explicitly refers to settlement instructions and electronic settlement links. But, let's face it - that is a stretch. The Bloomberg chart shows a "links to portfolio accounting" although the cynical amongst us may say that is only because Bloomberg already has a product that provides the link.

So, what do the accounting vendors that tout their systems as STP ready or STP compliant have to say? Eagle Investment Systems, a whole owned subsidiary of Mellon, in their entire marketing spiel about their accounting system, STAR, has this to say about one module: "Through Eagle STAR's Workflow Manager component you can view and edit exceptions quickly and easily, transferring the error submit corrections back to Eagle STAR, which backs out and reprocesses the trades automatically. Designed for STP, Eagle STAR's Workflow Manager includes an inference engine capable of analyzing a transaction and selecting a processing solution without the need for manual intervention - saving you time and the possibility of an additional manual correction." They also say, "Eagle STAR's message management features facilitate connection to inter-organization networks supporting your Straight Through Processing needs based upon SWIFT, ISITC and FIX message formats." But in reality, at most institutional investment managers (especially larger organizations), the Trade Order Management System (TOMS) is expected to fill that role. Believe it or not, this is not intended as a shot at Eagle. In fact we believe that their accounting engine may be the next major step in the evolution of portfolio accounting.

Princeton Financial Systems (PFS), developer of PAM for Securities® and PAM for Mutual Funds®, says, "The PAM family of portfolio management and accounting systems' comprehensive functionality automates the entire investment process, fully integrating your portfolio management, trading, operations and reporting functions to facilitate Straight Through Processing of your investment operations. Because you no longer need separate systems that must then be reconciled, PAM enables you to streamline your front, middle and Back Offices to improve the efficiency of your operations and achieve greater control over your business. With PAM's single database, open systems approach and ease of interface development to other systems, it represents the best straight-through-processing (STP) solution for leading global institutional investors. PAM's Front, Middle and Back Office STP capabilities give you the tools you need... From your portfolio management and trading functions to your middle- and Back Office operations and reporting needs, PAM's robust straight-through-processing capabilities give you the functionality and technology to handle changing global market requirements as well as complex new investment products." The key PFS assumption is that you use PAM, its tools, interfaces, and your personal development with their Software Developers Kit (SDK) as a monolithic solution. Few organizations I know work that way; best of breed is far more typical.

SS&C Technologies, Inc. says that "it has championed the concept of 'Straight-Thru Processing' for investment management with a suite of software solutions that provides total integration of Front-end trading and modeling... straight through to portfolio management and reporting... to Back Office processing, clearing, and accounting." But in the sales materials related to CAMRA®, their self-proclaimed flag ship product, the STP concept is not mentioned. STP as described by SS&C is similar to PFS; STP is about using their other products and does not have an explicit accounting focus.

SunGard, an industry leader for both the buy-side and the sell-side, has this to say about their Invest One® product:

"Processing over $8 trillion in portfolio assets, SunGard's INVEST ONE® is the most widely used global investment accounting solution for the eWorld.

- INVEST ONE is utilized by over 175 mutual fund groups, 16 of the top 20 U.S. banks and 11 of the top 50 world banking companies. Our worldwide client base represents more than 30,000 portfolios in client locations including Australia, the Bahamas, Bermuda, Belgium, Canada, Cayman Islands, Channel Islands, England, Germany, Hong Kong, Ireland, Japan, Luxembourg, the Philippines, Singapore and Spain.

- INVEST ONE accounts for U.S. and non-U.S. mutual funds, hedge and bank commingled funds, pension funds, master trust accounts, offshore trusts, U.K. unit trusts, OEIC's, money market funds, insurance portfolios, separate and private accounts. INVEST ONE's investment accounting system capabilities include a fully integrated general ledger, multi-currency accounting, mutual fund accounting, multiple class and master/feeder accounting. INVEST ONE accounts for virtually all security types."

Maybe we missed it, but STP never is even mentioned. Even in their description of the Phase3® offering, which extensively touts it's STP capability, accounting is mentioned as a core feature, but there is no clear link drawn between STP and accounting.

So we seem to have a situation where some of the leading vendors of investment accounting systems[42] like the notion of using the STP buzz words, but they have not defined what accounting and STP have to do with one another. If they can't do it, who can? Do STP and accounting actually relate?

Classic Definition of Accounting: Point in Time and Period-to-Period Measurement

Before we can begin to answer the above questions we just asked, we need to have a clear definition of what exactly we mean when we use the term accounting. As consultants to the investment industry, we are continuously amazed at what constitutes "accounting" at various firms. Not wishing to start a controversy over what is and is not accounting, here are two definitions right out of dictionaries:

- The bookkeeping methods involved in making a financial record of business transactions and in the preparation of statements concerning the assets, liabilities, and operating results of a business. [43]

- The system of recording and summarizing business and financial transactions and analyzing, verifying, and reporting the results; also: the principles and procedures of accounting

  - Work done in accounting or by accountants

  - An instance of applied accounting or of the settling or presenting of accounts[44]

Typically when accountants talk about financial records and statements, they are referring to three main documents: the Income Statement, the Balance Sheet, and the Statement of Cash Flows. In order to make the preparation of these financial statements manageable, an Italian named Luca Pacioli, (AKA the Father of Accounting) developed what we know as the start of modern accounting in 1494. His book, "Everything about Arithmetic, Geometry, and Proportions" was the first book written on double-entry accounting. The truth is that he wasn't really the father of accounting. While Brother Luca (Pacioli was a monk) is often called the "Father of Accounting," he did not invent the system. Instead, he simply described a method used by merchants in Venice during the Italian Renaissance period. His system included most of the accounting cycle as we know it today. For example, he described the use of journals and ledgers, and he warned that a person should not go to sleep at night until the debits equaled the credits! His ledger included assets (including receivables and inventories), liabilities, capital, income, and expense accounts. He demonstrated year-end closing entries and proposed that a trial balance be used to prove a balanced ledger. Also, his treatise alludes to a wide range of

---

[42] A system produces actual debits and credits ideally for a feed to a corporate general ledger.

[43] The American Heritage® Dictionary of the English Language, Fourth Edition. Copyright © 2000 by Houghton Mifflin Company. Published by the Houghton Mifflin Company.

[44] Merriam Webster Collegiate Dictionary 11th Edition © 2003 by Merriam-Webster, Incorporated

topics from accounting ethics to cost accounting.[45] You will note that the concept of Straight Through Processing is not mentioned, except for the part about not going to sleep before debits equaled credits – work straight through until they do equal!

While this may be more about accounting history than you ever thought you needed to know, the most important point you should take away from the previous paragraph is the notion of an accounting cycle. Unlike trading and settling which is typically described as a process, from the beginning accounting was considered a cycle. The two are not the same.

When one looks at the three core accounting statement (income, balance sheet, and cash flow), two key points become obvious:

1) They are historically oriented and intended to reflect transactions over a stated period of time; and

2) Since the balance sheet, which is a point in time report, is inexorably linked with the other statements because of the double entry system documented by Pacioli and still in use today, one can conclude it's preparation was intended to be precise and with a thoughtful understanding of the transactions that lead to the balances.

With an historical perspective then, we can see that accounting was intended to be a cyclical process over certain periods of time: annually, quarterly, monthly, etc. Clearly accounting overall has grown more complex and the pressure by management and the other users of financial statements to shorten the reporting cycle has increased tremendously. Most recently, the Securities and Exchange Commission (SEC) finalized rules concerning Acceleration of Periodic Report Filing Dates and Disclosure Concerning Website Access to Reports.[46] The table below summarizes the SEC mandated changes:

FOR FISCAL YEARS ENDING ON OR AFTER	FORM 10-K DEADLINE	FORM 10-Q DEADLINE
December 15, 2002	90 days after fiscal year end	45 days after fiscal quarter end
December 15, 2003	75 days after fiscal year end	45 days after fiscal quarter end
December 15, 2004	60 days after fiscal year end	40 days after fiscal quarter end
December 15, 2005	60 days after fiscal year end	35 days after fiscal quarter end

Figure 57 – SEC Mandated Changes

The bottom line is that companies must be able by 2005 to do their 10-K's in sixty days and their 10-Q's in thirty-five days. For some companies this will present a huge challenge because information does not flow quickly enough

---

[45] Based upon materials published by Dr. L. Murphy Smith, CPA, Mays Business School, Department of Accounting, Texas A&M University (2002-2003)

[46] Final Rule: Acceleration of Periodic Report Filing Dates and Disclosure Concerning Website Access to Reports Securities and Exchange Commission. 17 CFR PARTS 210, 229, 240 and 249 [RELEASE NOS. 33-8128; 34-46464; FR-63; File No. S7-08-02] RIN 3235-AI33

into the accounting systems to allow for aggregation, management review, and audit. The rules and penalties imposed by the Sarbanes-Oxley Act, which makes management directly responsible for the accuracy of financial statements and reporting, will be a huge source of stress for those that rely on outmoded technology and practices to complete the accounting cycle. Then there are companies like Intel that have made a name for themselves by being able to close their books in a reported twenty-four hours.

Intersection of STP and Accounting

In reality, as the Bloomberg graphic on page one shows, there should be a connection between the investment process and the accounting for investment, portfolio, and investment related transactions. Without appropriate links, investment firms will be hard pressed to produce accurate financial statements, associated footnotes, accounting tests, have management reviews, and still have time to audit the final results. In fact, if one reads the official responses the SEC received when the acceleration of reporting deadlines was first proposed, common themes develop: increases in staffing, costs, decreases in accuracy, insufficient time for management review and so forth. In our personal opinion the objections raised, many by financial services firms and insurance companies, demonstrates "dinosaur" thinking. That is, these individuals have not embraced the technology and the reengineering necessary to take investment accounting into the 21st century.

Like it or not the SEC rule is final. Like or not securities analysts want better information and they want it faster. Even the general public, which grows more web savvy each day, does not understand why it takes so long to report results – and they don't care about the excuses. It is all about the ultimate adoption of an attitude that would make Nike proud: Just do it. No excuses, no weasel words, just give us the facts quickly and accurately.

So faced with new reality what should investment firms do? We have a few thoughts based upon the better practices we have observed by various institutions in the marketplace today:

Forget the traditional monthly, quarterly, and annual accounting cycles. Accounting for investment activity needs to take place in near real time and that implies an automated electronic process. At a bare minimum this means a daily accounting cycle. This process must have automated control procedures and tests built into the data exchange from transaction systems to accounting systems, because there will not be sufficient time later to do all the accumulated work of a month or whatever the accounting cycle is.

The first item implies a significant change in the workflows, procedures, and tasks of the accountants. This is a move from the routine of most accounting tasks to an exception based analysis of transaction or other activity flagged by the automated testing.

Based upon the second item, financial firms must upgrade the quality of their accounting personnel and the firms must continuously invest in ongoing training. The term "accounting clerk" should have died in the 1950's, but many money managers think of their accounting staff as nothing more than a bunch of clerks with green eyeshades accumulating information and manually transforming the information into debits and credits. In short, accountants don't get any respect – just like Rodney Dangerfield. That is, until something goes wrong. Then they become important potential scapegoats.

As financial instruments have become more complex, as have the trading strategies that use these instruments, a higher caliber of personnel is required. Considering the dynamics of the financial marketplace, even the best people in this field need to stay on top of the changes and the impact of those changes.

The accountants must be partners in the investment process. Accountants need to be in the loop early about new instruments a firm may use as well as new strategies that a firm may utilize. Why? Remember the automated controls mentioned above? Somebody with considerable knowledge must build the automated controls and have sufficient time to do so. (By the way these automated controls make auditing easier as well as making compliance with Sarbanes-Oxley easier.)

If the automated testing flags something, accountants need access to the resources best able to help clarify what has happened and why. Firms can no longer tolerate an atmosphere where traders, their assistants, and other settlement people are "too busy" to respond to a query. Ultimately it is the people at the top of the organization that will be betting their careers (and pocketbooks) on the effectiveness of their accountants down in the trenches. Just consider the complexities with FAS 133 and 149.[47]

Accountants and accounting systems needs better and faster access to reference data, also known as security master file data. This runs the gamut from complete call and put schedules (in order to determine appropriate amortization periods and amounts), to corporate actions, to quantitative data such as PSA's, SMM's, and CPR's (for securities subject to prepayment risk) in order to comply with regulations[48] promulgated by the Financial Accounting Standards Board (FASB). FAS 91 requires firms to change the rate at which a premium or discount is recognized as income based upon actual prepayment experience. Wouldn't it be nice if the accounting staff could give management a heads-up on the financial impact of a change? Wouldn't it be even better if speeds could be updated on a frequent basis and thereby reduce the impact of a change in assumptions in any given period?

In conclusion then, firms must take the principals of STP and apply them to the accounting cycle. This has implications for staffing (not necessarily more, but better people), the tools and systems they use (more automated and flexible), and better access to both other departments of an organization and reference data in general. None of this will come inexpensively, but viewed in another

---

[47] Statement No. 149 Amendment of Statement 133 on Derivative Instruments and Hedging Activities (Issue Date 4/03)

[48] Statement No. 91: Accounting for Nonrefundable Fees and Costs Associated with Originating or Acquiring Loans and Initial Direct Costs of Leases—an amendment of FASB Statements No. 13, 60, and 65 and a rescission of FASB Statement No. 17

way it's less expensive to be proactive to avoid accounting errors, public embarrassment, and potential punitive fines for management. The bottom line for Sarbanes-Oxley compliance; fewer manual touch points mean better controls and easier, more rapid audits.

What does accounting mean in the securities business? Does it include reporting, analysis, performance measurement and compliance oriented activities?

We noted previously that as consultants to the investment industry, we are continuously amazed at what constitutes "accounting" at various firms. Some investment advisors consider a list of the assets in a portfolio (names and market values) along with some indication of the interest and dividends received more than sufficient "accounting." May the words "debit and credits" never darken their doorposts.

Humor aside, accounting does mean much more than the three basic financial statements (income, balance sheet, and cash flows) in the investment world, especially when reporting to investors. Suddenly accounting includes performance measurement (which is typically derived from accounting data about various cash flows and market values over a specified period of time), and it is crucial to reconcile the data to the accounting system. In fact many accounting system vendors have built performance measurement features into their offerings. Some vendors do it reasonably well; otherwise, you are better off with a system specifically designed for performance calculations.

Accounting can also play a significant role in compliance testing. At a high level there are two types of compliance tests that firms perform: exclusionary and concentrations. Exclusionary tests are fairly easy to comprehend and relatively easy to monitor in real time. Examples of exclusionary restriction tests can include:

EXCLUSIONARY TESTS	DEFINITION
Broker	Certain brokers cannot be utilized
Country	Securities from companies in certain countries are prohibited
Currency	Currencies denominated in certain currencies are prohibited
Duration/Maturity	Fixed income securities outside of established duration or maturity bands are prohibited
Industry	Purchasing securities of firms in certain industries are taboo, i.e., sin stocks
Ratings	Fixed income securities below a certain minimum rating are not permitted, i.e., non-investment grade bonds
Security Type	No Derivatives permitted (options, futures, swaps, etc.)
Transaction Type	No short sales

Figure 58 – Possible Exclusionary Restriction Tests

The reality is that most of today's better TOMS (Trade Order Management Systems) handle these types of test at various levels (business segment, portfolio, investor, etc.) rather well in general. With the exception of some calculations that are readily available to vendors in acquirable libraries, these are simple "yes" or "no" tests. There is usually not a lot of gray area; not a lot of manual intervention is required to stop an error from occurring.

Compliance becomes much more complex when considering the area of concentration tests. Simply stated concentration tests measure how much of something compared to a predetermined limit. For example, no more than twenty percent of a portfolio will be invested in equity securities. Concentration tests are much more challenging to test intraday because there may be a number of trades, either buys or sells, working that when completed may push a portfolio out of compliance with the established rules imposed by a client, prospectus, regulation, management, or some other source. Below are some common concentration tests that we have seen with our clients:

CONCENTRATION TESTS	EXAMPLES
Broker	Some buy-side firms get concerned when too many trades are placed through a single broker, especially if the trades are all initiated through one internal trader
Country	Many insurance companies have what are called basket restrictions imposed by the NAIC[49] on the amount of foreign securities they may own
Industry	No more than x% of the portfolio/fund may be invested in a single industry
Issue	The portfolio/fund may not own more than y% of the amount outstanding of a single security
Issuer	Total exposure across all asset classes may not exceed z% of the total portfolio/fund value
Ratings	No more than r% of the portfolio may be held in below investment grade securities
Security Type	No more than s% of the portfolio/fund maybe held in cash or cash equivalents
State/Regional	(Especially applicable to municipal funds)

Figure 59 – Sample Concentration Tests

The problem grows more complex when non-traditional accounting matters such as performance measurement and other forms of analysis intended to help the investor are considered. In a recent speech, Peter R. Fisher, Under Secretary for Domestic Finance, told attendees at an American Enterprise Institute conference:

---

[49] National Association of Insurance Commissioners

"To succeed, I believe that we must acknowledge the insufficiency of the accountant's mindset, which animates our existing disclosure framework, and focuses on identifying facts (about the past) that are precisely comparable between firms," he elaborated. "Investors have a different mindset and focus on comprehending the probabilities of likely and unlikely future deviations from particular desired or expected outcomes. We need to remedy this mismatch between what investors are looking for and what our disclosure regime provides."

"This information needs to be organized and presented to investors on a systematic basis," he insisted. "Some companies are doing this. More need to do this. To provide stronger incentives for companies to make these business value disclosures we need to improve the clarity of financial disclosures."[50]

The bottom line is that investors, both potential and current, want information based upon what the purists would call accounting. The demand is for risk management analysis, performance measurement, attribution, exposure reporting, yields, and a myriad of other information that has its root in accounting, but does not look like debits and credits, trial balances, and ledger. The challenge for accountants is to maintain the integrity and purpose of the accounting cycle as first envisioned by Pacioli while leveraging technologies and the benefits of STP to meet the actual information needs of the users of accounting based data.

Mutual Fund NAVs: The Industry's Dirty Little Secret

There is a dirty little secret in the mutual fund industry about how funds account for their valuation that, in turn, may impact the published Net Asset Values (NAVs) published in various newspapers, publications, and on countless web sites across the globe. Few people outside the horrific world of mutual fund accounting realize that investors at the end of the day are not necessarily getting a completely accurate valuation of their fund. How can we say such a thing? Well, the industry has adopted a unique accounting standard referred to by insiders as T+1 accounting.

Simply stated the mutual fund industry is allowed to use the portfolio composition as of the previous day with the current day's prices. To make this perfectly clear, let us assume you open your Wall Street Journal on Friday September 5, 2003 and flip to Section C to find the NAV of your favorite mutual fund. The NAV you read is based on the end of day portfolio from Wednesday September 3rd and "marked to market"[51] using the closing prices from Thursday September 4th. In short, yesterday's portfolio with today's pricing.

The mutual fund industry has long argued that any discrepancies caused by T+1 accounting are immaterial. Maybe that's true, but in a volatile market with a fund that has high turnover[52] can one absolutely be sure? The industry

---

[50] Source: Stephen Taub, CFO.com, September 05, 2003
[51] Mark to Market is the process whereby the closing price for a security is multiplied by the units held.
[52] High turnover basically means the fund has a lot of buying and selling taking place.

has long argued and bamboozled regulators in to believing that it is simply impossible for fund accountants to value the current day's portfolio with the current days prices. Let's ask a simple question: does anyone think that the portfolio managers and traders for a mutual fund are working with stale positions? The reality is that portfolio managers and traders have real time access to exact positions and they get real time pricing. At any point in time they know absolutely what they own and what their positions are worth based upon the last reported trade. If they can get that detail, why can't investors get better, more accurate NAVs?

This last question has an easy, one word answer: money. Cranking out NAVs at the end of the days is a labor intensive, ugly process that no children should be allowed to witness. Quite honestly a number of adults have been traumatized watching armies of fund accountants run from fax machine to computer printouts to terminals all the while screaming out things like, "Where are my prices?" Nothing strikes fear in the heart of a fund accountant when somebody yells out, "When is the IDS (or fill in the name of your favorite pricing service here) feed going to be loaded?"

The truth is that the industry overall works today more or less just like it did thirty years ago. In fact many of the same systems and vendors still dominate the mutual fund marketplace. STP and mutual fund accounting are completely foreign concepts. It is likely it will stay that way until the industry is forced, one way or another, to adopt state of the art technology for position tracking, income recognition, fee calculations, and pricing and NAV calculations. We say forced, because it is unlikely the industry as a whole would be willing to invest the considerable capital required to bring this process into the 21st century. After all, calculating NAVs is a cost of doing business; there is no value added. Or so they say.

If there were just one single area that could benefit from applying STP concepts to a daily accounting cycle it would be the mutual fund industry. Here then are our recommendations for changes in the mutual fund business:

- Kill the practice of T+1 accounting. It is completely out of step of the rest of the investment industry, it's unnecessary, and potentially inaccurate.

- Spend money on the technology to account for trades in near real time. We have all heard the excuses that accountants do not know how block trades are allocated to individual accounts until far too late in the process. That's what high speed computers are intended to do. Stop thinking in terms of manual effort and look to make procedures at least resemble better practices in the industry. We find it hard to comprehend how portfolio mangers and traders get real time information, but investors get NAVs based on stale data. If the managers and traders would not put up with it, why should the people whose money is on the line put up with it?

- The mutual fund industry as a whole must use its clout to get a better system of identifying securities, the exchanges where they are traded, and the appropriate mark to market price. (We will discuss reference data in detail a bit later as it relates to accounting.) The industry overall has simply not united and insisted on better standards and better communication protocols. Now is the time.

- Come to the realization that spending money on technology to produce faster and better NAVs is an investment. This investment pays back over time by increased efficiency, i.e., fewer people with less manual intervention.

- Stop viewing fund accounting as a necessary evil and a cost of doing business. Instead, when introducing new technology and new procedures seek to incorporate it into better client service as part of an overall Client Relationship Management (CRM) effort. Provide better, more useful, and in depth information in a timely manner that investors can really use to make purchase decisions.

Accounting Rules and SMF Data

Once upon a time in a life far, far away one of this chapter's contributors ran an investment accounting unit for a major financial services firm, and before that was an investment accountant and a financial statement specialist – whatever that is. The other contributor was for 6½ years the CIO [Chief Information Officer] for a multi-billion dollar, global hedge fund. From our personal experience and the experience that we have had with clients as consultants, we can both say with reasonable confidence that the single largest source of accounting errors come from bad data. We are not referring to someone entering a bad price on a trade or the wrong broker that will trigger the wrong commission schedule; those kinds of errors will occur and hopefully the full implementation of STP on the trading and operations side of the house will catch most if not all of these errors. The bad data we refer to is reference data otherwise known as Security Master File data. These are the bits of non-financial descriptive data that may or may not have financial implications. But somewhere, somehow, bad descriptive data always comes back to bite the backsides of investment accountants.

First let us consider the case of a floating or variable rate security. The payment rates on these securities are typically tied to some index such as Libor. Do you know how many Libor[53] rates there are? We know of at least four: the one-month, the three-month, the six-month, and the one-year. Did we say Libor? Did we really mean the Euro Libor rates of which there are also four? Many times errors in the base indices used for floating or variable rate securities are only caught when an actual payment comes in and the cash does not match the expected receivable.

The truly sad news is that because of a lack of advanced technology as well as overworked and under trained staff, many firms have raised the "permitted discrepancy tolerance" for transactions that do not match. One firm we know of has a five hundred dollar tolerance for interest payments. That means that if the cash is within five hundred dollars, plus or minus, of the expected amount,

---

[53] London Interbank Offered Rates

no investigation by staff is required. The difference is simply booked as a debit or credit to miscellaneous income. The rationale of this firm was that it was too costly to investigate and correct income errors of five hundred dollars or less; beside net-net the amount is immaterial – or so they say. Mediocrity allowed to run amok in the investment world.

As much as one would like to point the finger at management and blame them for shoddy practices, there are some core reasons for these issues that are difficult to tackle. In the most basic terms there are two major obstacles to getting accurate and timely reference data in to accounting systems. The first is the "internal politics" of many institutions.

As the old expression goes, knowledge is power. Areas of a company, or more specifically individuals within an area of a company, may be unwilling to share what they have in terms of data and may be reluctant in general to share what they know about data. Why? Because many of these people believe it will diminish their role or their importance to an organization. Forcing cooperation is nearly impossible. Senior management will call a meeting, all the right people will be in the room, and management will explain why cooperation is important and then will demand that it takes place. Everyone in the room will nod their heads in agreement and head back to their offices and nothing changes. This happens because in reality management is scared that the keepers of the knowledge may be irreplaceable. Hence the demands for cooperation rarely have any teeth.

The second major obstacle to getting accurate and timely reference data into the accounting systems lies at the feet of the data vendors themselves. The data business is huge and players try to show why their data is better than the competition. The absolute truth is all data vendors have holes; it is just a question about how huge those holes are. Since there is a lot of money at stake, data vendors have no incentive to cooperate with each other to provide a more comprehensive package. It almost appears to the outsider that data vendors go to extremes to make their data "look" completely different from every other data source. That is their "competitive advantage" in the marketplace – proprietary information.

It never ceases to amaze us that one major provider of market data and reference data even lacks internal consistency in the data provided. Some securities are presented one way and others are presented in a completely different way, and we are not talking about the difference between Equities and bonds.

The data vendors have been exceedingly slow in adopting a truly workable standard for XML feeds. It is clear they have little enthusiasm for standardization of data and are only responding because their clients are forcing them into it. Someday the current process of aggregating and disseminating market and reference data will need to undergo radical change. Data must be complete, homogenized, and less expensive then it is today.

In summary then the fragmented and poor reference data available to accounting systems today would benefit greatly from a reformed industry wide

STP process. Better data will lead to more accurate accruals, computation of accretion or amortization, yields and performance measurement. Most importantly, this will lead to less human intervention to correct, complete, or enhance the information required by accounting systems to fulfill their functions.

Accounting and Corporate Actions

We have deliberately elected to discuss accounting and corporate actions as they relate to STP as a unique subject. The unvarnished, harsh reality is that corporate actions are the Achilles heel of STP. We are not referring to mundane dividend announcements or routine stock splits; those are child's play in the world of investment accounting. We are referring to more sophisticated and complex corporate actions like certain spin-off transactions, corporate reorganizations, debt restructuring, partial calls, and a host of other events that do not fit neatly into the mold of the vast majority of investment transactions.

Ken remembers a time when he ran a securities operation group, where he did not process corporate actions until receiving the latest copy of "New Matters" from Commerce Clearing House – in the mail. CCH New Matters was the bible when it came to how transactions should be processed – things like were they taxable or non-taxable events, if it was taxable was it a capital gain or income, how should cost be allocated from the original securities to the new securities? For those veterans out there reading this book, who could forget the court mandated break-up of the old AT&T? All the "Baby Bells" were tax free spin-offs except for one (Ameritech if our memory is still intact – which for some strange and bizarre reason was a taxable income event). Back in those days (we hesitate to refer to them as the good old days), operations and accounting areas had time to gather the vital information necessary to make informed decisions about how to record these out of the ordinary transactions.

We are also not afraid to admit there were times when we sold bonds only to be notified by our custodian on settlement date that a portion of the position we thought we held had been called in a lottery process. Nothing makes an operations person sweat like the notice of a failed bond sale trade on settlement date. On the equity side, usually the worst thing that could happen was the broker would do a buy in to replace the share you failed to deliver. Of course, that could be bad if the price of the stock had risen between trade and settlement date.

But the corporate bond market is nowhere near as liquid as equity markets. Failed trades are to be avoided, because it usually ends up costing somebody a fair amount of money to rectify the situation – even if you have a friendly counter party that's willing to revise the trade. A number of companies have published estimates of what it costs to cancel and correct a trade. We are pretty comfortable that the cost is around two hundred dollars for a bond trade.

In all fairness the industry has come a long way in providing data more rapidly than in the past. Many services now provide at least the basics about corporate actions in some electronic format. But the sad truth is many large investors have whole departments staffed with a multitude of bodies to handle corporate actions. Unless somebody, somewhere, comes up with a solution, corporate actions will be the potential point of failure in an STP world.

FX Rates & Foreign Withholding Tax Expenses

If we go back and review the Bloomberg representation of STP, one will note that our friends, the custodian banks, play a major role in the process. One part of the equation that most of us would conveniently like to forget is that we are in a twenty-four hour trading world. Lots of those trades are in currencies other than the base currency of a fund or portfolio. This twenty-four hour world has placed new demands on accountants and has raised issues for which there is little, if any guidance.

Consider a rather simple scenario. It is December 31st, the end of the fiscal year for an investment manager. A significant portion of this manager's holdings includes securities traded outside the country, in currencies other than the base currency of the portfolio, and the portfolio needs year-end accounting. Here is an easy question, what foreign exchange rates do you use to value the foreign investments? Not so easy?

Well here are a few choices: the foreign exchange rate (FX rate) available as of the close of business local time, the closing rate on the FX market in the local country of each issues, a rate you may have locked in via an FX contract notional for some trade that used a forward when executed, or maybe a rate you get from a vendor that you don't have a clue what the source was. What if you can get a "better rate" in some other exchange market unrelated directly to the local or base markets? Time is up. And your answer is? The truth is companies make different decisions based upon the theory that if they are consistent and can document their process, whatever they decide is fine and dandy.

The truth is companies and their accountants are saddled with nearly incomprehensible rules for foreign exchange accounting. The truly sad part of these complex rules is that they give little tangible guidance to accountants, leaving considerable room for "management judgment and discretion" on such matters. This mess started with a nearly impenetrable pronouncement from the FASB known as FAS 52 back in 1981. I think almost every professional accountant that had some dealings with foreign exchange accounting sent in an objection letter during the comment period. Since it was adopted it is clear that the original left a lot to be desired. Here is a list of affects and interpretations generated over the years[54]:

---

[54] Source http://www.fasb.org/st/status/statpg52.shtml

Status of Statement No. 52, Foreign Currency Translation   Issued: December 1981

Effective Date: For fiscal years beginning on or after December 15, 1982

Affects:

Amends ARB 43, Chapter 12, paragraph 5

Supersedes ARB 43, Chapter 12, paragraphs 7 and 10 through 22

Supersedes APB 6, paragraph 18

Amends APB 22, paragraph 13

Supersedes FAS 1, FAS 8 , FAS 20 , FIN 15 , FIN 17

Affected by:

Paragraph 13 amended by FAS 130

Paragraph 14A added before paragraph 15 by FAS 133

Paragraphs 15 and 16 amended by FAS 133

Paragraphs 17 through 19 and 21 superseded by FAS 133

Paragraphs 22 and 23 amended by FAS 96 and FAS 109

Paragraph 24 amended by FAS96, FAS109, and FAS135

Paragraph 26 amended by FAS135

Paragraph 30 amended by FAS 133

Paragraph 31 amended by FAS 135

Paragraph 31 (b) amended by FAS 133

Paragraphs 34 and 46 amended by FAS135

Paragraph 48 amended by FAS 96, FAS 109, and FAS 142

Paragraph 162 amended by FAS 133

Issues Discussed by FASB Emerging Issues Task Force (EITF) - Affects: No EITF Issues

Interpreted by:

Paragraph 11 interpreted by EITF Topic No. D-55

Paragraph 13 interpreted by EITF Issue No. 01-5

Paragraph 15 interpreted by EITF Issue No. 96-15

Paragraph 21 interpreted by EITF Issue No. 97-7

Paragraph 26 interpreted by EITF Topic No. D-12

Paragraph 46 interpreted by EITF Issues No. 92-4 and 92-8 and Topic No. D-56

Abbreviations for Accounting Pronouncements

FAS - FASB Statements

FIN - FASB Interpretations

FTB - FASB Technical Bulletins

APB - APB Opinions

AIN - AICPA Interpretations

ARB - Accounting Research Bulletins

CON - FASB Concepts

EITF - EITF Issues

Q&A - FASB Implementation Guides

Figure 60 – Alerts and Interpretations

So why have we spent so much time going through such a boring topic (with sincere apologies to foreign exchange accounting experts who eat this stuff for breakfast)? We do so for two reasons:

1) It is both an example of the disconnect between the data available today, data vital for a true STP world, and the accounting cycle, and

2) It represents a tremendous opportunity to streamline and simplify the accounting cycle if only everyone could agree upon and understand some very basic rules and principals.

Here is an area where STP could help accounting tremendously – with everything from valuation to bifurcation of income.

This globalization of the investment industry has caused another problem, one that really hurts investors. It's a problem that the accounting world understands and handles well, but the operations world falls flat on its collective face when dealing with it. We are speaking of tax withholdings, tax expenses, reclaimable taxes, and costs associated with these items. Just about every country that has active securities markets has rules about "foreigners" paying taxes on interest and dividend income. These rules are widely published and easily available.

In short, each country demands that some amount of the gross interest of dividend payment be withheld. Most countries have some methodology for reclaiming at least some portion of the gross amount withheld. But truth is the process of actually claiming a refund and actually collecting it is an administrative and operational nightmare. As a result a few companies have sprung up around the globe that, for a fee, will handle all this messy work for institutions.

The great news is that because the necessary data about interest and dividends and withholding and reclaims is well known, accountants are more than capable of accurately accounting and recording these events. But because the manually intensive, non-standardized process of actually getting one's money back is so difficult, some firms have elected to not bother. That's right; some bright person did a cost benefit analysis and decided it just was not worth the time and effort to chase the cash. So, the accountants are generally forced into a situation to adjust what would be easy accounting to net out the lost cash. We were listening to some expert on this subject droning on about the problem on CNBC or some channel like it. For the most part, it was background noise until we heard the number. It was an amount so staggering that I hesitate to repeat here for fear of loosing all credibility. OK, twist our arms; here are some staggering statistics:

- "Over $6 billion worth of investor funds are being lost in un-reclaimed withholding tax on cross-border securities holdings, according to new research." The revelation comes from a ground breaking new report by industry tax reclamation specialist GOAL. According to GOAL, this situation has become of great concern to investors and their fund managers at a time of tightening asset returns and many are now demanding more effective tax reclamation services from their custodian banks. The GOAL research also reveals that leading custodians who are using automation to deliver profitable reclamation services can access a global earnings market worth billions of dollars.

- The annual tax withheld on cross-border securities dividends/income, at September 2002, amounted to almost $70 billion worldwide, of which just over $24 billion was reclaimable by investors and their fund managers.

- Custodians are estimated to have a potential income market from tax reclamation services of $483m across the globe.

- In major markets, an average of almost 8% of investors' returns from cross-border securities dividends/income are reclaimable.

- The report estimates that only 73 per cent of over withheld tax is actually reclaimed from foreign tax authorities each year, leaving over $6 billion dollars that are un-reclaimed in the last year.

- Fund managers and pension funds are coming under increasing pressure from investors to ensure that their custodian banks are efficiently and effectively reclaiming withholding tax, often now including automated reclamation capabilities in their RFPs.

- Fund Managers are now actively seeking automated methods of being able to predict investor portfolio returns, taking into account the effect of withholding tax reclamation cash flows.

Commenting on the findings, GOAL director of sales and marketing Wendy Cohen said: "The subject of withholding tax reclamation is often swept under the carpet because investors, their fund managers and custodian banks have no reliable data sources which indicated the true scale of losses being incurred. As returns from capital growth have largely disappeared from the Equities market, there has been an aggressive focus on dividend income and a move in portfolio balances towards fixed-income investments."

"Our first annual report on the withholding tax reclamation market provides investors and their service providers with benchmark metrics on withholding tax reclamation, so that they can manage their cross-border investments more efficiently. In this atmosphere, leading custodians have recognized the market opening represented by effective tax reclamation services, both for their fund management clients, and as an interbank services opportunity. Automated reclamation facilities have now made the provision of such services highly profitable, in a market climate where other revenue streams appear to be declining."[55]

If this is not a problem that STP can fix, then perhaps the whole concept of STP is a crack-induced dream. We'd like to believe that this is a situation where accounting is ahead of operations and that cleaning up operations via STP will permit both more accurate accounting and better returns for investors.

Accounting and true STP lead to homogenization of cross company comparisons & Electronic filing of financial data.

Hopefully, we have made the case that STP and accounting are not one and the same, but they are linked. Appropriate linkage can have benefits to investors via reducing costs, more accurate reporting and more useful information - plus

---

[55] ICFA, November 21, 2002, Copyright MSM International Ltd., Thames House, 18 Park Street, London SE1 9ER.

they will be able to get that information much more rapidly than today. Accounting by its very nature is a cycle not a process – and certainly not a straight process. It is supposed to allow for controls, analysis, sanity checking, and blessing by senior management. But just like operations where the process must be faster and require less human intervention, accounting must also shorten its cycle and reduce manual intervention and thus avoidable points of failure.

We also believe that there will be an unforeseen benefit to the investment community as a whole with the introduction of true STP and better, appropriate linkage to the accounting cycle. We firmly believe that standardized reference data and operational practices will absolutely lead to better, more rapid accounting. And since in an STP world this new and improved accounting data will be available in electronic format using some variation or dialect of XML, this could also lead to a better job of securities analysis by Wall Street, independent analysts, as well as in-house analysts.

By the very nature of better reference data and processing standardization, there will be a natural evolution towards homogenization of the data that feeds the analysis engines employed in shops around the globe. To the firms that employ these high priced analysts/soothsayers, they should realize significant increases in productivity. Studies have shown that analysts or their assistants spend nearly seventy percent of their time gathering and formatting accounting data before any real work takes place. Since everyone has, or claims to have, their own proprietary models the results may not be the same. However, investors may have greater confidence that securities analysts are starting on equal footing. Who knows? This may even restore some confidence to securities analysts.

About the Authors

The authors' biographies were presented in Chapter XII.

CHAPTER XVIII - STP AND FOREIGN EXCHANGE

By Larry Wentz, Managing Partner of Wentz Consulting LLC

Introduction

The advent of online foreign exchange trading in the 1990's has provided the impetus for the introduction of a variety of straight-through-processing solutions. These solutions have benefited both the organizations that initiate trades and those that make markets in various currencies. Providers of these STP facilities include various foreign exchange trading portals and platforms, treasury workstation vendors, companies that provide or operate trading software and other organizations involved in post-trade processes. Our objective here is to provide an overview of STP in the foreign exchange trading process.

Benefits

Various articles and product brochures discuss a multitude of benefits to be derived from STP. In general, however, these benefits fit into three categories, Error Reduction, Efficiency, and Timeliness. These benefits result in lower costs for trade initiators, market makers, and others involved in the execution of currency transactions.

Error Reduction

Why error *reduction* and not error elimination? This has to do with a pneumonic from the initial days of data processing, GIGO, also known as *"Garbage In, Garbage Out"*. Initially, almost all FX transactional data must be entered manually. An error made at the onset will be carried throughout an entire process until recognized and corrected. However, STP can eliminate most errors resulting in substantial savings for both trade initiators and the institutions with which they trade.

Efficiency

Foreign exchange transactions involve a number of steps carried out by various processes, often provided by multiple vendors. The ability to seamlessly link these processes improves the efficiency of the entire process. Once one step has been completed, data can be "pushed" out to the next process. In some cases, the next process is constantly polling for the data and "pulls" the data from the previous step as soon as it has been completed. In either case, the entire transaction process can be completed more efficiently.

Timeliness

Vendors will often claim to provide "true STP" or "real time" STP. What they are really talking about is the timeliness with which data is transferred from one application to another. As we will see, in some cases timeliness is very important, almost critical. The ability to provide updated information in a more timely manner to various foreign exchange processes results in the ability to increase revenues while mitigating risk.

FX Processes with STP

STP has evolved at virtually every step of a foreign exchange transaction, from the initiation of a currency transaction to its ultimate settlement. We will examine the following processes in a foreign exchange trade and discuss how STP has been introduced, benefiting the overall process by linking each stage.

- Trade Initiation and Execution
  - Reducing errors
  - Linking processes
  - Timely execution
- Position Updating
  - Risk Reduction
- Credit Checking/Updating
  - Allocated credit lines
  - Centralized credit
- Settlement Instructions
  - Reduction in the budget for Back Office errors
- Trade Confirmations
  - A "win-win" solution
- Post-Trade Analysis (treasury workstation)
  - Plug-and-play
- Trade settlement
  - Automating funds transfers
- Prime brokerage
  - Automating tri-party reporting
- Other STP Efforts
- Next Steps

The introduction of STP for the some of these processes is relatively straightforward and obvious. For others, STP has resulted in entirely new ways of conducting business. We will spend more time on these sections, providing specific examples. However, one constant remains. In each instance, the advent of Straight Through Processing has improved each step, resulting in benefits for all involved.

Trade Initiation and Execution

Trade initiation is the typically the first step in the execution of a foreign currency transaction. It is also one of the most error prone processes, creating significant risk for both the organization initiating the trade and the bank that is providing the exchange rate.

When a trade is executed over the phone, the trade initiator must communicate several pieces of information to the trader at the bank. Minimally, these include:

- Type of trade (spot, outright forward, forward swap, etc.)
- Currencies involved
- Value dates for forwards
- Transaction amount

Whether the currency is being bought or sold (a trade initiator will sometimes ask for a two-way price, further adding to the risk of error)

Organization name: a corporate trader may be trading on behalf of the parent company or on behalf of a subsidiary with a different credit line.

The price maker (bank trader) will communicate the rate information back to the trade initiator. This information may be as simplified as a single rate or as complex as multiple spot rates and/or forward points.

This verbal process is a breeding ground for misunderstanding and errors.

To resolve errors and misunderstandings, banks have invested heavily in recording equipment to tape all phone transactions with their traders. However, the investigation process requires time, an inefficient process in a market where rates in the major currencies change rapidly, often second-by-second. Errors and misunderstandings have resulted in large financial losses for one or both parties, late transaction settlements and damaged relationships.

With the advent of electronic trading, misunderstandings were largely eliminated because there was full accountability for which party provided each piece of information. However, errors, inefficiency, and time delays are still possible when humans are required to input trade data and currency rates.

Let's examine two case studies involving trade initiation, depicting how STP has improved the process and while providing the benefits previously described.

Error Elimination: The Credit Card Company

A leading credit card company nets international credit card usage on a daily basis, generating positions that must be settled by buying or selling the currency of various countries. This organization employs an electronic trading portal, originally

Waldron Management's *FX FOX* and now Currenex's FXTrades, the successor to *FX FOX*. On one occasion, this organization had to purchase approximately $1 million of an infrequently traded currency. Due to a lack of familiarity with the currency, their trader inadvertently entered an additional zero, thereby purchasing $10 million of that currency. By the time the error was discovered, the market had moved against the company. To avoid a further loss, they sold off their excess $9 million position, incurring a loss in the tens of thousands of dollars.

STP was introduced to eliminate the possibility of a recurrence of this type of data input error. The credit card company generated a daily data file directly from their internal netting system that included all of the relevant data to initiate their foreign currency transactions. Waldron, and later Currenex, developed a process to upload that data and format the information into preformatted trades. The credit card company trader simply has to log on and release each trade for pricing and execution. The possibility of input error has been virtually eliminated by the seamless transfer of information from one process to another.

Efficiency: The Treasury Workstation

FXPress provides their Foreign Exchange Risk Management System for corporate treasuries. The corporate treasurer inputs completed currency transactions into FXPress and the systems keeps track of open positions and indicates when various trades need to be executed. Prior to STP, this would require keying completed trade data into FXPress' system. It also involved taking trade data from FXPress to be executed by phone with the corporation's banks or re-keying that data into one of the electronic trading portals.

FXPress has made this process much more efficient, as well as error free. Working with both FXall and Currenex, two of the portals most favored by the corporate market, FXPress has developed Contact Creation Screens. This facility enables trades to be executed via FXall or Currenex *directly from the FXPress software*. The step of passing data from FXPress to the portal and then logging into the portal to execute the trades has been eliminated. Both treasury management and trade execution can be accomplished through the use of a single process.

Completed trades are immediately booked back into FXPress. They are also recorded in FXall and Currenex to facilitate post-trade settlement and confirmation functions.

Trade execution has also benefited from STP, enabling for improved pricing strategies as well as error reduction.

Error Elimination and Efficiency: Trading Software

Banks and other market makers provide pricing to customers through their own one-to-one currency trading systems or through one or more of the multi-bank portals. Currency rates entered manually by traders are susceptible to error and are not an efficient use of the trader's time for smaller transactions.

For that reason, the leading vendors of currency trading software such as Cognotec, PFS TraderTools (TradeTrac) and Reuters (TIBCO and AVT), as well as various bank proprietary systems have provided facilities to enable automated pricing of trades through one or more rate feeds.

The feed can come from various sources such as an internal bank feed, Reuters, EBS, or even another bank. More sophisticated software, such as PFS TraderTools' TradeTrac, enables multiple rate feeds to be employed with the best bid and offer rates selected for pricing. The feed can be marked up or spread according to various criteria such as currency pair, transaction size and customer quality.

As customers initiate trades, the trading software automatically develops rates for each particular transaction. The software controls how long a rate is valid, usually just a matter of seconds, before updating it or canceling it as required.

Some trading software, such as Dresdner Bank's Piranha system and PFS TraderTools' TradeTrac, provides streaming prices in which prices for major currencies are always displayed and updated as the market moves. Customers simply have to click on a rate to execute their trade. This feature appeals to Commodity Trading Advisors (CTA's), hedge funds and others that require the timely execution of their trades.

The ability to price trades in an automated manner not only reduces errors and provides greater efficiency. It also reduces the high cost of trading staff and trading desk infrastructure, as the most common trades can now be executed automatically through the use of trading software.

STP has also been introduced to simultaneously address both trade initiation and execution.

Error Elimination: Small Trade Processes

Many companies have small "nuisance" trades that they have to execute. Due to their size, the corporate trader's objective is to execute these deals quickly and accurately. Competitive rates are not required. The time spent on this activity can be used in more productive endeavors.

To address this issue, some banks with one-to-one trading solutions as well as multi-bank portal FXall have introduced a batch trading facility. Groups of trades can be uploaded automatically by the corporate trader from an internal system, from accounts payable software such as those of SAP or PeopleSoft, or even from a spreadsheet. Once uploaded, the trades can be priced, executed and automatically passed to the settlement process.

Timeliness: The CTA Model

Commodity Trading Advisors (CTA's) and hedge funds trade foreign currency for a single reason, to make money. Unlike corporations or fund managers, who execute currency transactions as part of an underlying business transaction, the execution of a currency transaction is the business of these organizations.

Several CTA's employ model-driven trading strategies. The computerized model maintains their open positions as current market rates flow into it. As the market moves, the model indicates trades that should be executed. Time is now critical. It is important for the CTA trader to execute trades before the market moves again. Using the phone or keying trades into an electronic trading platform like HotSpotFX, FXall or Currenex can be time-consuming. In a fast moving market opportunities can be lost in seconds while risks increase.

To address this issue, some CTA's and their electronic trading vendors have worked together to generate a STP solution directly from the CTA's computer-driven model to the trade execution process. The model indicates trades to be executed. These are immediately transferred to the electronic trading platform where they are automatically executed. All of this occurs with little or no human intervention. A computer initiates a currency transaction and another computer executes it. Can a Terminator-like world run by machines be far behind?

The following schematic provides a generic depiction of how STP has become integrated into the process of initiating and executing foreign exchange transactions:

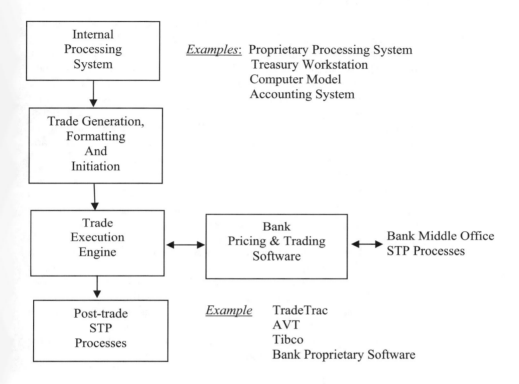

Figure 61 – FX Processing

Position Updating

Maintaining accurate currency positions is essential for bank traders. Bank traders deal these positions to generate revenue and to avoid risk. Electronic trading and STP have enhanced the accuracy and timeliness of this activity. Bank trading systems (Cognotec, TradeTrac, AVT, etc.) automatically update internal bank deal capture systems as soon as a trade has been completed through API's (Application Program Interface). Sophisticated deal capture software, such as that provided by Wall Street Systems, can then provide traders with positions on a local, regional or global basis, performing sensitivity analysis and enabling risk managers to deal with position risk on a more timely basis than previously possible.

When customers perform post-trade activities such as rolls (a spot position may be allocated into various spot and forward dates), portals such as FXall can update positions through their Quick Connect feature. The original position is reversed and replaced by the rolled amounts. These position updates can be sent to banks in real-time or on a pre-arranged basis, depending on the requirements of the bank and the size of the positions.

Credit Checking/Updating

The early days of electronic trading provided benefits while creating challenges in this area. The ability to automatically check credit lines and update them was an improvement over the manual lookup process. However, as customers began trading through multiple channels, credit lines had to be allocated to different processes. For example, a customer would require part of their credit line for trading by phone, another part for trading through a bank's one-to-one trading system and yet another in order to use a multi-dealer trading portal. Allocating a portion of the customer's line to each process is an inefficient use of credit and increases the difficulty of managing and monitoring the entire line. A customer could be prevented from executing a trade through a multi-dealer portal even though available credit existed in their total line.

Enhancements in Straight Through Processing have been able to resolve this issue. Bank Middle Office processing systems such as Wall Street Systems provide a credit API to any application that requires it. This enables multiple channels to access a consolidated credit tracking facility. Credit can be checked prior to trades being executed and updated once a transaction has completed. Wall Street Systems provides features that allow banks to enable designated customers to exceed their credit, up to a certain amount. Alternatively, alerts can be sent to electronically to credit managers enabling them to analyze specific situations. The credit process can be managed as a centralized facility, updated on a real time basis by any application connected to the credit API.

Settlement Instructions

Along with trade initiation and execution, the settlement process has traditionally been the most error prone area of foreign exchange trading. Settlement instructions must be complete and accurate. Funds must be delivered on the agreed upon settlement date. Banks have long maintained large budget items, often in the millions of dollars, to compensate customers for Back Office errors.

Nowhere is the accurate, timely settlement of currency transactions more important than in the institutional market. Large mutual funds are constantly trading in foreign Equities and Fixed Income instruments. In most cases, the underlying currency transactions are accumulated (netted and accumulated together) into a single block trade (spot or forward) executed in the name of the holding company. Forward swaps for hedging purposes may also be executed as a bulk trade across various funds or accounts. Once the trade has been executed, various amounts must be allocated to the underlying funds and accounts managed by the company. As a result, in this world, the need for accurate settlement often outweighs the desire for competitive pricing.

State Street's FX Connect is a multi-dealer foreign exchange portal that has successfully focused on the needs of this market, with trading volumes now exceeding $20 billion daily. After an institution executes a trade with an FX Connect participating bank, the trade is automatically passed to a settlement process that performs all of the post-trade allocations to various funds and accounts, required for supporting the required daily valuation process. It is efficiency of its post-trade STP allocation process that has enabled FX Connect to become the dominant FX portal in this market.

The Currenex FXtrades portal also provides a variety of STP settlement features. Customers can store fixed allocation algorithms within the service. An algorithm can then be selected at time of trade execution, providing the ability to automatically allocate the trade once it has been executed. Alternatively, customers can upload allocation instructions with the trade details, again streamlining the allocation process.

Currenex offers its customers and participating banks three ways of using STP to deal with settlement instructions:

- Standard delivery instructions (SSI's) can be uploaded into its FXtrades system to be stored and maintained.

- Non-standard instructions associated with a specific trade can be uploaded from a customer's in-house system along with trade execution details.

SSI's can be applied automatically using predefined defaults after a trade has been executed.

The benefit here is that errors are greatly reduced. Instructions are stored in a single place, making them easier to update. It is not necessary for banks to mail or fax their updated SSI's to each customer for updating in multiple customer internal systems. Similarly, it is no longer necessary for customers to key their SSI's for each trade and to update them for each bank with which they trade.

Perhaps the most interesting undertaking in this area is FXall's Settlement Center, which has been established as a separate application. It can be used in conjunction with the FXall multi-dealer trading system or as an independent service, accepting input from other sources including phone trades, bank one-to-one systems and other portals.

The Settlement Center provides a variety of STP related services. Transactions processed in this application are SWIFT compatible, and important consideration for asset managers and others. It provides full STP to and from customers and their banks. This provides it with great flexibility as users can use all or some of the functionality provided. If a specific user prefers to perform some post-trade functions in-house, they can obtain the data electronically at any point.

One of the Settlement Center's objectives is to establish a central database for customer standard settlement instructions (SSI's). Corporations and institutional customers typically maintain 5-10 banking relationships. Each bank must maintain a database of its customers' SSI's. By providing a central database for these instructions, instructions can be applied from a single source with bank databases updated from the same source.

STP related features of FXall's Settlement Center include:

- Trade confirmations (to be discussed separately)
- Rolling of completed trades into various value dates
- Splitting of bulk trades into individual transactions
- Application and maintenance of customer SSI's
- Application and maintenance of bank SSI's
- Prime brokerage linkage (to be discussed separately)
- Settlement Netting (to be discussed separately)
- Custodial advisement (to be discussed separately)

A case study provides an example of the benefits derived from this approach to STP.   Prior to the advent of the Settlement Center, one of FXall's customers performed settlement functions and confirmations by phone with each of their trading banks. This process took approximately three hours every day. Additionally, the customer is based on the West Coast and most of the leading foreign currency banks are based in the East. This meant that the Back Office staffs of each of the customer's banks had to stay an additional three hours to participate in this process. The introduction of this STP functionality has enabled FXall's customer and their banks to now complete this process in fifteen minutes.

The following diagram provides an overview of the various STP facilities offered via the Settlement Center.

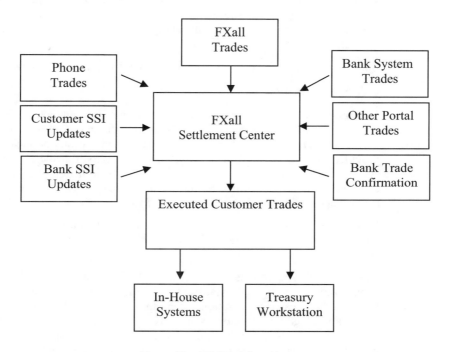

Figure 62 – FXall Relationships

Trade Confirmations

No one likes trade confirmations. Banks don't like them. Customers don't like them. However, they are a necessary evil because both the bank and the customer must agree on what they transacted before their respective Back Offices can process it. Traditionally, confirmations were done by phone or fax. This meant that the customer had to be available to confirm trades with the Back Office of their banks by phone or to sign and return faxes.

Early attempts at automation provided some relief, but were often viewed as cumbersome by both banks and their customers. Recent STP efforts have enabled this process to be automated.

FXall's Settlement Center accepts input files of completed trades from their participating banks. These are matched electronically to the trades input to the Settlement Center. Any mismatches are reported back to the bank for corrective action. Since most trades can be confirmed automatically, only the mismatches require further investigation and customer follow-up.

Wall Street Systems uses a similar method for both settlement and confirmation. However, instead of passing data *to* a portal such as FXall, Wall Street System's provides banks with a Back Office solution that accesses portals on a real-time basis, pulling trade data *from* the portals. The settlement and confirmation matching is then done within the bank's software.

Both solutions provide the same functionality using different approaches.

Post-Trade Analysis

Customers perform post-trade analysis activities through a variety of treasury workstation applications. Some of the more prevalent are FXPress, Trema, XRT, Wall Street Systems, and various applications provided by SunGard Treasury Systems, the market leader. These systems keep track of currency positions, recommend hedging strategies, supply accounting functions, perform mark-to-market calculations, and support accounting regulations such as FAS133.

Virtually all treasury workstation applications now employ STP to move data to and from trading applications. This is typically done through API's.

One interesting effort is that of the TWIST group, the Treasury Workstation Integration Standards Team. This goal of this organization, led by the treasury operations department of Royal Dutch Shell Corporation, is to develop standards for integration to treasury workstations and other applications. This is an ambitious task to develop true plug-and-play integration, where various applications apply the same integration standards. This will take time. Some vendors have been resistant to the idea of making it easier for competitors to replace their applications. According to Greenwich Associates research (*e-Forex magazine, July 2003)*, the volume of online currency trading is growing; however, they project that only 40% of currency volumes will be transacted online by the end of 2003. As online volumes continue to grow and electronic trading matures, standardization could become a reality.

Trade Settlement

FXall appears have taken the lead with respect to the actual settlement of currency transactions. They offer a number of solutions including:

Settlement Netting

Customer payments to and receipts from the same bank in various currencies are netted into a single payment. FXall's Settlement Center then employs STP to initiate wire transfers via SWIFT formatted instructions.

Custodial Advisement

Asset managers maintain accounts at their custodial banks. Once the asset manager has completed their trades, FXall then sends

SWIFT formatted MT200 transactions to their custodian bank automating the payment of funds from their asset management account.

CLS Integration

The CLS (Continuous Linked Settlement) Bank became operational late in 2002. The objective of this "bank" is to provide for T+1 settlement of currency transaction through its member institutions. The simultaneous settlement of currency transactions in the CLS Bank will eliminate settlement risk, the risk that now occurs when currency transactions settle in different time zones. FXall is one of the initial organizations to provide STP generated messages to both the customer's lead bank and the bank with which the customer has traded indicating that a trade is to be settled through the CLS Bank.

Prime Brokerage

The use of prime brokerage has grown in recent years. In this arrangement, a customer enters into an agreement with a large financial institution such as Deutsche Bank, JPMorgan Chase, Bank of America, AIG, or ABN Amro to act as its prime broker. This enables the customer to execute trades, up to a specified daily limit, with various other banks designated by the prime brokerage agreement. Essentially, the customer is leasing its prime broker's balance sheet as a form of credit. This arrangement is typically used by CTA's (commodity trading advisors) and hedge funds.

When the customer executes a currency transaction with one of its approved banks, the customer is obligated to report the transaction to its prime broker on a timely basis to enable the prime broker to monitor credit limits. This has been accomplished by phone or through a Reuters messaging terminal. The bank with which the customer traded also must report the trade to the prime broker in a "give-up" arrangement in which the bank settles the trade with the prime broker. As the use of prime brokerage has grown, the timely reporting of these trades has become problematical.

STP solutions implemented by Currenex and FXall have resulted in timely, accurate reporting of prime brokerage transactions. In the Currenex implementation, the customer selects its prime broker and an executing bank. It then executes a currency transaction. Currenex then sends a "give up" message to the prime broker and generates back-to-bank trade tickets between the customer and the executing bank, the customer and the prime broker, and the executing bank and the prime broker. The prime broker can log into Currenex on a regular basis to download these tickets into its in-house system.

The FXall solution provides similar functionality as well as confirmation matching. Both the customer and the executing bank send confirmations that are matched. The prime broker can then access and approve the matched deals within the customers credit limit. Both solutions have improved the timeliness of prime brokerage reporting and processing.

Three prime brokerage banks (Deutsche, JPMorgan Chase, and AIG) have recently joined forces to create a prime brokerage messaging solution hub called Harmony, built by Traiana, Inc. FXall has already announced that they will link to this system to support customers that have prime brokerage arrangements with these banks.

Other STP Efforts

As electronic trading of foreign exchange transactions continues to grow, new ways to employ STP will also evolve. FXall's integration of payment advices to risk managers' custodial banks is one example of a unique STP application.

Wall Street Systems has also advanced its STP effort by linking its bank Back Office applications directly to their accounting systems. They have not stopped the process at the foreign exchange "border," but continued the process beyond the trading room. It is not unusual for a Foreign Exchange Department to maintain its own internal financial reporting system. Because this system does not reflect the official books of the bank, debates often occur between the FX and Accounting departments. With Wall Street Systems solution, everyone is on the same page. There is no need to "reconcile" two different accounting systems. The entire process has been taken through to its logical conclusion.

Next Steps

Over time, the STP applications mentioned here will obviously be improved and adapted by ever-larger numbers of customers and their banks. New forms of STP will also be introduced.

In interviewing various market participants, two applications that have yet to benefit from STP were mentioned. Order management has yet to be fully integrated into the world of electronic trading. While some portals, such as Currenex, provide for the input of orders, links do not yet exist to provide the necessary integration from the bank's order management application back to the originating system. Once that occurs, other safeguards will be required to ensure that duplicate reporting to Back Office systems from both the order management system and the foreign currency trading system does not occur. The only vendor that has solved these issues is PFS TraderTools, which supplies both order execution capability and an integrated order management solution.

Another potential future STP application is the automated reconciliation of customer foreign bank accounts (nostro accounts). As the number of electronic transactions increase, we can expect to see this function also benefit from STP.

Summary

STP applications in the foreign exchange market have come a long way in a relatively short time. Online currency trading was first introduced by a few banks in the 1980's. The first multi-dealer system did not appear until 1994, less than ten years ago. Virtually every phase of a currency transaction now employs some form of STP. Millions of dollars are now saved annually through error reduction, efficiency, and improved timeliness as a result of STP. Those multi-million dollar bank budget items for Back Office errors have been significantly reduced.

In the next ten years, we will see fewer new forms of STP. What we will see is continual improvements in those STP applications that have already been introduced, as a larger number of banks and customers adapt their systems to integrate to them.

About the Author

Larry Wentz is Managing Partner of Wentz Consulting LLC, which specializes in the development of e-commerce business opportunities. Wentz is also President of Direct Foreign Exchange Inc., which provides currency services for the retail and small business markets.

Wentz has over twenty years of experience in the area of e-commerce business development. As the president and founder of Waldron Management Services, he developed the first multi-bank foreign exchange trading platform, *FX FOX*. At the end of 1999, he sold Waldron Management and *FX FOX* to a group of investors who renamed the company Currenex, moving the service to the Internet and re-naming it FXTrades. Wentz remained with Currenex before founding Wentz Consulting in 2003.

Prior to starting Waldron Management, Wentz spent fifteen years at Citibank in various capacities. He spent a number of years in the Latin American Banking Group, working on the financial staff. He followed that assignment by using his financial and systems skills to build and market on-line services for financial information, money markets and currencies.

Larry Wentz graduated from Rutgers College with a degree in mathematics and subsequently obtained a Masters degree in Computer Science from the University of Pennsylvania and an MBA from the University of Connecticut.

wentzconsult@aol.com or lwentz@foreign-currency.com

CHAPTER XIX - STP AND AUTOMATED RECONCILIATION

By David Flinders, Head of Securities and Derivatives, City Networks Limited

Introduction

Automated reconciliation systems have been around for many years, and many have matured into fully-fledged business control systems. The leading suppliers have generic systems capable of wide application through the business; there are also still a large number of niche products designed to address specific business requirements such as nostro reconciliation. The aim of this article is to explore some of the issues involved in reconciliation and to assist the reader in selecting an appropriate system for the needs of the business.

Despite the enormous advances made in reconciliation systems in the last few years, prospective users still frequently express a requirement for a "matching engine." A reconciliation system is a lot more than just a matching engine, for two main reasons:

- Matching is just one part of what modern reconciliation systems do. Although generally very sophisticated matching is becoming an increasingly smaller component as these systems develop, incorporating such features as problem analysis, automated workflow management, and so on.

- Most of the work of a reconciliation system is to do with controlling accounting information. There are some exceptions to this in the earlier part of the trade cycle, but in most reconciliations it is now common for transactions to be reconciled within positions or balances. It is crucially important to maintain the correct relationship between these, as you would expect to do in an accounting system. This includes restricting the ability of users or the system to match transactions across instruments or other important accounting sub-divisions within a reconciliation.

An "appropriate" system for the business does not necessarily mean the one with the most features or the greatest capacity. Some leading systems have a bewildering degree of bells, whistles, and configurable rules. At the risk of stating the obvious, these are only of value to the business if they save human effort, make things possible, or reduce operational risk. Most users' volumes may easily be handled by most of the available systems; it is generally only when volumes get very high or when business requirements dictate that large workloads be completed very quickly that the field of available systems narrows to those capable of multi-threaded, high performance processing.

The article explores in as much depth as the space allows:

- The scope of modern reconciliation systems and the relevance of some of the areas covered.

- The issues involved in business process control – what can go wrong and where, and the impact of processing errors.

- How an automated reconciliation system, intelligently applied, may be used to deliver the assurance to management that their main business processing systems are working correctly and are fully under control.
- Specific issues surrounding securities and Derivatives reconciliation, in particular the treatment of instrument associations.
- Specific functional attributes that may be essential in a reconciliation system, depending on the users' requirements.

Why Do We Reconcile?

Let's start by looking at why we reconcile things. The answer may seem obvious to anyone whose career has involved either auditing or business control activities, but sometimes it's not as obvious as it seems. Consider the following statement by the head of operations at an asset manager.

"We hold client securities in segregated accounts with our custodians. There is a cost to this compared with holding them in pooled accounts, but it improves control and our clients like it. We only need to reconcile the holdings once a month at balance level because each individual holding tends to have only a few transactions per month, and if anything goes wrong it's easy to find out why. The key thing is to have the holdings agreed."

It contains an argument in favor of not reconciling underlying transactions and an attempt at justifying the reconciliation of holdings on a monthly basis. Examining whether or not we think these are valid arguments will help us reconsider why we perform reconciliations.

Frequency of Reconciliation

Frequency or performance of any business control should be dictated by the chance of something going wrong and the estimated impact if it does. Let's say that this asset manager's internal system is reckoned to be very effective and that the chances of a transaction processing error are low because:

- His internal security and segregation of duties mean that opportunities for fraudulent transactions are insignificant.
- His global custodian is highly efficient and rarely makes mistakes.
- Clients do not see their holdings on-line, but are sent a statement after each month end's reconciliation.

If all of these things are true, then a monthly frequency is possibly reasonable because its main purpose is not to trap errors but to provide final verification of the state of the holdings. If any of them are not true then the frequency is inadequate.

Level of Reconciliation

This is more to do with efficiency than actual control in this particular business case. Let's say our asset manager thinks seriously about the points above. He decides that he has good segregation controls. He estimates that the efficiency of internal transaction processing systems is such that there might be 100 instances of incorrectly processed transactions in a month. These might affect up to 100 holdings. Since there are a total of 500,000 transactions per month and a total of 100,000 holdings, only five transactions on average will be involved in a holdings break investigation. If there is a break, his staff is able to access the custodian's system on-line and quickly get a transaction list that they can check against their own system. However, his clients access their holdings on-line at any time and it is therefore vital that their correctness is verified daily.

Therefore he decides to switch to a holdings level reconciliation on a daily basis because this offers the most efficient way of meeting his particular business control objectives. He is now able to say:

"We hold client securities in segregated accounts with our custodians. There is a cost to this compared with holding them in pooled accounts, but it improves control and our clients like it. We automatically reconcile the holdings daily because although the likelihood of a discrepancy is low, a high level of certainty is critically important to us. We don't reconcile transactions because each individual holding tends to have only a few per month, and if there is a discrepancy it's easy to review the account activity. The overall cost of this is lower than full daily transaction reconciliation.

Understand Your Objectives

The key point in the above story is that any business control activity should arise from a clearly understood objective. A statement to the effect that "we reconcile holdings to ensure that our systems agree with the custodian" is clearly not any kind of understanding. The fact is that:

- Many reconciliations are performed because the data is available, not because a business control requirement dictates that it is necessary.

- Conversely, there are business control activities that need to be performed but are not.

What might be the reasons for not performing apparently necessary controls? There are several possibilities, and none of them stand up to scrutiny.

- First, innocence. Management is not aware of a particular area of risk. There is a process that has apparently worked fine for years and apparently doesn't need controls. But conditions may change, so that potential for breakdown is increased. The change in conditions doesn't have to be anything as visible as a change in systems; it could be the pattern of business or a change in personnel.

- Second, ignorance - the worst case. Management is aware of potential risks but prefers to ignore them. They are just "not on the radar right now."

- Third, unacceptably high cost. This is understandable in a way, but the answer to the problem is to make controls more cost-effective rather than to fail to implement them at all, and this can be done with automated reconciliation systems and some thought.

To achieve this, the design of efficient business controls must flow from a complete and well-documented understanding of the firm's internal systems. This should include an assessment of the likelihood and potential or actual impact of the business process breakdown. Controls should be designed to have the maximum cost-effectiveness and wherever possible should be applied automatically, which in turn guarantees that they are systematic. Cost effectiveness will only be achieved by understanding the process and careful targeting of control activity. Controlling "everything that moves" is simply not an option.

The Impact of Errors

Before moving on to business control design, we'll eliminate any doubt over the necessity for sound and comprehensive control by looking at the potential damage resulting from a processing error in an asset manager's system.

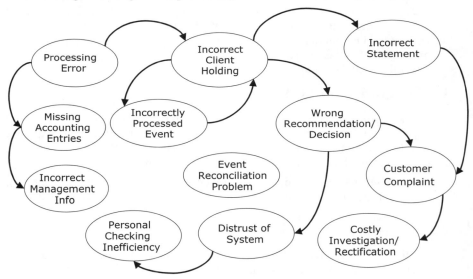

Figure 63 – Sample Error Flow

- The processing error causes an incorrect client holding. This goes unresolved and soon thereafter, a corporate action event is processed, compounding the error and creating an event reconciliation problem.

- A client manager relies on information from the system to make investment decisions and as a result of using incorrect information he gives incorrect advice. At the same time the client is sent an incorrect statement.

- One of the results is that the client manager starts to distrust the system and as a result gets less efficient because he feels he has to check everything before giving advice.

- There are also incorrect or missing accounting entries, so the financial accounting and analysis people are working from incorrect information.

- If the client makes a complaint it has to be investigated, and the cost can be enormous. It needs highly skilled resources who understand the system and have both analytical and communications skills - and it takes time. If such errors accumulate in a system, these resources are quickly overwhelmed. On occasions, often at the insistence of the regulators, new resources are brought in. These are frequently both expensive and ineffective.

This is not a fictitious or theoretical example; it has happened repeatedly in firms around the world. In some cases firms have been closed or forced to sell because they were unable to escape the downward spiral initiated by the twin effects of defective processing and lack of internal controls.

Implementing Efficient Business Controls

Why Do Processing Errors Occur?

Don't assume that processing errors are more or less likely to occur in computerized processes than manual ones. Essentially they are the same apart from one feature – which is that a human is capable of making mistakes that are not connected with his or her understanding of the business logic but are simply down to fatigue.   Both manual and computerized processes involve the same processes and can go wrong in similar ways. The illustration below shows a simple manual process.

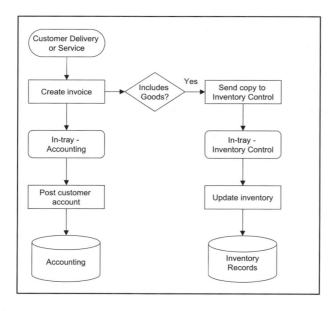

Figure 64 – Simple Manual Process

First an invoice is created and immediately the decision has to be made as to whether it involves any inventory movements.

Assuming it does, there are then two streams of activity, each of which starts with a 'request' for further action being placed in an in-tray in a specialist department.

There are then sequential activities (in this case only one per stream) that apply business logic to the incoming request and perform the required updates to the accounting and inventory systems.

Automating Controls

If this process were computerized, the Accounting and Inventory Control departments would be specialized sub-programs (or classes in an Object Oriented system) and the in-trays would be request queues of some kind.

Various things could go wrong in the manual version, all of which have parallels in a computerized system:

- The decision as to whether the Inventory Control department needed to receive an update request might be made wrongly.

- The staff in either of the departments might be absent or asleep.

- Someone might encounter a situation for which they have not been trained. They might reject the item and leave it in the in-tray, which could result in:

  - Tasks performed incorrectly because the item looks like something they can deal with but actually has specialized characteristics.

  - Rejected items in the in-tray might not be monitored and might simply go unprocessed.

  - Performance of a task might require reference data that cannot be found for some reason.

Business Process Analysis

Here is a simple part of a business process, included because the principles of controlling it will apply to real, much larger processes. We have a single activity performed on a population, resulting in the creation of a new one. In the context of the securities industry, Population 1 might be fulfilled orders and Population 2 might be trades.

Let's say that it is crucial that this one activity is performed completely and correctly because there are downstream sub processes that depend

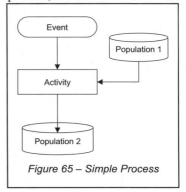

Figure 65 – Simple Process

on it and errors are intolerable. We, therefore, need to establish a control that compares the attributes and numbers of transactions in the two populations.

In the days when cost and efficiency were less important than they are today, we might have seen clerks performing one-to-one checking of transactions like these; it used to be quite common. Such controls have tended to disappear entirely because of cost pressure, which of course is not the right response if the control is genuinely important.

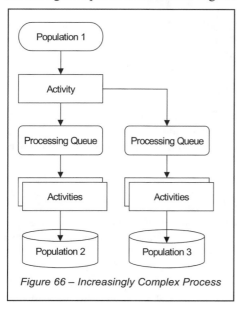

Figure 66 – Increasingly Complex Process

Here's a slightly more complex process that is more illustrative of real life situations. We have a population of transactions, the complete processing of which results in the creation of two populations. Each time an item in Population 1 is created, an activity creates a request for a new piece of specialized processing that will produce the final outcome.

Let's say that we can identify a direct relationship between Population 1 and the final outcomes in Populations 2 and 3. If this is the case we don't have to concern ourselves with what happened in between. This is the ideal situation when it comes to designing controls, and one should always aim to find the points of control that offer the maximum coverage for the minimum effort. There might of course be more relevant relationships between Populations 2 and 3. It is only by understanding and documenting business process flows that this will be understood.

The choice of control points and the design of controls will depend to a large extent on the level of detail required when discrepancies are reported. In the above process there are a number of sequential activities involved in the production of each outcome population. Because each activity performs some sort of conversion or transfer of information it is capable of adding its own errors. We want to know not only that there has been a problem somewhere in the overall process, but also to know where it has occurred, in order to get it rectified as quickly as possible. There are two ways in which we might do this:

If at all possible, we identify characteristics of breaks between the two outcome populations that point to different types of error. As an example, let's say that population 1 in this example is "Trades" and that populations 2 and 3 are holdings in a Front Office and a Back Office system. We choose to compare multiple attributes of the holdings, which include the Quantity and accumulated Profit and Loss. If we see a break in which the quantities disagree, we are probably missing a trade in one or the other. If the quantities agree but the Profit and Loss does not, this could be because a trade has been entered at the wrong price. We are, therefore, able to some extent to classify the break and in turn get the right person to investigate and rectify it.

If we need greater detail than this, we must start to reconcile "upstream" and almost certainly at the transaction level, but as in the asset manager example in the introduction to this article, this has more to do with investigation efficiency than control.

Business Control Activities

There are essentially two types of business control activity, Reconciliation and Exception Monitoring. Reconciliation is about comparing two or more populations and is generally performed for one of two reasons.

To control assets

This is the most common reason given for performing reconciliations of holdings with custodians. However let's be quite clear about something. The asset manager in the example above was able to point to a high level of internal security and segregation. If this was not true and one individual was able to create a fraudulent transaction that impacted both the real world holding and the internal records, there would be no point whatsoever in reconciling for this purpose.

To control processes

Wherever we have a business process that divides into separate legs, there is an opportunity for them to be processed inconsistently. Most business processes do this at some point or other; for example every time we send an instruction to a custodian or bank to move an asset, we are delegating part of a business process. Reconciliation of the outcomes gives us some comfort that the processing was consistent. Here's another thing to be clear about; because our version of a holding agrees with that of a custodian it doesn't mean that everything underlying that holding is in order. One of the main reasons that our asset manager was able to justify reconciliation of holdings only, was the fact that the accounts were segregated down to beneficial holder level. If he had been running any kind of pooled or clearing accounts, this argument would not have been appropriate because agreement at the balance level would have been potentially meaningless.

Exception Monitoring is about reviewing in some way a single population, comparing the attributes of each member with "acceptability" rules. These rules might be based on attributes of the item itself - "Is value A greater than Value B?" or on group attributes – "Items where a value is more than n% different from the group average for that value," or by reference to baseline criteria maintained within the reconciliation system. This type of business control will work in situations where reconciliation has no applicability – for example, where processing results in the modification of one population – and needs to be addressed by reconciliation systems if they are to be used as comprehensive operational risk control systems.

Performance and Documentation

Controls that are poorly performed or documented may as well not exist at all – in fact they can be worse than non-existent controls because they give a completely false sense of security.

If a control is being performed by a human being, using a tool that allows data to be manipulated in any way, then any review or sign-off of the results must involve at least periodic and complete re-performance if the control is to be relied upon, otherwise those results might be complete fiction. This is something that auditors have always understood but which most users of spreadsheet-based controls have conveniently ignored. If you are a busy manager under constant time pressure and you are presented with a printed spreadsheet reconciliation or other kind of business control for sign-off, you are highly unlikely to recheck the addition of all of the columns of numbers. You are almost certainly unlikely to re-analyze whole populations of underlying detail in order to double-check a summary report.

This is an area in which automated reconciliation systems add significant value to the whole internal control process. Not only do they perform their work systematically and routinely, but their results are immediately available to management and cannot be manipulated – provided that is, that the mistake is not made of transferring things back to spreadsheets before reporting them! The lure of the spreadsheet is magnetic; it is at the same time one of the cleverest and most dangerous business tools ever invented. Put spreadsheets in their place and do not rely on them for business critical control purposes.

In addition, recon systems usually include integrated exception management facilities enabling a consolidated view to be taken of all control issues throughout the enterprise.

Control Automation

To summarize, we have several clear reasons for comprehensive automation of business controls:

- To ensure that they are applied routinely and systematically.

- To ensure that their results are permanently documented and cannot be manipulated
- Cost effectiveness – or even feasibility or performance.
- Comprehensive exception management.

We have identified two ways in which reconciliation controls might be applied to populations in a process; to perform end-to-end verification of completeness and correctness, and to provide cross-verification of the outcomes.

We have also identified cases in which exception monitoring is relevant.

Both activities are capable of being implemented within an automated reconciliation system provided it has the range of capabilities required.

High Level System Requirements

As an introduction to the more detailed analyses of system features, here is an overview of the high level requirements that a user may have, and an appraisal of the system features that might be required to support them. It is not exhaustive, but a similarly business focused requirements list will help considerably in the system selection process and will avoid the 'Desired features' list that populates too many RFPs.

BUSINESS NEED / DRIVER	REQUIREMENTS
Need to obtain data from many sources, together with inability to produce stipulated file formats.	Recon system external interface that will handle any format of incoming data, including formatted reports designed for human consumption and other forms of highly structured message or file.
Handle inconsistent data content on each side of reconciliations, for example different trade price and date formats	Ability to manipulate data during or after loading, so that data elements may be converted into compatible forms.
Handle inconsistent data level on each side of reconciliations.	Structural flexibility. Ability to aggregate transactions and / or positions Ability to maintain running positions from transactions.
Control business activity across multiple instrument types and asset classes	Integrated system with common processing, enquiry and reporting across all reconciliation types. Strong support for instrument cross-referencing.
Control non-accounting business process flows, for example pre-settlement reconciliations for trades. Handle transactions other than accounting postings, for example open items, trades, status messages	User defined transactional behavior by reconciliation, or type of reconciliation, to include ability to supersede or to cancel without a new event from the supplying system.
Control over the lifecycle of business transactions.	Ability to store basic business transaction data. Strong ability to control and maintain both source and common referencing of incoming data. Without this, lifecycle management cannot work effectively. Integrated system.
Reduce or eliminate the time taken to investigate position breaks	Integrated Position and Transaction reconciliation. Strong tracking of position breaks over time.

BUSINESS NEED / DRIVER	REQUIREMENTS
Centralize operational control.	High capacity performance. Segregation of operational units' data and users.
Offer reconciliation as an ASP service to operational units.	As above, plus segregated, parallel streaming of reconciliation processing.
Operational Risk Analysis; ability to analyse exceptions and provide useful feedback.	Automated classification of breaks during the matching process and by user input. Statistical analyses.
Handle high incidence of exceptions.	Automated routing and subsequent escalation of exceptions. It should be added that a more intelligent response to a high exception rate would be to look seriously at the business processes being controlled, rather than to automate exception handling.
Integrity. A Reconciliation system must be able to control its own integrity if it is to be relied upon as a business control system.	Robust source data validation Audited changes Internal defense of accounting integrity where reconciliations involve transactions within balances or positions.
Detect exceptions in single populations	Ability to compare the attributes of an item with business rule generated comparators, based on lookup data and item attributes.
Process high volumes (e.g. > 500,000 per day), or moderate volumes (e.g. < 200,000 per day) with time-critical performance requirements	Parallel reconcilements engine processing capable of using multiple processor machines.

Figure 67 – Systems Requirements

Structural Flexibility

Populations to be reconciled are not always conveniently symmetrical. Here are some typical situations that might arise.

One side of a securities reconciliation consists of pooled holdings. The other side consists of individual client account holdings that must be aggregated to reconcile in total to the pooled side.

On the external side of a reconciliation getting positions from a CSD is too expensive to do daily, so they must be maintained from transactions and periodically audited against a position download. On the internal side the source system cannot supply transactions at all, so they must be implied from position movements to give the external transactions something to match against.

Transactions on one side of a reconciliation are bulked and must be matched on a one-to-many basis against the other side.

Always consider the data available on each side of a reconciliation, and look carefully at any situation in which they appear to be asymmetrical. Without the necessary features to handle these situations you might find that your attempts at automation are defeated.

Transaction Behavior

From the point of view of reconciliation systems there are essentially two types of transaction.

Accounting Events

Events occur and are reported once. Typical examples of events are account postings and bank statement entries. Reversals in the system of origin give rise to a second, reversal event. Events are the most common form of transaction and are handled effectively by all reconciliation systems.

Open Items

These inform on the current state of one or more aspects of a business transaction. A typical example would be a report of the current status of a settlement instruction, e.g., "cannot settle – insufficient securities." They differ radically from events in that the same transaction will be reported by a source each time its status changes, when other sources may report nothing new because the status has not changed from their viewpoint. We always wish to attempt to reconcile the latest versions against each other; therefore, we need to have robust ways of:

- Telling the difference between a new version of an existing transaction and an entirely new transaction. This is not as easy as it might seem. Some senders of information might have reliable referencing systems, for example transaction 123456/1 when superseded becomes 123456/2, others might not. Either way, because different suppliers will use different referencing systems, it is often necessary to use sophisticated rules-based data manipulation facilities to achieve effective transaction supercession.

- Automatically unwinding previous matches if a new version of a transaction arrives, so that they may be superseded and submitted for re-matching.

Some reconciliations may involve "snapshot" reports of large numbers of open items from accounts in one source system against parallel populations from another. Each recon event is distinct from the previous one and entirely supersedes it to give the latest position, rather than transactions being individually superseded. In many cases the transactions will be supplied along with balances that should represent their totals.

Matching and Exception Analysis

These are two sides of the same coin. All users wish to maximize automated transaction matching rates, which often require a degree of sophistication, including:

- The ability to associate transactions with each other on the basis of pseudo as well as actual references.

- The ability to compare any number of transaction attributes or pseudo attributes in different ways, including tolerances.

You may also need to compare multiple attributes of balances or positions.

As important as maximizing matching rates, is establishing why items failed to match. The number of possible reasons increases with the number of comparisons that are made. If you are simply associating transactions on the basis of a reference and are then comparing the values, there is a very limited range of possible match failure reasons. If on the other hand, you are comparing multiple attributes, then the number of possible reasons expands somewhat – mathematically the number of possible combinations, but in business reality a smaller number!

The ability to establish automated problem categorization for patterns of match failures is frankly unimportant if you have few exceptions, but you will probably still need the ability to assign user-defined categories manually in any case. If you have more than a handful of exceptions every day, automation is highly desirable because this is a key enabler in automating the distribution of problems to users.

Specific Securities and Derivatives Reconciliation Issues

Most users seeking to automate securities reconciliation do so because they wish to move from periodic positions only, to positions plus underlying transactions on a daily basis. There are several potential issues in this area, all of which need to be properly addressed by the selected system if the implementation is to deliver completely on its promises.

Security Identifiers

Holders and senders of securities data use different coding conventions.

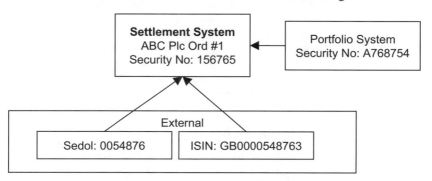

Figure 68 – Security Identifier

Some of the better known of these are ISIN, CUSIP, and Sedol, which tend to be used when sending information to third parties. In addition to this, many if not most securities processing systems use their own internal unique coding standard and maintain cross-references to external standards, as illustrated below.

These relationships need to be maintained in the recon system, so that it can correctly associate holdings and transactions on each side. This needs to be done reliably, particularly if a reconciliation involves both holdings and underlying transactions, in order to maintain accounting integrity between different securities. This is generally achieved through cross-referencing within the recon system, which is far from straightforward and is discussed in more detail after the next section on the topic of accounting integrity.

Accounting Integrity

Users will reasonably expect to be able to drill down into a position level break and see one or more unmatched transactions that explain it. This seems a simple enough concept, but it requires enforcement of accounting integrity:

- Transactions must be closely and unambiguously associated both with their parent (source) positions and with the common security identifier.

- It follows that neither transactions nor holdings can be allowed fully into the system as valid holdings until they have been assigned a common security identifier.

- It must not be possible under any circumstances to match transactions across holdings.

- The recon system must be capable of validating incoming data by source, regardless of how or when the data arrive. There are always at least two sources in a reconciliation – maybe more. If validation is not performed at source level, then situations will arise in which unmatched transactions do not account for balance level breaks and it is difficult or sometimes impossible to find out why. Securities reconciliation data do not usually arrive in the form of a convenient statement with opening and closing balances; holdings and transactions generally arrive in separate messages, and some providers of custodial services frequently deliver transactions that do not sum to the movement between last and current reported holdings.

Cross-Referencing Issues

Cross-referencing needs to be as automated and as reliable as possible, otherwise reconciliations will constantly contain items that have to be associated manually, leading to the possibility of this being done incorrectly. Two typical ways of automating the process are:

- To have one authoritative source of securities from which all cross reference data in the recon system are routinely maintained – typically by sending file of securities and all known codes from a central securities database or the settlement system. Incoming data are then "hooked" onto existing cross-references provided by this source.

- To have the system "learn" about cross-references as reconciliation proceeds. This requires one of the sources to send its own code together with information about the coding standard that is used on the other side, along with its reconciliation data.

In either case it is essential that the system knows, for each sender of information, the type of coding standard used and doesn't simply rely on the code itself, because the same code might exist in more than one coding standard.

It is also essential for cross-references to be maintained at custodian / sender system level. There is a significant problem in that some coding standards are less specific than others, so global cross-references across the entire recon system cannot deliver the required degree of accuracy. Take the case of a dual quoted security. In each of its quoted forms it will probably have a different Sedol code and internal system code, but the same ISIN code. If you have holdings with different custodians for each country / exchange, both of which use ISIN code, you will need a separate cross-reference for each custodian, each pointing at a different internal security.

It can be worse than this. You might have a global custodian reporting holdings in the two securities, each identified by the same ISIN code, in the same message. Depending on how your reconciliation system behaves this might result in either of the following:

- The holdings being aggregated under the one ISIN code and being associated with one of the internal holdings, or...

- One of the holdings being taken to be the "latest" one and being associated as above.

In either case artificial breaks will result. The only solution to this is to have the custodian supply distinct and reliable descriptions and to use these as well as the ISIN codes to create cross-references.

A further problem arises out of inconsistent degrees of accuracy. Take the case of a corporate action involving a capital reconstruction. Let's say that we have been reconciling a holding in ABC Plc #1 Ordinary Shares between an internal system and a custodian and that there is a two for one stock split. The custodian uses ISIN and the internal system uses its own more accurate standard. When the corporate action is processed in the internal system, a new security is created to represent ABC Plc Ord 50p. This is essential because not all client holdings are necessarily processed at the same time, particularly in a complex corporate action, and it is necessary for both the old and the new version of the security to be able to co-exist in the system. However in the outside world the security continues to be referenced using the ISIN code, with no change.

Here's the sequence of events.

EXISTING ASSOCIATION:	EXTERNAL CODE	EXTERNAL HOLDING	INTERNAL CODE	INTERNAL HOLDING	UNMATCHED TRANSACTIONS
BEFORE STOCK SPLIT – PERFECT MATCH	GB0000548763	5,000	156765	5,000	None
CORPORATE ACTION	GB0000548763	+5,000	156765	-5,000	
RESULTING HOLDINGS		10,000		0	2
NEW SECURITY					
CORPORATE ACTION			175342	+10,000	
RESULTING HOLDING			175342	10,000	1

Figure 69 – Process Sequence

A new security is created in the recon system because of the new internal code. The external holding continues to be associated with the old internal security reference, the holding for which has now been reduced to zero, and there is a break. In order to repair this, the recon system must have a mechanism through which the existing association may be broken and a new one created. This seems simple enough, but there could be a whole history of matched transactions behind the old association. It is therefore essential that the system "journalize" the re-association properly in order to maintain accounting integrity. In the case above, any transactions and holdings up to the point where the corporate action occurred must be left in place under the old association. The transaction that moved the external holding from 5,000 to 10,000 must be moved, and a pair of journal transactions must be created to explain the movement of the original 5,000 from one to the other. If this is not done properly, there will always be situations in which accounting integrity is breached.

Derivatives Reconciliation

With Derivatives reconciliation, cross-referencing problems are exacerbated. A future will be identified by an exchange allocated Product Code and an Expiry Date, which will generally appear in different positions on an incoming file. An exchange-traded option will be identified by the combination of Product Code, Exercise Date (or month), Option Type, and Exercise Price, again appearing in different places on an incoming file. To perform a 'positions plus transactions' reconciliation these identifier elements will need to be assembled together as data are loaded, to create unique instrument identifiers; it isn't enough simply to treat them as separate matching fields because this will open up the possibility of users matching across instruments. The problem is further complicated by the widely varying conventions exchanges have for expressing Prices and Dates, so that business rules almost always have to be built to achieve compatible formats across a reconciliation, for example: 14Q (London Traded Options Market) needs to be converted to 14.25 to match against an internal system.

Accounting Segregation

SEC Rule 15c3-3 states that:

- At all times, the firm must know which of the securities it holds belong to their clients and which belong to the firm...
- All securities fully paid for by the client must be fully segregated from the firm's positions and those in the course of settlement.

If you are an asset manager or broker conducting private client business, you may well have reconciliations to perform in which there are tens if not hundreds of thousands of individual client accounts that should be segregated. It is clearly not feasible to do this by setting up static data within the reconciliation system; the idea of having tens of thousands of individual account reconciliations is almost unthinkable and in any case the population is highly dynamic. Therefore your system needs to have a way of both automating and enforcing account segregation below reconciliation and instrument level, in much the same way as is done for individual instruments.

Zero Balances

In securities reconciliation it is quite common for transactions to exist without positions, for example, where a position is reduced to zero by the most recent transactions, or in trading accounts that always start and end the day at zero. The reconciliation system must be capable of maintaining these implied zero balances.

When positions only are being reconciled (i.e. without transactions), a zero position will be evidenced only by its non-existence in the latest set of positions from a given source. There are various ways of managing this, some of which work better than others. Suffice it to say that a method that relies on SWIFT messages will not be generally applicable, so if you have position reconciliations such as those between internal systems, you will need to know that the reconciliation system can supersede old balances with zero balances where necessary.

Problem Management

Tracking Position Breaks

When you move to daily reconciliation you will have position breaks that persist over time. If you compare positions in a simplistic way, matching each day's data load in isolation, you will have one break per position per day. This of course is not the real business situation; what you actually have is a position break that occurred on a particular business day, persisted for several days possibly changing along the way, and was finally resolved some days later. The recon system must be capable of tracking positions over time so that it can present you with an up to date picture of each position break, accurately age that break, and allow you to track, investigate and annotate one problem.

Tracking Open Item Transaction Breaks

Tracking positions is relatively simple, because a position is always identified by its source, an instrument identifier and possibly a sub-account identifier below that level. Tracking open item transaction breaks is a quite different matter because we are then down to the level of transaction references, which as discussed earlier, may well be unreliable. That having been said, provided that references may be established that allow a particular open transaction to be tracked from one reconciliation to another, the requirement and the mechanism is essentially the same as for tracking position breaks; they are in effect mini positions, and you should expect it to be possible to track them.

Automated Problem Assignment

A number of vendors now include, or have as optional modules, automated workflow engines capable of handling the routing of problems to appropriate users. These generally incorporate the ability to define business rules that, inter-alia allow the user to:

- Define initial allocations of problems to users based on attributes of a break. These could include, apart from attributes of the positions or transactions themselves, the value of the break and the problem classification (whether automatically or manually assigned).

- Define subsequent escalation rules based on age and value. These in turn require the ability to:

- Flexibly define an organizational model so that the system knows to whom a problem should be referred if it remains unresolved.

- Age items correctly regardless of the type of item. Age, in the case of "event" transactions will be based on the date of the event (which could be a logical business date or value date, or the event date), and is generally handled well by most systems. In the case of positions and open transactions the quality of aging depends entirely on how well the system tracks these types of break.

Some Generic Recon Scenarios

This article takes it for granted that reconciliation system users will wish to automate Cash Account and Holdings reconciliations. The final section explores some of the business scenarios that go beyond those areas, in particular concentrating on general business controls.

Accounting Process Control

Scenario

You have an accounting system that maintains both open trades and balances. When cash is received and posted to an account, a separate sub process also updates the open trades, like this:

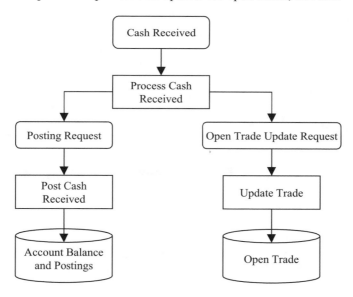

Figure 70 – Automated Processes

The sum of open trade values should equal the account balance for any given account and instrument. Because of occasional processing problems it is possible either for the account posting or the update trade legs to fail.

Recon Solution

In principle this is a clear case of comparing two outcome populations, but it's complicated by the fact that there could be any number of individual open trades comprising an accounting balance. We need to take in the open trade values on one side and treat them as sub-balances, automatically aggregating them to balance level to compare the resulting balances with those on the other side. We also need to retain the detailed open trade information at sub-balance level for audit purposes so that its relationship with the source data remains intact. Here's how it looks in terms of reconciliation structure:

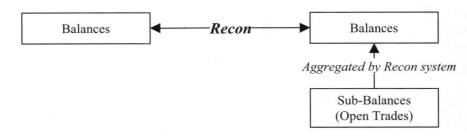

Figure 71 – Reconciliation Process

Extended Accounting Control

Scenario

Let's say that in the above example there are deficiencies in the account posting processing in that occasionally an account balance may move in a way that is not explained by its postings. This may seem bizarre, but it has been seen.

Recon Solution

The solution above may be extended by feeding in both the postings and the balances from the left-hand source, allowing the recon system to validate the two against each other. However this would give a one-sided population of transactions with nothing to match against on the other side. The solution to this is:

- To have the recon system generate implied transactions to account for the daily changes in constructed balances on the right hand side

- To build matching rules that will automatically match in bulk the detailed actual account postings against the implied movements provided that they are the same in total. They will only fail to match if there is a problem with the maintenance of the balances in source A.

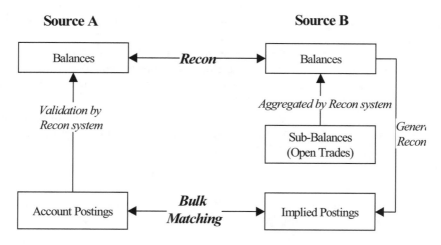

Figure 72 – Accounting Control - Reconciliation Solution

That way you get all the control you need in one recon event. If there is an account posting problem in source A, it will be reported as a source validation problem, distinct from a problem related to the agreement of the two systems.

Offline Open Item Accounting

Scenario

You have a settlement accounting system in which most, if not all accounts, are maintained on a rolling balance basis – i.e. there are no facilities for maintaining sub-analysis at business transaction level. Each month end accounting and other staff spend hours analyzing movements in and out of certain accounts in order to establish what the balance is made up of. This is a common situation applying in particular to suspense and corporate action process control accounts. Even where an accounting system does provide open item accounting it is often too rigid to be able to handle all situations – for example it might be based on one particular reference field.

Recon Solution

This is an area where a recon solution may offer massive return on investment, because it is able to:

- Receive all of the account posting events from selected accounts, possibly with the account balances.

- Maintain its own accounting balances and check these against the supplied balances, to prove its own integrity and the completeness of the incoming account postings.

- Perform automated matching of the transactions within each source account, using rules that are considerably more flexible and powerful than those (if any) available in the source system.

- Enable users to maintain in a controlled audited way, the manual matching of suspense items that were unable to be matched automatically and the re-opening of inaccurately matched items.

- Present at any time an up to date analysis of the open items that comprise the balance, with the assurance that the two will always agree.

Open Items Reconciliation

Scenario

You have two systems in which the same population of open trades should be present. The processing of these trades originates from a single Front Office source, but at some point middleware is used to route information to the two systems. You need to know that open trades are present in both populations and have the same attributes.

Recon Solution

Each day, you feed the populations into your recon system as open items. They are associated with each other across the reconciliation by reference, and several comparisons are performed on various bases, in some cases on multiple combinations of fields using complex user-defined business rules.

Each comparison may have its individual tolerances and rules.

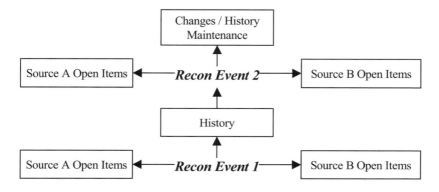

Figure 73 – Open Item Accounting - Reconciliation

On each recon event the breaks are compared with the previous situation for each reference, enabling the system to highlight new, cleared and changed problems.

Conclusion

The examples above probably only begin to scratch the surface of what is possible in terms of internal control implementation with a competent generic recon system. A little thought through one's own business processes together with some analysis of the control tasks that are currently performed, will almost certainly reveal a business case for cost-effective automation of a wide range of business control tasks in addition to the traditional reconciliation areas. Carrying this through to implementation will yield both tangible benefits in terms of reduction of performance costs, and intangible but nonetheless crucial benefits in terms of reductions in operational and reputational risk, and evidenced and auditable controls.

About the Author

David Flinders is Head of Securities and Derivatives at City Networks Limited and is based at its London office. A UK Chartered Accountant, his career history includes Audit responsibility for securities firms and Operational and Financial Management within large stockbroking organizations, together with wide consultancy experience. He is currently responsible for the management and strategic direction of the CityNet Enterprise Reconciliation product.

dflinders@citynetworks.co.uk

PART V - CONCLUSION

As we've seen, there are many solutions currently available to assist firms in improving their level of STP. While no firm has achieved 100% STP, it is possible to improve by using the concepts that are presented.

However, knowing the goal and implementing the processes to achieve the goal are very separate activities. In most cases the goals as obvious while identifying and implementing the solutions are very different. In this section we present two views of how to implement STP concepts.

CHAPTER XX - PRACTICAL GUIDE TO IMPLEMENTING STP[56]

By George Bollenbacher, President, G. M. Bollenbacher & Co., Ltd

Introduction

The concept of Straight Through Processing (STP) has gained wide acceptance throughout the investment industry, among broker/dealers, investment managers and custodian banks. Its conceptual popularity is due to several factors:

- The increasing complexity and volatility of securities markets
- Impending moves to longer trading hours and shorter settlement cycles
- An increasing emphasis on cost containment throughout the securities business
- A blurring of the organizational lines dividing the front and Back Offices

However, as popular as the concept of STP is, its attainment is much more problematic. This is also due to several factors:

- Each securities transaction necessarily involves several entities, each of which has its own objectives and constraints
- Each security type and client set has a different processing work flow
- Certain aspects of securities transactions may require human intervention under any workflow
- Much of STP depends on technology interfaces, which are notoriously difficult to manage

In addition, many firms have taken what amounts to an impractical approach to implementing STP. These firms have formed STP Task Forces, STP Committees, or STP Working Groups, whose memberships cut across many departments. Because of that makeup, these groups often attempt to attack the STP issue across all the securities, geographies, and/or functions the firm does business in. In all too many cases, these "boil-the-ocean" efforts run out of steam or are sidetracked before any real benefits can be realized.

The Practical Approach

What is needed is a practical approach to STP. That approach probably begins with changing the frame of reference. Instead of Straight Through Processing, we might better focus on what James Hartley of the Securities Industry Automation Association calls Securities Processing Automation, or on becoming the most efficient and effective processor of securities transactions in our peer group. Once liberated from the specter of STP, we can free ourselves from the endless debates about whether a particular process is really straight-through, or from fruitless efforts to quantify the percent of our transactions that actually are straight through.

---

[56] Originally published in *The Journal of Securities Operations*, Summer 2002, Summit Press

When we start thinking outside the STP box, we can focus on meaningful processing improvements, useful metrics, and measurable benefits. Thinking about it that way, we can take the following approach:

Pilots – we can identify subsets of securities categories and geographical regions for initial implementation, and roll out the implementations to the larger universe after they have been tested.

Models – we can build a model of a specific securities process, encompassing workflow, metrics and systems, and use the model to prioritize and redesign process components.

Workflow Mapping – we can map the workflows from the beginning of a securities transaction to the end, and relate those maps to the metrics.

Metrics – we can measure processing performance, both before and after projects have been implemented to ensure that we have properly prioritized our efforts and gotten the expected results.

Prioritization – based on the workflow mapping, the metrics, and the model, we can identify the processes and parts of processes for improvement that give us the best cost/benefit ratio.

Root Cause Analysis – once the processes are prioritized, we can perform root cause analysis on the highest priority problems in the workflows

Process Design – we can redesign these workflows using a methodology like normative modeling, so as to maximize their efficiency and throughput, and minimize their error rate and cost.

External Entities – we can involve external entities in our process design to the extent possible and to the extent that their involvement will facilitate process improvement.

Technology – we can utilize available technology to support or enable the process improvements and execution of the projects.

Iteration – finally, we can go back to the beginning of this list and look for the next opportunity, using some of the benefits from this effort to help pay for the next one.

Let's look at each of these components in more detail.

Pilots

The first suggestion is that you not try to cover all the securities in all the geographies you process. Instead, choose a type of security or geography that is small enough in volume to handle with the resources you have but important enough to justify the resource commitment. A good candidate would be a security which has moderate volume and complexity, but which requires manual effort out of proportion to its trading volume.

But you really should tailor your pilots to your own needs. For example, a major global securities dealer chose two securities types and regions to pilot its approach to STP. These were US Listed Shares (not including syndicate transactions) and Finland Equities. The pilots were chosen for quite different reasons. US Listed Shares processing, while high volume, was too manual and error-prone. Finland Equities, while much lower in volume, represented the processing architecture the dealer expected to adopt in the future. Thus US Listed Shares represented a challenge to STP, while Finland Equities represented a possible solution.

On the other hand, a large US money manager chose mortgage-backed securities settlements as their pilot program, because the current processing was heavily manual, error-prone, and constrained their ability to manage these securities. This pilot was more complex than other possible choices, but the tremendous benefits of streamlining the processes justified the larger commitment of resources.

Models

Once you have selected your pilot(s) the real work begins. Because this kind of process modification is fraught with costs and risks, it is essential to build a model from which to work. The model should contain the following components:

- Workflow maps
- Metrics and benchmarks
- Prioritizations and expected benefits
- Root cause analyses
- Workflow redesigns

Some firms divide the process(es) themselves into component parts and attack each component separately. They map each component, establish metrics for each component, and redesign each component. While this appears to break the task into manageable pieces, it actually makes the job harder to do. This is because the process itself doesn't function in parts, but as a whole. The types of risks this chronological fragmentation faces are:

- Incorrect handling of recycled trades
- Higher automation rates early in the process at the expense of higher error rates later in the process
- The inability to determine root causes of manual steps because those causes are embedded in another component

This last point is especially important because root cause analysis is critical to successful implementation. In particular, there are two kinds of root causes for manual processing in transactions. The first cause would be something built into the standard operating procedure. An example would be the manual matching of client account allocations for block executions. The second root cause would be exceptions, such as breaks or cancellations and corrections. These two kinds of causes have different kinds of metrics, and respond to different kinds of process redesigns. The model should keep these two types of causes separate, so they are not likely to be confused.

Workflow Maps – Handoffs and Recycles

You must document the workflows in your pilot, both to verify the assumptions already made and to identify bottlenecks. In mapping the workflows, look for four things:

- Inputs from, and outputs to, external entities like clients, agents or CSDs
- Manual steps that are menial or rote in nature
- Exceptions causing the process to recycle to a much earlier point
- Exceptions requiring manual processing in downstream steps

These all signal process improvement opportunities. Conversely, a manual step that sends the process back into an automated flow may not be a high priority for redesign.

The following is a typical process map, in this case for DTCC-eligible Equities. This process is so complex that it requires a three-page map, of which this is the first page.

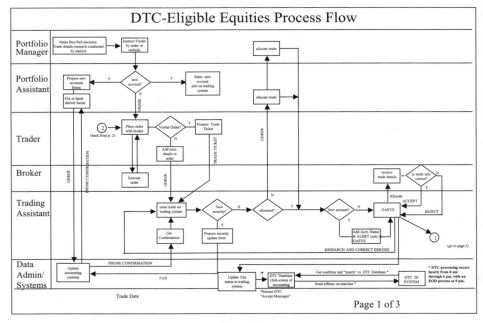

Figure 74

This method of workflow mapping is particularly useful for this purpose because it highlights the handoffs and inter-enterprise interfaces that are critical to automating trade processing. Here we can see what looks like a very convoluted process, but many parts of it are actually quite efficient. The improvement opportunities in these maps are often hidden just under the surface.

Of course, workflow mapping only tells part of the story. For example, in the above mapping the broker's trading assistant handles every trade the same, no matter whether it is electronically or manually entered. However, the amount of effort required of the TA may be very different, depending on how the order is received. To find that out, we must look at the metrics.

Metrics – Benchmarks and Diagnostics

First you need to identify the metrics you plan to use, and then where those metrics reside. There are two kinds of metrics you will need, benchmarks and diagnostics.

Benchmarks show you how well you are doing in achieving STP, both against internal objectives and against industry standards. Benchmarking against industry standards does more than tell you how you are doing. It also starts to tell you about the root causes. If your metrics are low and the rest of the industry is high, it's an indication that you have a process flaw. If the industry metrics are uniformly low, it means that there is a flaw in everyone's process, often originating with the client or perhaps with regulations. In this case, working with your competitors to alleviate the bottleneck may be the only approach.

Diagnostics give you insights into the root causes of your benchmark performance. While benchmark metrics are usually obvious, diagnostic metrics are often anything but obvious. In some cases you will have to get several sets of diagnostics, if the first set doesn't point you to the right bottleneck.

Once you know which metrics you plan to use, you need to find out where you can get them. In particular, you need to know where you can get them on a regular basis, without an inordinate amount of work. Static or one-time metrics have very little value for our purposes. We need time series to make rational decisions, and we will need to keep getting these metrics after the implementation is complete, both to gauge how successful we were and to keep us on target for the future.

Here is a typical list of metrics for the listed shares pilot we mentioned before. Some of these were needed for benchmarking, and some for diagnosis. Can you tell which was which?

Order Handling

- Electronic transmission by client – percent of orders transmitted by clients electronically

- DOT executions – percent of trades executed through DOT
- Electronic transmission to client – percent of executions transmitted to client electronically

Trade Booking – Client Side

- OASYS allocations – percent of block trades that are allocated via OASYS
- Other electronic allocations – percent of block trades that are allocated via other electronic feeds
- Manual allocations – percent of block trades that are manually allocated
- T+1 release – percent of block trades not released to the trading system until T+1
- Cancellations – percent of account-level trades that are cancelled without use of the error account

Trade Booking – Street Side

- Floor breaks – percent of floor trades that don't compare
- Floor corrections – percent of floor trades that must be corrected
- T+1 compares – percent of floor trades that compare on T+1

Client/Street Break Resolution

- Total breaks – percent of account level trades where there are breaks between client side and street side
- Street side wrong – percent of total breaks where street report is wrong (Top five reasons – the top five reasons with percentages)
- Client side wrong – percent of total breaks where client report is wrong (Top five reasons – the top five reasons with percentages)

Pre-Settlement

- Affirmed by noon on T+2 – percent of trades affirmed by client before noon on T+2
- Affirmed after noon on T+2 – percent of trades affirmed by client, but not by noon on T+2
- Not affirmed, but good for settlement – percent of trades not affirmed by client, but correct for settlement
- Not good for settlement – percent of trades where something must be changed in the instructions in order for settlement to occur

- Affirmed but not authorized for ID settlement – the percent of 5.1. that is not authorized for ID settlement

Settlement

- ID night cycle attempted – percent of account-level trades entered into the DTCC ID night cycle
- ID night cycle successful – percent of 5.6. that settled successfully
- R&D attempts – percent of account-level trades attempted for settlement in the R&D cycle
- Fails – percent of trades attempted for settlement that fail to settle
- New Fails – percent of trades with today's settlement date that fail to settle
- Fail Persistence – number of fails older than 10 days and 20 days

Interestingly enough, every one of these metrics was available from either an in-house system or the depository.

Prioritization

The combination of workflow maps and metrics gives you a picture of all the things that need to be fixed in the process, or the building locks for prioritization. Armed with the metrics and the workflows, you can identify the highest priority process changes. These would give you the maximum economic benefit for the lowest expenditure of resources. Because this prioritization can be an emotional topic, it is best to use a rigorous method of deciding. Below is the comparison sheet used by one asset manager for prioritization, and one of the underlying analysis sheets.

Investment Operations	
Cost / Benefit Analysis	
Comparison Sheet	
Region and Product _____	
Process Change	Cost/Benefit
1.	
2.	
3.	
4.	

Figure 75 – Sample Comparison Sheet

Investment Operations
Cost / Benefit Analysis

Process Change 1. _____

Benefits

Step Removed: _____
Hours/Week   _____   Cost/Hour   _____   Annualized   _____
Step Removed: _____
Hours/Week   _____   Cost/Hour   _____   Annualized   _____

Exception Removed: _____
Exceptions/Week   _____   Cost/Hour   _____   Annualized   _____
Exception Removed: _____
Exceptions/Week   _____   Cost/Hour   _____   Annualized   _____

Collateral Benefit: _____
Benefit/Week   _____   Annualized   _____

   TOTAL BENEFITS   [_____]

Costs

Redesign   Hours   _____   Cost/Hour   _____   Total
Implement   Hours   _____   Cost/Hour   _____   Total
Technology   Hours   _____   Cost/Hour   _____   Total   _____
Purchased Software   _____

Total Technology   Total   [_____]
Training   Hours   _____   Cost/Hour   _____   Total   _____
Marketing   Hours   _____   Cost/Hour   _____   Total   _____
Technology   Hours   _____   Cost/Hour   _____   Total   _____

TOTAL COSTS   [_____]

Cost/Benefit Result   [_____]

The result is expressed as a monetary benefit if the benefit exceeds the cost, or as years-to-recover if the cost exceeds the benefit.

Figure 76 – Sample Cost/Benefit Analysis

Of course, this is a simplified analysis, but even this kind of metrics-based prioritization not only gathers support throughout the organization for the choices made, it also sets the stage for measuring the results after the implementation is complete.

Root Cause Analysis

Root cause analysis (RCA) has been part of process design almost since its inception, but this is one of those cases where familiarity breeds, if not contempt, at least short shrift. Many attempts at RCA are cursory and only scratch the surface. In other cases, process participants, and even their management, may try to steer the analysis away from causes they don't want discovered. Finally, firms in a hurry to get on with the design phase may shortcut this stage. All of those mistakes expose you to erroneous process designs and wasted time and money.

What is needed is a rigorous RCA, one that starts with the benchmark metrics, moves to the diagnostic metrics, and finishes with some serious detective work. For example, in the U.S. Listed Shares example previously mentioned, a high priority was placed on the fact that the firm averaged more than 200 aged fails (open more than 10 days) on the books every day. Our detective work turned up the fact that the largest single category of aged fails included those that opened after settlement date. In other words, these trades first settled, and then failed.

Needless to say, this finding caused great consternation in the operations area of the firm. How could so many trades that had settled open up as fails? Further research showed two major causes for post-settlement fails: a valid one and an invalid one. The valid reason was money managers who discovered compliance problems with purchases that had already settled. In these cases, the money manager put through a cancellation and rebooked the purchase into another account which didn't have the compliance problem. That cancel and rebook opened a new fail to receive and a new fail to deliver on the broker's books. In some cases, it took several weeks to get the securities back from the wrong account's custodian.

The invalid reason, by far the most common, resulted from a client's request for a duplicate confirm for a trade that had already settled. The broker's support staff, instead of accessing the trade in the system and requesting a duplicate confirm, sometimes canceled and rebooked the trade to force the system to print a new confirm. Of course, this opened two fails on the broker's books. The staff would offset the fails by doing a pair-off in the system, but sometimes the firm's efficient delivery process would attempt to deliver against the sell-side fail before the pair-off could be entered. So there was good news and bad news out of this RCA. The bad news was that the firm had some sloppy practices in its operations area. The good news was that these fails, at least, weren't real and didn't expose the firm to error or loss. Sometimes what looks to be bad news is actually good news in disguise.

Process Design

Based on the prioritization and RCA, certain processes will be chosen to be redesigned. Because many processes involve multiple constituencies within the enterprise, and possibly within other entities, the redesign methodology employed must reconcile and resolve objectives and constraints across many constituencies. The best methodology for such redesign is normative modeling.

Normative modeling employs the following steps:

- Identifying constituencies
- Identifying constituency objectives
- Developing optimal processes for each constituency
- Reconciling optimal processes
- Identifying constituency constraints
- Applying constraints
- Identifying Constituencies

The first step in process redesign is identifying all the constituents. A constituency is any group, department, or external entity that has a stake in the process, whether as a contributor, user of output, or monitor. The identification includes what they contribute, use, or monitor.

Identifying Constituency Objectives

The next step is identifying the objectives of each constituency, both valid and invalid. Valid objectives are those the constituency would voice in an open forum. An invalid objective is one the constituency may have, but wouldn't voice in an open forum. It is important to identify any invalid objectives because ignoring them may cause the constituency to resist the new process at the point of implementation.

Developing Optimal Processes

In this step, we develop the optimal process for each constituency's valid objectives, without regard for any other constituency's objectives, and without regard for any constraints. It is important that the optimal process is designed for the constituency's valid objectives, but not for the invalid objectives, to the extent that the invalid objectives are detrimental to other constituencies. The optimal processes are all documented in the same format.

Optimal Process Reconciliation

In this step, we will reconcile the various optimal processes into one. Where all constituents have the same valid objectives, the solution will be easy. Where their valid objectives differ or are in opposition, we will resolve those differences using one of several time-tested resolution methodologies. This step will give us the optimal process for all the constituencies, without regard to constraints such as cost and technology.

Application of Constraints

In this step we will apply all the constraints we face. Technology constraints will include the estimated date of availability for the appropriate technology. At the end of this step, we will not only have the optimal process for all constituents, given the current constraints, we will know which constraints have which effect, and when their removal would occur or how much it would cost.

At the end of this normative modeling, we will have the best possible process for all the participants, given the constraints we face. In addition, we will know exactly what prevents us from making the process better, giving us a roadmap for the future.

External Entities

It is a little known rule of process design in the securities world that the more our design work incorporates interaction with external entities, the more likely it is to succeed. Of course, process design has involved external entities from the very beginning. Professor Mike Hammer's original article on the subject in the early 1990's used as an example the Ford Motor parts ordering process, which was redesigned in cooperation with suppliers. But, somehow the latest efforts in this industry seem to spend little, if any, time and effort incorporating external entities.

For institutional securities processing, the main classes of entities are: brokers, asset managers, custodians, and depositories. Each of these classes of entities has performed specific functions for many years, so many that most market participants assume that they have an inalienable right to fill that space. But the fact is, times are changing. For example, brokers and custodians now own asset managers, asset managers and brokers now act as custodians, and depositories are edging into the custodian field.

What this all means is that process designers need to think creatively about how they interact with external entities. As an example, there is generally no statutory reason that a large asset manager couldn't become a member of a depository. This arrangement could expedite both trade settlement and corporate actions notification. Clearly, such an arrangement would raise questions about the custodian's role in the process, but any business whose role is simply to take information from one entity and pass it to another needs a better business model. Suffice it to say that the drive for speed and efficiency in trade processing will place great pressure on the current roles of market participants. Those who adapt will survive and thrive. Those who don't, won't.

Technology

Like external entities, technology has been in the background of the discussion up to now – implied but not invoked. Although technology is often mentioned as an enabler in securities processing, many people in the industry will tell you it is actually a disabler; preventing them from getting where they want to go. In many ways, the whole history of STP has been one of the business people pushing the envelope and the technologists holding it back. There are several reasons why this view prevails:

Vendor Competition – As technology vendors struggle for competitive advantage, the main casualties are standards and interoperability. The result of this competition is often the perpetuation of technology silos and the proliferation of expensive integration jobs. Only if their clients get together and opt for standards-based products will some tech vendors get the message.

Application Databases – Most trading applications come with their own database, complete with unique field names and attributes. Thus getting trades through the cycle often means translating the same data element several times. In addition, and often worse, the trade cycle often requires trade enrichment via data queries to downstream systems. In these cases, the query may have to be translated into the downstream data format, and the response back into the upstream format. Finally, these different data formats can make data maintenance a nightmare.

National Requirements – As much as the capital markets are global, their supervision and regulation are often national. Whether the national rules pertain to secrecy, public reporting of trade prices and volumes, or access to settlement entities, they often serve to complicate the job of technology. Until the world's securities regulators begin to see their jobs as having global impact, the technologists may have to be the grease for some very squeaky wheels.

Iteration

Once the pilot programs have been put into production, it's time for two much more pleasant tasks – quantifying the results and identifying the next iteration. In many cases, the quantification of benefits has initially been disappointing. Often this is because the business unit has resisted the last of the changes necessary to realize the largest benefits. In these cases, the project team needs to do one last round of root cause analysis, and one last presentation to the project's management. In the mortgage-backed case I mentioned earlier, we recognized that the biggest benefits required a change in the way traders and operations staff related to each other. Management initially resisted these changes, but, to their credit, they saw the light before we went live. As a result, during the first month under the new process they made enough incremental trading profits to pay for the software purchase. Results like that leave everyone anxious to find the next pilot, which is the real point of the whole approach.

About the Author

George Bollenbacher is President of G. M. Bollenbacher & Co., Ltd., which supplies management consulting and project management services to the investment industry. Among its client list are Alliance Capital Management, Putnam Investments, Thomson Financial, Goldman Sachs, and Franklin Templeton.

Mr. Bollenbacher spent 20 years in the investment industry, from 1967 to 1987, 10 years in the technology industry, from 1987 to 1997, and has been President of G. M. Bollenbacher & Co., Ltd. since 1997.

He is the author of three books: The Professional's Guide to the U. S. Government Securities Market, The New Business of Banking, and Banking Strategies for the '90s, as well as numerous journal and newspaper articles. He has taught at Marymount College, The New School, The New York Institute of Finance, and Securities Operations Forum.

CHAPTER XXI - ESTABLISHING AN STP PROCESS

By Hal McIntyre, Managing Partner, The Summit Group

To establish an effectively engineered process that will lead to STP we have to establish goals and consider a variety of factors that can affect how we work. These categories include:

Input time - When is the transaction available and how long does it take to input?

Volume – How many total transactions are there, and how many are there at the peaks? When are the peaks?

Content – Does the message contain the information needed to process it or do we have to access other sources? Are these sources in electronic form?

Repair – How will we know that an error has occurred, and how will we fix it?

Mix of work – Will work arrive in batches of similar transactions, or will the transactions arrive randomly?

Manual processing required – What is automated, and what remains to be automated? Why is it still manual?

Processing steps required – What steps are conducted by a single person, and what handoffs are needed?

Procrastination – Does the transaction have to be processed as received, or can people decide to delay?

To evaluate these categories, we need to obtain information about our internal processes. Internal information can be gathered either manually on a daily, weekly or monthly basis and can be automated in a batch or real-time. This management information is typically gathered by Management Information Systems (MIS). MIS reports should focus on:

- Trends
- Peaks
- Variance to standards
- Comparisons
- Industry benchmarks

And, as we review the processing MIS that is collected, the information itself should cause us to focus on specific areas within the process flow to identify potential trouble spots, such as:

Bottlenecks – Where do they occur, and why?

Volume sensitivity – What level of volume can we process in a given amount of time, and what happens when volume increases or decreases slightly, or significantly?

Handoffs – How many hand-offs are there in the process, and why?

Redundancies – Are there similar functions that are being performed in different processing areas? Is there a good reason for the redundancy?

Points of increased errors – Are there units or processing points that have a significantly higher error rate than other areas? Why?

And, an evaluation of IPO (input process output) with the times and sequences that the transactions are input and output.

As a result of answering these questions and evaluating the Management Information that is discussed later in this chapter, we can decide whether the problem relates to the:

- Type of transaction
- Source of the transaction
- Generic errors that affect multiple transactions

Once we understand why we don't have STP, we can develop a strategy to resolve the problem.

Strategy Development

A firm has a variety of resources that it can call upon to develop a strategy. There are a limited number of generic strategies, and there are several tactics that are available to support multiple strategies. The available tools can also support multiple tactics.

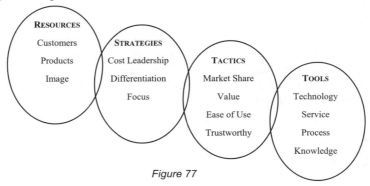

Figure 77

Once the business strategy has been developed, the firm can look to strategic solutions to the problems and opportunities that are needed by the business. The primary Operations and technical strategies are:

OPERATIONAL	TECHNICAL
Re-engineering	Network
Outsourcing	Central Applications
Merging	Central Database
	ASP

Figure 78 – Operational Strategies

Re-engineering

The re-engineering pendulum has finally begun swinging back to where operations managers have known it should have been all along. Operations managers have known that their primary job has always been to maintain a high level of control and quality while improving efficiency. However, for the last few years, this focus has been confused as multiple consultants and academics have promoted Downsizing and Business Reengineering.

Recently, senior managers were too quick to apply the techniques behind reengineering, and the consultants and academics were too busy delivering services to notice that firms were misapplying the concepts and damaging themselves in the process. The academic approach that is based upon complex teams and massive reorganizations was appealing to senior managers because it promised a panacea - and quickly. Instead, firms created a demoralized, fragmented workforce that was being asked to do more work with the same tools they have always had.

At last, the person who was probably the most responsible for the downsizing of the American workforce, Michael Hammer, the author of *Reengineering the Corporation: A Manifesto for Business Revolution*, has stated that he realizes that the most important factor in process change is the people involved in the process.

This new understanding is spreading rapidly. "People are starting to realize that changing how people work is more important than reengineering," says Thomas Davenport, a professor at the University of Texas. For operations managers who are engaged in the day-to-day task of changing their processes every day, that does not come as a surprise.

Firms cannot change their organization or their process without also altering the tools their people use. Throughout the industry firms have cut layers of management without redefining the survivors' roles and without altering the flow of work. This has led to situations where managers above and below the eliminated layer have had to assume the responsibilities of the manager who was eliminated.

This has led to longer hours, and if that was not possible, some things have just been dropped. While much of what has been dropped was no longer necessary, the selection of what would be dropped was not usually made as a conscious decision. It was often made by individual managers as they passed their saturation point.

This has led to increasing operational risk and to an environment where managers began to feel that they could decide what to do and what to drop. This is one contributing factor to the increased level of control and operational problems that have plagued firms recently.

The need for reengineering isn't dead, nor is the concept. What we will see over the next few years are some new buzzwords and some repackaged ideas. Firms are just now beginning to realize that the real objective of reengineering is to increase the profitability of the firm while managing risk, not to merely downsize. The new focus hopefully will have as much focus on increasing revenue and on decreasing costs.

The objectives and most of the techniques won't change, but it will give academics and consultants something new to talk about.

Identifying the Problem

When a firm is conducting a re-engineering project, we are normally making improvements to an existing, semi-automated process. In this case, we usually focus on automating problem areas. Frequently, we are only able to recognize problems after they occur. Problems are usually recognized because of the following:

- Financial loss
- Error rates
- Quality indicators
- Timeliness indicators
- Client complaints
- Internal complaints

Naturally it's better to identify these potential trouble spots before they occur and fortunately there are some ways to focus on mass. In general if we create the proper management information systems, we can identify problems as they are developing.

Processing Strategies

There are number of successful time sensitive process strategies. These include:

- "If I knew then what I know now"
- Parallel processing
- 80/ 20
- Staffing for peaks
- Filter input redirect
- Define expectations
- Do it once
- Prioritize - There are number of different kinds of priorities that can be considered:
    - Relative
    - Sequential effort
    - Sequential finish
    - Allocation
    - Categories

Over the last thirty years, operations and systems professionals have automated most of the functions in securities processing. However, many areas within a firm have been historically difficult to automate. Sometimes there isn't sufficient volume to justify the cost of automation; sometimes the rules have seemed too complex to specify; and sometimes the effort required to conceptualize the entire change has been overwhelming.

Vendor Applications

Vendors are developing applications that can be transformed into solutions for most of these problem groups. Software application vendors must design a generic application that can be easily replicated in order for them to make a profit, and then these vendor applications need to be applied to specific business problems in order to be useful. This usually requires a systems integrator who understands the technology, the application and the industry. In order to provide solutions for today's institutional client, a software vendor must:

- Articulate how their solution will merge with existing systems' architecture
- Offer complete support (installation, training, and development)
- Provide flexible, modular packages of services
- Support a variety of user skill levels, with minimal impact on IS
- Demonstrate client reference sites of quality and breadth
- Provide a comprehensive set of complementary products that can be used to enhance the productivity gains even further
- Have established relationships with software partners and integrators who completely understand the industry
- Provide an efficient way to thoroughly test the application in the client's environment

Automating Exception Processing

It has always been easier to develop processing systems that address the routine flow than to automate the processing of exceptions. Typically, firms have concluded that if they try to identify all of the exceptions and automate them in the first release of a new application, the new system may never get completed. So, the usually process is to automate the high volume, repetitive functions first and come back to exceptions later.

It is also typical that each exception has such a low volume that it may not be economically appropriate to enhance the processing system to accommodate each exception. So, once a system has gone live, it becomes difficult to justify the enhancements that automate individual exceptions.

What Goes into the First Release?

Since users and systems development people both know that enhancements are difficult to justify, they are often at odds with each other over what should be included in the first release. The systems staff would prefer to keep the application as simple as possible so that they can deliver it faster and it has a greater probability of working correctly; and the users try to get in as many functions as possible in the initial release because they don't know if the budget will still be there or if some other project will take priority over their enhancements.

This conflict is typically complicated by the fact that exceptions are often caused because of rapidly changing or evolving rules. Defining these rules is difficult for the users, and hard coding these changing situations is impractical.

However, with some of today's tools, it is possible to establish a table of rules that can be maintained by users as these rules change, and to embed these rules into the process flow itself.

Exceptions Occur Throughout the Process

Exception processing is usually found in areas such as:

- Transaction initiation
- Client investigations
- Fails processing
- Error re-entry
- Corporate actions
- Reconcilements
- Etc.

While systems have existed for years that record the number and type of investigations or the rate of fails, very few systems have taken on the task of automating some aspects of exception processing itself.

One way of implementing exception processing is within a workflow process. However, whether exception automation is embedding into workflow, or it is established as a standalone process, there are some guidelines for implementation.

Rules for Establishing Rules

With the new tools, a platform is established, with a small set of rules that evolves as the team begins to understand the opportunities. The project teams should realize that rather than attempt to identify every single rule, they should identify the situations that the application is likely to encounter, and then establish a series of rules that begin to cover each situation. If a proper foundation is established, additional rules can be added to the process as additional exception situations are identified once the application is in production. If a proper foundation is established, additional rules can be added to the process as additional exception situations are identified once the application is in production.

At some point, advanced technologies such as neural networks will also have evolved to the point where they can be self-teaching, and can learn new relationships and new rules without human instruction. Until then, we can still make significant advances in productivity by isolating and eliminating pockets of exception processing.

Types of Re-engineering

There are two major categories of reengineering that managers have been engaged in: Process Redesign and Business Redesign. All too often, managers in the financial industry have seen the term Reengineering, and focused on operations, rather than on the entire business. The day-to-day role of the manager is to constantly reevaluate the efficiency of their operation and constantly engage in Process Redesign. There are a number of very specific tools and techniques that can be used in this level of redesign: all of which revolve around the concepts of Measure, Manage, Monitor.

Reengineering at the business level is more complex, and has usually been less successful since it involves multiple disciplines, and an in-depth understanding of the trends that are driving the industry, what your clients want, and how your competition is preparing to deal with the future. Business Redesign requires firms to make major changes to their assumptions and to their habits. These are the areas that Hammer and Champy were really driving towards - a fundamental and radical change in the way businesses behave and in their role with their clients.

There are two major categories of reengineering. One focuses only on operations and the other considers the entire business.

Process Redesign

As previously stated, the day-to-day role of the manager is to constantly reevaluate the efficiency of their operation and constantly engage in process redesign. There are several very specific tools and techniques that can be used in this level of redesign: all of which revolve around the concepts of Measure, Manage, and Monitor.

Process redesign requires that managers establish some measurement tools so that they know what they are doing. Knowing volumes, timeliness, error rates, sources or errors, etc., is essential to defining possible solutions and improvements. Once a new process is implemented, the manager must continue to monitor the process to verify that the situation actually improves. If not, try another adjustment.

Business Redesign

Reengineering at the business level is more complex, and has usually been less successful since it involves multiple disciplines, and an in-depth understanding of:

- The trends that are driving the industry
- What clients want
- How the competition is preparing to deal with the future

Business Redesign requires firms to make major changes to their assumptions and to their habits. These are the areas that Hammer and Champy were really driving towards - a fundamental and radical change in the way businesses behave and in their role with their clients - not merely cutting operational costs.

Project Management

Managing Project Risk

Managing Operating Risk has become increasingly important as the potential impact of unmanaged processes has grown. In the past, if someone made a processing mistake, they could lose their job. In today's networked and highly leveraged processing environment, one person's mistake can cost hundreds of jobs. For example, Barings' failure to exercise adequate controls over its Singapore office resulted in many people looking for new career opportunities.

Before we can measure - manage - monitor risk, we have to be able to define it. There are several major categories of operating risk, including:

- Daily processing risk
- Periodic processing risk
- Project risk
- Oversight risk

The most important risk category for the purposes of implementing STP is Project Risk.

Categories of Project Risk

One way to categorize Project Risk is shown in the following table.

Types of Project Risk	Cancelled During Development	Go Live - Cancelled Before Payback	Go Live - Success	Go Live - Blow Up
1. Project is Late and/or Over Budget	1A	1B	1C	1D
2. Project is On Time and Within Budget	2A	2B		2D

Figure 79- Categories of Project Risk

This chart shows that there are really seven different categories of Project Risk. All of the Group 1 types of risks are the kind that we all know too well. Complex technology projects are not always completely on-time and completely within budget unless considerable effort has been spent dimensioning the potential impact of unknown events. We can always account for the possibility of events we can foresee, but it takes a lot of experience to build in contingencies for events that we do not understand.

Within Group 1 Type 1A risk includes projects that were started but which are canceled during the development. This typically results from projects that were not adequately defined, or where management or users did not really buy into the concept, or where the business has moved faster than the development cycle. That is a better result than type 1B, where the project has been completed and has gone through the agony of going live only to be canceled before it has met its objectives. This type of problem wastes a lot of time and money.

Type 1C is probably familiar to most developers. The project team completes their work, only it takes a little longer and costs a little more than expected. Usually these projects are still considered a success because each level of management above the project team has probably built in their own time and money cushion, as experience has dictated.

Type 1D is the risk that everyone works the hardest to avoid. It is the disaster that can ruin businesses and careers. Usually this results from inadequate testing. Almost everything else that can go wrong in a project, from insufficient requirements, to incomplete design to incorrect technology to poor development can be identified and resolved during the testing phase.

There is another category of risks - Group 2. In Group 2, although the project is on time and within budget, we see some of the same types of problems. Type 2A says that everything was going fine during development, but either the users were not sufficiently on board or the business has substantially changed. Type 2B also says that the development team did their job, but the project was poorly conceived.

There is no risk resulting from Type 2C since that is everyone's goal - On Time, On Budget, Live, and Performing as it should.

Type 2D is a terrible outcome. The project is on time and on budget, but then it blows up. Once again, inadequate testing is usually the cause of this type of problem.

As we can see, there are many ways that a project can go wrong. What are some of the ways that we can prevent these problems? Over the years, experience has taught that there are five areas to examine:

User Involvement

We are all told this over and over again. Without a significant amount of user involvement, projects are doomed. No matter how smart the development team is, and no matter how well they build the system, if the ultimate user doesn't accept and use the system properly, the project is a failure. Users must be involved from the Requirements Phase through to User Acceptance Testing and Implementation. The requirements must be clear. Senior Managers must be on board. The users must be committed to make it work, and the project must meet a real business need.

Business Knowledge

It is not enough to think that you understand your current business; you also have to understand the environment in which the new system will operate in the future. This evaluation of trends should be accomplished during the requirements phase.

Team

While teamwork is becoming more of a requirement throughout the industry, most people have not been trained in how to actually work with a team. Each of the people on the team has to bring their own knowledge and experience to the task and to respect the skills that the other people bring. No one can know everything when we develop solutions to complex business problems, so we have to rely on each other.

There have to be enough people on the team and there should be some consequences for failure. If the team members are told that their primary job remains their number one goal, each one will only give their second best to the team. This is a classic recipe for failure.

Project

Managing a project requires a specific set of skills and the project managers must acquire them wither through experience or training. Projects cannot be too long or the business will evolve away from the project goals. Complex projects should be broken into parts that can be understood by the team members. Prioritization and phased delivery are almost always required for large projects.

Sometimes the users or the development team will try to stuff in as much as possible into the first phase because they know that the later phases cannot be cost justified. If so, those deliverables should be dropped - they are not worth doing, no matter how attractive.

The project cannot be managed on an ad hoc basis. There must be a development process, usually called a Systems Development Life Cycle that is used to identify the various steps of the project and the tasks that are to be performed. Plan for contingencies, and then, test, test, test.

Technology

All too often, new technologies become solutions in search of problems to solve. If the problem is not one that is important to the business, it runs the risk of losing management attention - and budget - before it is completed.

The technologists must understand the technologies to be used. If not, a significant amount of time should be built in for the learning curve. And, the technical solution has to fit within the firm's overall architecture or technology infrastructure. One-off projects using untested technology, with inexperienced people, will fail.

As described, there are many ways that projects can fail, and many areas to examine if your goal is to prevent the failure. And, it is up to each team member to prevent the TEAM's failure.

Management of Risk

Categories of Risk

USER INVOLVEMENT	BUSINESS KNOWLEDGE	TEAM	PROJECT	TECHNOLOGY

Clarity of requirements
 	
Senior Management Commitment
 	
User Commitment
 	
Project meets a real business need
	Industry
	
	Application
	
	Institutional culture
		Team Coherence (Teamwork)
		
		Adequacy of skills
		
		Adequacy of staffing
		
		Team size
		
		Consequences of failure on the:
		
		   - Business
		
		   - Team
		
		   - Individual
			Project Management Skills
			
			Size and Length of project
			
			Complexity of project
			
			Phased delivery?
			
			Can some elements be deferred?
			
			Are the elements cost justified?
			
			Is there an SDLC process?
			
			Is the SDLC used?
			
			Depth of Acceptance Testing?
			
			Contingency Planning
				Experience with the development tools
				
				Use of CASE tools
				
				Experience with CASE
				
				Experience with the selected Technology
				
				Experience with the methodology
				
				Is there an application architecture?
				
				Experience with the target architecture

Figure 80 – Managing Risk

Measure - Manage - Monitor

The primary goal of operations managers is to manage! That should not be a surprise to anyone; however, all too many managers spend the bulk of their day resolving problems. That is not what managers should be doing. Managers should be preparing their staff to resolve the problems, and the managers should be focused on preventing the existing problems from reoccurring, and new problems from surfacing.

Measurement

Before we can manage something, we have to be able to measure it. Measurement includes counting, qualifying, dimensioning, sizing, evaluating, comparing, etc., and then it involves analyzing the data. The most common tools that are used to analyze operational data are comparisons, ratios, percentages and trends.

These tools are then organized into one of several reporting techniques, most commonly charts, graphs, tables, and matrices. One of the most effective matrices for evaluating errors is called a source/cause report. It shows one dimension of activity across the top (departments, clients, geographies, etc.) that is the source of the error; and a second dimension down the left side (incomplete form, incorrect data from client, incorrect data entered by operator, etc.) As the number of errors is entered into the various cells, mangers can begin to select the areas that produce the greatest number of errors, and which should therefore be addressed first, if at all possible.

Measurement tells managers what they do, and helps them identify where they should look to prevent problems.

Management

Management is the process of effecting change. The most effective way of producing change is through your staff, or through people over whom you have some influence. Managers identify potential problem areas, obtain and allocate resources, motivate their staff, evaluate the effectiveness of machines, and keep superiors, subordinates and peers informed.

Manages are always responsible for maintaining (or improving) client satisfaction by maintaining processing quality and timeliness; and for improving the efficiency of their process by reducing the number of errors, and the overall cost of the process.

Since managers must always be alert to shifting patterns of quality or control, they must continue to monitor their processes.

Monitoring

The same tools that were used to measure a process should now be used to ensure that the process remains in control. However, good managers do not only rely on their reports to monitor the effectiveness of their department. They need to talk to clients (whenever possible) and to their peers, to determine how their organization is perceived by other functions.

Most importantly, managers need to receive feedback directly from their staff to identify potential problems in areas that are not being actively measured. This concept, called Managing by Walking Around, is more effective than it appears. A good operations manager can spot potential problems very quickly by watching how their staff is responding to the workload, by observing the cleanliness and orderliness of the workplace, and by asking questions.

While managers are responsible for their equipment and process flow, they are the most responsible for their people. The most successful managers are those who communicate the most with their people.

Contingency Planning Tools

In the past, most managers developed contingency plans because they were told to, or because they knew that the auditors would look for them. Few of us ever thought that disasters would happen to us.

As our businesses become more interdependent, we increase the number of potential points of failure; and as technology becomes more complex, we increase the probability of some type of failure.

Why should we worry?

Disasters can affect us all. Most recently, we have seen fires, floods, terrorists, earthquakes, and even squirrels bring down the biggest firms.

- There was a major fire several years ago in lower Manhattan that put many banks, brokers and financial firms out of business for some period of time. The full damage was not repaired for four days (Monday through Thursday). It was a very long week.

- Chicago had a flood, and lower level data centers, generators and telecommunications connections were affected.

- Both tragedies at the World Trade Center affected firms that were tenants, and had a ripple affect as other firms provided resources to prevent a wider impact on the financial industry.

- The San Francisco earthquake caused considerable disruption but was not devastating because businesses there were becoming more prepared.

- NASDAQ was humbled twice a few years ago as squirrels nibbled through phone wires and caused some disruption.

This list shows that Murphy's Law is ever present, and will become more important as the industry becomes more automated and interdependent.

The industry has a goal of Straight Through Processing, and this goal comes closer to a reality everyday. However, as business connect to each other and send rapidly increasing amounts of data to each other, the potential for disruption will grow.

In the days of glass houses, central computer departments managed one or two mainframes, which hopefully had built-in redundancies and off-site back up. Our business could survive problems - even if we didn't think they would happen. And, one or two central people made it their job to ensure that if processing had to move off site, it could do so quickly. After all, everything we needed was in the mainframe.

Today, even if a business has a mainframe, it almost certainly has some amount of processing on servers or directly on PC's. Each PC becomes its own "data center" and requires backup and its own contingency plan.

Contingency Plans must account for all of the process that is conducted and the firms has to be prepared to move it all, quickly and efficiently. How many C drives contain information that is needed to conduct business? How long would it take to reestablish your LAN(s) in another location? Do you even know how each of your PCs is configured?

Preparing for disasters cannot be solely the job of one or two experts in a central IT department. Line operations managers will have to take control to ensure that their functions will continue when a problem occurs.

Preparing for disasters takes longer than it did in the past and costs more. And, all of that investment in time and people is totally wasted - unless you need it. Then is it priceless.

Testing Tools

Several Schwab clients recently felt the impact of insufficient user testing a few years ago when they awoke to find that their Mutual Funds had been drastically under-priced. A program change caused the system to not recognize several of the Mutual Funds that were owned by Schwab clients. Tracey Gordon, Schwab spokesperson, said that: "We were making some systems changes when there was a program error."

As applications become increasingly complex, the need for thorough testing becomes ore important. In the Schwab example, the clients were concerned, and inconvenienced, but Schwab has promised to reimburse any client who traded based upon the inaccurate data. What is more important is the impression these clients and potential clients have regarding Schwab's overall accuracy. Do you want to deal with a broker who has inaccurate information? This could seriously affect their business for months.

It could have been prevented with a better testing program. Study after study has clearly demonstrated the need to test early and often. A famous MIT study found that the difference between fixing an error during the unit testing phases and fixing it after the application has moved into production was 100/1. That is, for every $1.00 it cost to fix the error during unit testing, it will cost $100.00 after the system goes live.

DEVELOPMENT STAGE	COST
Coding / Unit Testing	$ 1.00
Integration Testing	10.00
Acceptance Testing	40.00
During Installation	60.00
In production	100.00
	Source: MIT

Figure 81 – Cost of Identifying and Repairing Errors

The Summit Group wrote a book about testing that is available as a guide, *Software Testing for Financial Services Firms.*[57]

About the Author

The author's biography is included in Chapter I.

---

[57] This book can be ordered from the Securities Operations Forum website, www.soforum.com.

CHAPTER XXII - SUMMARY

By Hal McIntyre

In this book, several industry experts have united to identify the current opportunities to begin implementing STP through a series of continuous process improvements. While neither the industry nor individual firms can afford to make sweeping changes to the processing infrastructure at this time, we can all afford to make incremental changes. Of course, each of these changes must be cost justified.

The next significant change to the securities industry is likely to be related to outsourcing to a centralized processing utility. In an article in *the Journal of Securities Operations* I pointed out that:

"It is time to expand the role of the DTCC to include supporting processing functions that no longer provide any competitive advantage for banks and brokers, and which can significantly reduce their processing costs when centralized. The dream of a common back-office for Wall Street has been discussed for many years but was perceived as impossible due to the competitive nature of the business and the people involved. This dream could now become reality if the industry would empower the DTCC to fully assume the technical support role for ALL of the common, non-competitive, processing functions that are performed by firm after firm throughout the US. The time for this change has come.

In the past, firms were able to differentiate themselves by the quality of their processing. As firms have increased their level of automation, the quality of their processing, and the mutual use of many processing applications provided by third party vendors, this is no longer the case. The similarities in processing are significant and the differences are in small details.

Banks and brokers all have many similar processing activities that could be centralized within the DTCC, which would free up redundant resources in virtually every firm in the industry. Every firm has to price its positions, every firm has to maintain corporate action information, every firm has to maintain securities information, etc. The only reason to continue processing these activities in-house is ego and in a few cases to capitalize on market process inefficiencies. It certainly is not good business for the industry.

This strategy could be implemented in a series of incremental steps, starting with the centralization of some specific categories of data and expanding to support the related processing functions. DTCC could develop and run the necessary applications without assuming any additional processing risk." [58]

But, firms should not wait for this to occur. Outsourcing of non-differentiating roles to vendors and other firms offers an immediate opportunity to reduce some costs, and the solutions presented in this book can be used to make processing more efficient.

---

[58] Expand the Role of the DTCC to Reduce Cost and Risk in the Securities Industry, Hal McIntyre, *Journal of Securities Operations*, Fall, 2002

ABOUT THE EDITOR - HAL McINTYRE

Hal has over 30 years of management experience, including 16 years at Citibank. He founded The Summit Group in 1991. Prior to establishing The Summit Group, Hal managed numerous banking and securities functions for Citibank, including marketing, operations, and technology. During his last four years at Citibank, he managed an Applications Development Division of over 300 people who supported Citibank's worldwide securities processing applications.

While at Citibank, he worked for four years in Zurich as the head of Operations and Technology for Citibank's Swiss Investment and Private Banks, and was the Chief Administrative Officer for Citicorp Investment Bank.

Hal is a Managing Partner of The Summit Group, which, with over fifty employees, is active in consulting to major banks, brokers, investment managers, and other financial institutions, and provides comprehensive services in Management Consulting, Market Research, and Systems Integration.

A former Air Force officer, Hal has a Bachelor of Arts in Industrial Psychology from Miami University and an MBA from Southern Illinois University. He has taught graduate and undergraduate courses at Fairleigh Dickinson University, and has been a guest lecturer at the University of Massachusetts. He is frequently quoted in publications such as American Banker, Trends and Institutional Investor, is a regular speaker at securities industry conferences around the world, and is the author of How the US Securities Industry Works and the Securities Operations Glossary.

hal@tsgc.com

ABOUT THE SUMMIT GROUP

The Summit Group has extensive international experience in numerous banking and securities processing activities, and has a unique ability to support business managers by quickly identifying effective solutions to complex business problems and opportunities. TSG is adept at selecting and using the most efficient technology alternative to implement optimal solutions, and has an overall goal to help clients increase profitability by building new revenue sources and reducing expenses.

Constant changes in the business climate, competition, and client needs require banks to adapt quickly to capitalize on dynamic conditions and opportunities. The Summit Group can help businesses respond effectively in this environment, identify and develop new revenue opportunities, and significantly reduce their cost structure. TSG has experienced professionals, the tools, and the methodologies that can provide support in the very complex tasks of systems implementation, and that can ensure each client's success.

To support this success, The Summit Group seeks on-going relationships where it can periodically supplement their client's team and assist managers when additional resources are needed to meet the shifting requirements that are common in today's minimum staff environments.

The Summit Group's Financial Services clients consist of leading firms such as Citibank, JPMorgan/Chase, Deutsche Bank, UBS, Bankers Trust, IBJ Schroder, PIMCO, CalPERS, DTCC, etc. And, TSG is frequently provides their securities industry expertise to other firms such as Sun Microsystems and Sybase.

TSG specializes in helping firms plan and implement STP solutions, SWIFT and Middleware programs, Cost Reduction efforts and Testing of new applications. Current clients include major securities firms such as Citibank, State Street Global Advisors, Alliance Capital, Deutsche Bank, AIG, and Thomson Financial.

A subsidiary of The Summit Group, Securities Operations Forum, is a leading supplier of educational services to the securities industry. SOF publishes two on-line newsletters for over 4,000 readers worldwide; Securities Operations Letter focuses on the US industry, and Global Custody News concentrates on international securities processing. SOF also conducts open enrollment and customized training classes for over 2,500 people each year throughout the US on processing topics such as Derivatives, Corporate Actions, etc., and annually presents three to four major conferences on key securities industry issues.

www.tsgc.com

PART VI - ADDITIONAL READING

This book has attempted to summarize the issues surrounding STP and to provide some immediately available solutions. Considerable work has been completed by other firms and industry associations that also should be reviewed. Several of these are listed in the first section of this part of the book, and we have included overviews of two of the important Group of Thirty Recommendations in the second section, and in the third section we've included a summary of an equally important US-based White Paper, the VISION 2000 report.

WHITE PAPERS

There are several articles and White Papers that the reader should consider when learning about implementing STP:

"Recommendations for Securities Settlement Systems"

Jointly published by CPSS and IOSCO in January 2001, and available at the IOSCO website (www.iosco.org).

The specific address is:

http://www.iosco.org/library/index.cfm?whereami=pubdocs

"The Securities Settlement Industry in the European Union – Structure, Costs and the Way Forward"

By Karel Lanoo and Matthias Levin, published December 2001, and available at www.ceps.be.

"Cross-Border Clearing and Settlement Arrangements in the European Union"

Published in November 2001 by the Giovannini Group, which was formed by the European Commission in 1996 to advise on efficiency issues in the EU financial markets.

http://europa.eu.int/comm/economy_finance/publications/economic_papers/20 02/ecp163en.pdf

"Second Report on European Union Clearing & Settlement Arrangements"

Published in April 2003, the Giovannini Group's second report is also available.

The first "Giovannini Report", published in November 2001, identified 15 barriers on the road to an integrated capital market infrastructure for the European Union. The follow-up report, released on April 16, 2003, presents a strategy for the removal of those 15 barriers. It recommends a sequence in which they should be dismantled, who should take responsibility for the action required, and the time frame envisaged to complete the work.

The report emphasizes the importance of a concerted effort involving both the private and public sector to ensure success. It concludes that the removal of the 15 barriers will lead to an integrated market place, which, in turn, will accelerate the pace of consolidation of the market infrastructure.

The report (56 pages) is available at:

http://europa.eu.int/comm/economy_finance/giovannini/clearing_settlement_en.htm

ISSA Report on Global Custody Risks 1992

This ISSA report is available at:

http://www.issanet.org/pdf/GlobCustRisk-92.pdf

"Standards for Securities Clearing and Settlement Systems in the European Union"

Published in July 2003 by a working group of the ESCB and the CESR, and is available at:

www.europefesco.org

SIA STP White Paper

The SIA's STP White Paper is available at:

http://www.sia.com/stp/pdf/Buy-SideWhitePaper.pdf

GROUP OF THIRTY

Although the Group of Thirty's recommendation is often seen to apply to only cross-border processing, in fact they are designed to guide the evolution of each country's processes, including the US.

The Group of Thirty (G30) is a group of international financial services professionals that has produced two reports and sets of recommendations:

Group of Thirty (1989)[59]

"Clearance and Settlement Systems in the World's Securities Markets"

Full copies of the Report are available for $60.00 from the Group of Thirty at *www.group30.org*

---

[59] Source: Group of Thirty

Background

In the mid-1980's, a group of thirty retired CEO's of worldwide Bank and Brokerage firms formed with the goal of improving the way that securities were settled across borders, reducing the risk associated with cross-border trading, and streamlining the overall settlement process to improve efficiency.

Recommendations

The group created nine recommendations in 1989 in a report titled *Clearance and Settlement Systems in the World's Securities Markets*. Each of these recommendations was established with the expectation that Working Groups in every country with a securities market would adopt them. In the US, the securities industry already complied with the majority of the recommendations.

Trade Comparison

1. By 1990, all trade comparisons should be accomplished by T+1

By comparing a trade as soon as possible after the trade has been completed, firms are able to identify mismatches early in the clearance and settlement cycle and correct the details to avoid a fail. There are two sides to the trade comparison, the street-side and the customer-side. The street-side of the trade is compared through the various clearing agencies for the securities they process and the customer-side for institutional trades is matched through the DTC for the instruments handled by the DTC.

2. By 1992, all indirect participants should join a trade comparison system

The inclusion of the indirect participants, which are the Investment Managers, in the trade comparison process improves the ability of the industry to ensure that trades settling at Custodians are processed efficiently.

Central Securities Depository

3. By 1992, each country should have a central securities depository

The Depository Trust Company is the primary securities depository in the US, and efficiently immobilizes certificates and allows automated settlement.

Netting

4. By 1992, each country should consider and install a netting system

Netting is the method most used by clearing agencies in the US to reduce the number of individual street-side trades that must be processed.

Deliver vs. Payment

5. By 1992, all settlements should be DVP

In the US, the process of exchanging cash for securities is accomplished through a process called Deliver versus Payment. Many countries did not have a linked process for settlement, and instead delivered the securities separately from the cash in a process called Deliver Free.

Same Day Funds

6. All settlements should be made with Same Day Funds

The US at the time of the G30 report had two types of money that could be recorded on a firm's books, Fed Funds and Clearing House Funds. Fed Funds is money that is usable when it is received, in contrast to Clearing House Funds, which were only usable on the business day after they were delivered. In 1996, the US eliminated the use of Clearing House Funds and all transactions today are made in Fed Funds.

Settlement Period

7. By 1992, all settlements should be finalized by T + 3

At the time of the G30 report, the primary settlement period in the US for most instruments was five days. In the 1920's, most securities settlements in the US occurred in one day, but as the volume of transaction grew; the settlement period was extended day by day, until in the 1960's it was five business days. At that time, the volumes again grew dramatically and the industry began to automate.

Applications were written for individual departments to help ease the clerical burden of processing large quantities of securities, and over time, the stand-alone applications were linked. This automation allowed the firms to process more efficiently, but it also firmly established the five-day settlement cycle.

In 1995, after a significant industry-wide effort, the US moved to a three-day settlement cycle for most type of securities.

Securities Lending

8. By 1990, remove all barriers to Securities Lending

Securities Lending is an effective way of reducing fails, and is an important part of an efficient settlement process. While Securities Lending overall is a very profitable business, each individual transaction could only be for a few days, and the profit margin can be very thin.

In some countries around the world, a Stamp Tax was assigned by the government for each trade, regardless of whether it was a regular purchase and sale or a temporary Securities Lending arrangement. This tax prevented the establishment of a viable market for loaning securities. The G30 proposed that countries modify their regulations to eliminate the tax and encourage securities lending.

Standards

9. By 1990, each country should adopt ISO standards

The G30 also recognized the importance of establishing standards as one key building block for automation, and recommended that each country adopt the ISO set of standards. The US was already using ISO standards for securities numbering and processing.

Overall, the US securities industry was happy with the G30's recommendations since the US already complied with most of the recommendations. The only two recommendations that the US had to improve were three-day settlement and the use of Same Day Funds. Both of these recommendations have now been implemented, and processing of securities that are held at the DTCC is basically accomplished with STP after the trade is completed. The US continues to work on extending STP within firms and into the Pre-Trade processes.

Implementation of these recommendations in other countries around the world has been inconsistent, and cross border processing remains inefficient and risky. Emerging markets have been quick to implement the standards since they had very little existing infrastructure to change, while the established markets had to make major investments to modify their processes and infrastructure and have been slower to adapt.

Group of Thirty (2003) [60]

" Global Clearing and Settlement: A Plan of Action"

This report is available at www.group30.org

This second G30 report created twenty updated recommendations:

CREATING A STRENGTHENED - INTEROPERABLE GLOBAL NETWORK

1. Eliminate paper and automate communication, data capture and enrichment.

2. Harmonize messaging standards and communication Protocols.

---

[60] Source: Group of Thirty

3. Develop and implement reference data standards.

4. Synchronize timing between different clearing and settlement systems and associated payment and foreign exchange systems.

5. Automate and standardize institutional trade matching.

6. Expand the use of central counterparties.

7. Permit securities lending and borrowing to expedite settlement.

8. Automate and standardize asset servicing processes, including corporate actions, tax relief arrangements, and restrictions on foreign ownership.

MITIGATING RISK

9. Ensure the financial integrity of providers of clearing and settlement services.

10. Reinforce the risk management practices of users of clearing and settlement services providers.

11. Ensure final, simultaneous transfer and availability of assets.

12. Ensure effective business continuity and disaster recovery planning.

13. Address the possibility of failure of a systemically important institution.

14. Strengthen assessment of the enforceability of contracts.

15. Advance legal certainty over rights to securities cash, or collateral.

16. Recognize and support improved valuation and closeout netting arrangements.

IMPROVING GOVERNANCE

17. Ensure appointment of appropriately experienced and senior board members.

18. Promote fair access to securities clearing and settlement networks.

19. Ensure equitable and effective attention to stakeholder interests.

20. Encourage consistent regulation and oversight of securities clearing and settlement service providers.

VISION 2000 [61]

On January 26, 1994, representatives from the Boards of NSCC and DTC met at the direction of their full Boards of Directors with the following mission: *Create an industry vision for the next decade that would focus on eradicating inefficiencies, maximizing use of technology, eliminating redundancies and reducing costs*

---

[61] Source: Vision 2000 Report, 1994

Members of the Task Force agreed to recognize and acknowledge certain conditions in identifying opportunities and approaches that will help to turn the Vision into reality. These assumptions included:

- Expiration of NSCC & DTC leases at 55 Water Street in 1997
- The possibility of consolidating NSCC's and DTCC's four data sites
- The possibility of NSCC and DTC sharing contingency liquidity resources (if found to be feasible)
- The potential for joint project planning in the introduction of new products and services, recognizing the strengths and weaknesses of each organization
- The overlaps in NSCC's and DTCC's participant bases
- NSCC's and DTCC's proven ability to work together or defer to each other in providing solutions to industry needs, e.g.:
- Cooperation on Same-Day Funds, "Flipping" and Cross-Collateralization
- NSCC's deferral to DTC in creating a system for settling commercial paper
- DTCC's support of NSCC's money settlements
- DTCC's display of NSCC's settlement members on its PTS system

Key Findings

The Task Force has recognized the following potential opportunities for greater cooperation among industry providers of services:

- NSCC and DTC should back each other up on a contingency basis for liquidity needs
- NSCC and DTC should develop a joint strategy for negotiating new agreements
- NSCC, DTC and SIAC should share data center sites
- Development of joint strategies for immobilization and elimination of physical certificates
- Establishment of a joint long-range planning group among clearing agencies and depositories

Summary of Recommendations

Having examined the issues that came within its mandate, the task force makes the following recommendations:

I. Certificate Immobilization

Establish common facilities and procedures for the receipt, delivery and distribution of securities that are not eligible for depository services.

Consider instituting a system for netting the settlement of institutional transactions done on a Delivery vs. Payment basis between

Broker/Dealers and Custodian Banks to reduce the need for movement of certificates.

Develop common vault facilities for the safekeeping and management of securities that are not eligible for depository services.

II. Certificate Elimination

A Mandatory Electronic Securities Ownership Program ("MESOP") should be created as an alternative to the Investor Registration Option ("IRO"). A task force of major industry, organizations should be established to analyze requirements (MESOP) and structure a proposal for implementation.

III. Cross Collateralization

The industry should build upon the National Securities Clearing Corporation's (NSCC) Collateral Management model to create a Collateral Management System. This system should far exceed the current and planned capabilities of the NSCC model to:

- Recognize the collateral requirements, risk management policies, procedures and assumptions of all participating agencies and standardize them as much as possible.
- Net the overall collateral required of each participant.
- Allocate on a book-entry basis the collateral required of each participant to the appropriate participating agency.
- Allow for the interactive and electronic management of collateral within the system.

IV. Common Industry Utilities and Structures

A Joint Rationalization Oversight Board (JROB) should be established by the Boards of Directors of common industry utilities (DTC, NSCC, SIAC et al) to identify overlaps and potential overlaps among the utilities, and determine where outsourcing or consolidation would better serve the industry and the investing public.

This was accomplished this year as the DTC and NSCC announced their plans to combine their efforts within a new holding company.

V. Cross-Border/Non-US Dollar Support

Recommendation # 7 of the Group of Thirty is critically important to the growth of cross-border markets ("A Rolling Settlement system should be adopted by all markets. Final settlement should occur by T+3").

The ISCC, SWIFT and other industry groups in the G7 countries should work to enforce global messaging standards. A board of industry experts from these countries should be convened to act as advisors to the many emerging markets' stock exchanges and depositories. The SIA should then enlist the aid of the New York Federal Reserve Bank to work with other central Banks to enforce the standards in their respective countries.

The SIA, PSA, and other key industry associations should work with SWIFT, the ISCC, CUSIP and other vendors and utilities to develop common methods of securities identification and description and standard global message formats for securities activities across national borders.

In parallel with the efforts described above, the same organizations should form a working group to define the critical design features of a global trade capture and comparison system.

Institutional investors as well as Brokers and dealers should implement stronger internal controls to ensure that accurate settlement instructions and security descriptions are relayed to settlement agents the first time around.